Fire and Spice

Jacki Passmore

Macmillan • USA

MACMILLAN

A Simon & Schuster Macmillan Company

1633 Broadway

New York, NY 10019

MACMILLAN is a registered trademark of Macmillan, Inc.

Library of Congress Cataloging-in-Publication Data
Passmore, Jacki
    Fire and spice / Jacki Passmore.
        p.   cm.
    Includes index.
    ISBN 0-02-860282-x (alk. paper)
    1. Cookery, Oriental. 2. Cookery (Hot peppers) I. Title.
TX724.5.A1P39   1996
641.6'384—dc20   96-9907
                                                             CIP

ISBN: 0-02-860282-X

Manufactured in the United States of America

10 9 8 7 6 5 4 3 2 1

Design by Rachael McBrearty

*D*edicated to the members of my International Curry Lovers Club, many of whom would follow me to the deepest depths of a Sarawak jungle or the highest mountains of Sichuan, if they knew there were chilies at the end.

(Write to P.O. Box 5049, West End, 4101, Q, Australia for information on The Curry Lovers Club!)

Acknowledgments

I wish I could remember the name of my grade school geography teacher who pointed out the legendary Spice Islands, the Moluccas, on the globe in our classroom one chilly winter day. I sat through the lesson mesmerized, learning of ancient merchant vessels, of trading monopolies and political intrigue, of religious domination and of men who were prepared to die in their efforts to control the spice trade. I'd like him to know just how significant that one short class became to me. Just as soon as I was old enough to travel overseas alone, I was off to Indonesia to meet my destiny. Now, twenty or so cookbooks later, I am just as excited when I see an Asian destination printed on an airline ticket, and know I'll never lose the thrill of my lifelong committment to the wonderous kaleidoscope of flavors, textures and colors that is Asian cuisine.

I did not come to understand and appreciate the food of Asia without the encouragement and assistance of the many cooks, chefs, teachers and restaurateurs who have helped and inspired me over the years. *Fire and Spice* is my tribute to the Daljits, Wangoos, Jayanthas, Auyeungs, Amatyakuls, Yeos, Singhs and Fernandez of my hot and spice food world. I offer you thanks for inviting me into your kitchens and your hearts.

For my daughter Isobel and son Peter I say thank you for being there—one day I'll put roast lamb on the table, I promise! Thank you Jenny for trading many patient hours of recipe testing for the reward of a lifetime of chili addiction.

My deepest appreciation to Judith Weber for her continuing support, editor Justin Schwartz for his confidence in my work and for envisioning the zappy format of *Fire and Spice*, and copy editor Alexandra Greeley for her patience with the tedious but vital attention to editing detail.

iii

Contents

Introduction

Passionate Foods from Asia

Asia is the ultimate destination for those hooked on spices and intoxicated by the incendiary pleasures of eating chili. Asian food is an irresistible melange of tastes, textures, aromas and vibrant colors. It isn't all hot, but there's plenty that is. They've had a love affair with chilies that's spanned five hundred years. Asian food isn't all spicy, but when they spice it up, they do it with panache. I crave chili and spices. That's why I made Asia my home for twelve years, and I still can't stay away.

Asian cooks use a spectacular range of sweet and hot spices, native fruits and vegetables, and exotic indigenous seasonings that range from breath-catchingly offensive to seductively aromatic. Employed with flair and understanding, these add the magical, musical notes that make their food incomparable. Asian cooks rarely measure in the kitchen. A pinch of this, a handful of that, a splash of sauce sizzled onto a hot pan, a jumble of seasonings and spices. They cook with senses on full alert, constantly checking the aromas as they develop, observing the softening of textures, the melding of spices with the gravy, the thickening and enriching of a sauce as it bubbles in the curry pot or wok. It's as entertaining to watch as it is rewarding to sit down to the finished dish.

Fire and Spice is a celebration of the passion and fire of the cooks of Asia: a collection of recipes for dishes that have inspired and excited me during my many years of living, traveling and eating there, and now are often on my table at home. They are recipes with flavors that jump right off the page or out of the pot: bold, intense, hot, and hugely, deliciously appetizing.

I've been knocked out by chilies since my first breakfast in Indonesia,

1

a bowl of rice, a fried egg on top and three fresh green chilies on the side. What zing and zap they gave to the day! What pep and sparkle they lend to a dish! What a thrill they are on the palate!

I've been mesmerized by spices for as long as I can remember. It might have started with a stunning ginger cake made by my grandmother, or the cloves and cinnamon stick that made our corned beef taste so much better than our neighbors'. My olfactories went into overdrive when I ground *garam masala* at my first-ever Indian cooking class, and they haven't stopped sniffing out a good, spicy dish since.

You have the book, now here's how to add fire and spice to your life.

It often amazes someone unused to chilies to see the quantity a chili freak can consume without (apparent) adverse effect. Too many spices can be aggressive on an uninitiated digestive system. Trainee spice-aholics and apprentice chili fiends should start slowly. The chili-heat factor is indicated on each recipe, so begin cautiously, and serve yogurt, milk or coconut milk as extra fire insurance. You don't have to make an entire meal of hot or spicy dishes. Perhaps start by introducing just one hot or spicy dish into the meal. Next try some of the fiery little dishes from the section we have titled On The Side (page 243). Then slowly build up to an all-out chili blast as your palate adjusts.

Asian meals are not usually structured into courses, and this presents the cookbook writer with the dilemma of how to categorize dishes. First Flavors includes some feisty soups and salads to serve as first courses. Next I have listed the smaller dishes that would suit as first courses under the heading Other First Flavors. Salads to serve as first courses, come next, along with some feisty soups. The chapter entitled More First Flavors groups together delightful small eats that are Wrapped, Battered, Stuffed, Skewered and Dipped. Enjoy these as first courses, and don't overlook them when you entertain. They are great party eats!

Main Flavors are the larger dishes, which I have sectioned into Flavors of the Sea, Chicken and Other Birds, and Beef, Lamb and Pork. Asian cooks usually serve more than one main dish at a meal and you may want to do the same. Servings indicated are for small servings on the assumption that at least one other main dish will be served, in the Asian way.

Great Grills is a hot and spicy tribute to outdoor cooking, and Greens and Grains includes some of my favorite vegetable and vegetarian recipes, to go with main courses or to be enjoyed on their own.

All the fiery, soothing, crunchy, sweet or tangy little flavors that complete a menu are listed in On The Side. Find here curry pastes and powders, spiced salts, dressings and vinaigrettes, chutneys and

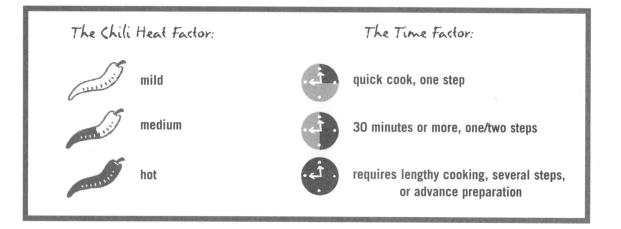

The Chili Heat Factor:

mild

medium

hot

The Time Factor:

quick cook, one step

30 minutes or more, one/two steps

requires lengthy cooking, several steps, or advance preparation

pickles, relishes and *sambals* to make your hot and spicy meals even more buzzy, peppy and absolutely sensational. And now you're all fired up, add on one of the perky afterthoughts listed as Final Flavors. There's ice cream with a precocious kick, some smooth and creamy tastes to knock out afterburn, and puddings with a provocative punch to extend palatable pleasures to the last bite.

Chapter 1

Glossary of Ingredients

Aamchur (**India**): Ground dried green mango. An enzyme component makes this an effective meat tenderizer when used in marinades. In sauces it imparts a pleasing tartness. Substitute tamarind or lemon juice.

Asafoetida (**India**): A resin used in cooking to aid digestion, it also helps to highlight flavors. Omit if unavailable.

Bean Pastes (China): Salted and fermented soybeans are ground with chilies, garlic and other ingredients into a range of strongly flavored seasoning pastes. **Soy bean paste** is predominantly salty; **chili bean paste** is hot and salty; **hot bean paste** is hot, salty and garlicky. Japanese red miso, combined with mashed garlic and chili, can substitute.

Black Beans, Salted (China): These wrinkled dried beans are salt-fermented soy beans. They are a popular Chinese seasoning ingredient which should be rinsed, dried and chopped for use. They can be kept for a year or so, in a spice jar.

Candlenut (Indonesia): The *kemiri* nut is a dry-textured nut inedible raw, but ground to use for thickening and enriching curry sauces. Macadamia nuts are the best alternative, but raw cashew nuts and almonds could be used.

Cassia Bark (Southeast Asia): A fragrant spice used as an alternative to cinnamon. The red-brown strips of bark are sold in Chinese stores and should be stored with spices and kept dry. Use whole chunks, or grind to a powder.

Chilies: See pages 36–37 and chili guide, page 10.

Chinese Cooking (Rice) Wine (China): A mild, clear-to-light amber colored wine made from fermented rice. Cooking wine may have up to 5 percent added salt. Alternatives are *sake* and dry sherry or Japanese *mirin* when a sweet taste is acceptable.

Cilantro: See *Coriander, Fresh and Ground*

Coconut (Southeast Asia): Cooking in many parts of Asia would have taken a totally different direction without coconuts. **Coconut milk** is the creamy extraction of grated fresh coconut flesh combined with water.

Cream of coconut, otherwise known as **coconut cream** is merely a more concentrated formula. It is the rich, creamy base for curry sauces, a refreshing drink over ice, the prime ingredient in many desserts. Coconut milk/cream is most accessible from the can, its chief drawback being that it does not keep for more than a day in the refrigerator once opened. The compressed block and powdered coconut creams make up in practicality what they lose in quality. You can't beat the fresh product, made by finely grinding, diluting and straining the peeled white flesh of a fresh coconut. Try it in your food processor, using the metal blade.

Coriander, Fresh and Ground (Southeast Asia): Coriander (also known as cilantro) is as integral to certain Southeast Asian cuisines as are ginger and coconut. The fresh plant is an intense and quite pungent herb used extensively as a garnish and flavoring; the seeds, a sweet, lemony aromatic spice, are a foundation ingredient in most curry powders and pastes. In Thailand even the fleshy, cream-colored roots are ground into curry pastes. Fresh coriander is becoming more readily available, and once purchased, can be kept for up to five days rolled loosely in paper and stored in the refrigerator with the vegetables. Whole coriander seeds are a better buy than ground seeds. Grind as needed, and toast in a dry pan before use to intensify their flavor.

Curry Leaves (Southeast Asia): Despite their name, curry leaves are not an ingredient of curry powder, but are used in curries for their subtle, earthy flavor. These small, pointed leaves look like miniature bay leaves arranged in neat formation along a slender stem. They grow and are used extensively in Sri Lanka and southern India. Curry leaves should be cooked briefly, so are added to curries in the final stage of cooking, or are fried in oil and stirred into or poured over a finished dish. They are sold dried, frozen and fresh, the fresh being infinitely better than the others. A bay leaf for every four to six curry leaves is a reasonable substitute.

Curry Pastes and Powders (Southeast Asia): Commercial curry pastes are easy to use and last well if properly stored, preferably in the refrigerator in warm climates. The best will introduce complex, authentic flavors to your curries. See our recipes for Thai Red Curry Paste and Madras Curry Paste on pages 248 and 249. Curry powders are less reliable as ground spices rapidly lose their fragrance. The yellow color of a spice mixture indicates the inclusion of turmeric, which can overpower more subtle spices. Choose curry powders packed in jars, or decant your purchase into a spice jar and seal tightly. If possible, buy curry mixes composed of whole spices to grind at home. See *garam masala*, below, and our recipe on page 247.

Dashi **(Japan):** A distinctly flavored stock made from an infusion of

katsuobushi (dried bonito fish) and *kombu* (a type of seaweed). *Dashi* is sold as powder or granules that mix instantly in hot water. Use a ratio of 1 teaspoon dashi in ³/₄ to 1 cup of water. A well-flavored fish or seaweed stock can be used instead.

Fish Sauce (Thailand/Vietnam): Also known as *nam pla* and *nuoc mam*, it is a clear, amber-colored sauce used in the same way as soy, as a condiment and seasoning. It is salty, and has an unpleasant pungency which disperses on cooking. Fish sauce gives a unique taste to Thai and Vietnamese food, which cannot be substituted, but it need not be as fish sauce is now readily available and keeps for many months without refrigeration.

Five-Spice (China): This fragrant combination of spices is unique to China. Cloves, fennel, Sichuan peppercorns (pages 56, 180–81), star anise (page 9) and cassia bark (page 5) are the constituents, ground to a fine powder that gives a delicate, pepper-anise flavor to stir-fries and braised dishes. Readily available. Store with other spices, keeping it dry.

Galangal (Southeast Asia): *Galangal* is popularly known as Thai ginger, because of their preference for this subtly flavored cousin of fresh ginger. Slightly harder than ginger, the rhizome can be identified by its pink shoots and brown skin. Shred or slice finely to use, and store wrapped in paper in the refrigerator for up to three weeks.

Garam Masala (India): An aromatic spice blend used to season curries and as a condiment to sprinkle over finished dishes. Recipe page 247.

Ginger, Fresh (throughout Asia): The unique flavor of fresh ginger rhizome is characteristically Asian. When buying ginger root, look for a smooth, buff-colored skin. Peel before using in chunks, finely sliced, shredded, very finely grated or minced as the recipe requires. Fresh ginger keeps for ages, and is best refrigerated to prevent dehydration. **Pink Preserved Ginger** is sliced or shredded ginger preserved in a mild, sweet vinegar solution. Readily available, it is best refrigerated or kept on a cool shelf. Ground ginger is rarely used in Asian cooking.

Herbs: Cooks in southeast Asian countries lavish their food with fresh picked herbs, particularly cilantro (fresh coriander), mint and basil. Indigenous aromatics include *bai manglak*, Thai lemon-scented basil; *bai krapow*, holy basil; and *rau ram*, Vietnamese mint-basil.

Hoisin Sauce (China): This sweet, brown paste is added to sauces, braised dishes and stir-fries for its rich, complex flavors, and is used as a condiment for dipping roast meats. Readily available, it keeps for many months and is best refrigerated in warm conditions.

Kaffir Lime (Thailand): A highly aromatic member of the citrus family, the kaffir lime tree grows unique two-tiered leaves which are added to soups

and sauces for their intense lemony flavor. The fruit is tiny, with knobbly dark-green skin and is used primarily for its aromatic skin as it has little juice. The fruit is rarely available, so can be substituted by other limes. The leaves are sold fresh, which are by far the best, and also frozen and dried, which should be rehydrated in hot water before use.

Lemon Grass (Southeast Asia): Recognize this fragrant herb by its tapering, pale-green layered stem. It is the compacted lower section that gives citrus flavors to curry pastes, soups and hotpots. Used whole, it should be slit lengthways and bruised to release its powerful flavor oils. It is also finely shredded into salads, dips and dressings. If not available fresh or frozen, look for the dried product which should be rehydrated in hot water before use, or bottled sliced lemongrass.

Mirin **(Japan):** A clear, sweet liquor brewed from fermented rice. It has a smoother, richer flavor than *sake* which could be substituted. Readily available, but on the expensive side.

Mustard Seeds (India/Malaysia): Brown mustard seeds are commonly used in Indian-style cooking for the searing heat and pungency they impart. To achieve their full potential as a spice, they are usually fried or toasted until they pop and splutter in the pan.

Palm Sugar (Southeast Asia): The liquid sugar extracted from palmyra and sugar palms is heated to form crystals which are compressed into cylindrical logs or cup-shaped blocks. It varies in color from white through ochre to almost black, the darker having a more intense smoky flavor. Unless specified, choose a light to medium color and shave or crumble the sugar before use. Any full-flavored brown sugar can substitute, as can *jaggery* made in India from cane sugar.

Pepper: See pages 180–81.

Rice Flour (Southeast Asia): A fine white flour milled from rice or glutinous rice which is sold in Asian stores and specialist groceries. Rice flour gives crisp batters and is used extensively in Asian desserts. Unless specified, use plain rice flour, as glutinous rice (conversely gluten-free) cooks to a thick and glue-like paste.

Sambal Ulek **(Indonesia):** A potent blend of crushed fresh red chilies and salt. Sold in bottles, it should be refrigerated after opening. To prevent oxidation cover the surface with a film of vegetable oil. This hot chili product can be used in any recipe requiring chili paste.

Shallots (Southeast Asia): The sweeter, milder members of the onion family. Asian cooks prefer these small onions that resemble overblown garlic cloves sheathed in red or copper-colored skins. The smaller they are, the milder their flavor, which is the objective. They store well in a cool, dry cupboard or hanging basket. Avoid refrigerating them as they may sprout.

Shrimp Paste (Southeast Asia): Shrimp paste is considered a good protein source; it is also one of the most interesting and little-understood flavorings in Asian cooking. Small, whole shrimp are salted and left to decompose in deep vats, then ground to a paste. It is then used "fresh," as a soft gray-pink mass, or dried and compressed into blocks. The former is *kapee* in Thailand where they prefer the softer paste, the latter *blacan* or *trassi*, in Malaysia and Indonesia. When this offensive-smelling seasoning hits the pan, it transforms into a powerful aromatic which adds depth and complexity to a dish, and highlights the natural flavor of the other ingredients. It should be kept tightly capped in a jar, and cooked in a well-ventilated kitchen. Compressed dried shrimp paste lasts for years, while "fresh" shrimp paste should be kept in the refrigerator and used within a few months. **Dried shrimp** are small, sundried, shelled shrimp that have many uses in Asian cooking. Add whole or chopped to stuffings and a variety of braised dishes. It is frequently used in rice and noodle dishes. **Shrimp floss** is made by grinding dried shrimp in a blender or food processor, to produce a fluffy mass which can be used as a seasoning, or sprinkled on a finished dish as a garnish.

Sichuan Peppercorns: See pages 180–81 and 56.

Sichuan Sauce (China): Like the *sambal ulek* of Indonesia, Sichuan sauce is a fiery blend of chilies and salt, with the addition of mashed garlic. Store the jar in the refrigerator and use it judiciously.

Soy Sauce (China): For general cooking, use the standard soy sauce which is salty, but light in color. Where a dark color is expected in a dish use the thicker, darker soy which is less salty. **Sweet soy sauce** is the *kecap manis* of Indonesia. It looks and tastes like thin molasses, and is used as a seasoning and condiment.

Spices: See pages 116–17.

Star Anise (Southeast Asia): Something that looks this cute must taste as good. This elegant star-shaped pod infuses any dish in which it's used with its delightful, intense, licorice-like flavor, giving superb depth and flavor dimension. Use a whole star, break off a point, or grind to a powder as the recipe dictates. Whole star anise keeps indefinitely in a well-sealed spice jar.

Tamarind (Southeast Asia): It is commonly accepted in Asia that tamarind helps retain the nutrients in vegetables with which it is cooked. Tamarind is principally used for tenderizing meat and for its pleasantly tart flavor, which makes it useful in sauces and marinades. Bought as "pulp" that contains both tamarind flesh and numerous smooth seeds, it must be softened in boiling water, the pulp mashed and the seeds and skin strained off. Pure tamarind is seedless, but the pulp must be mashed in hot water to remove the skins. **Tamarind concentrate** is easiest to use and can be added directly to a dish. **Tamarind water** is the mixture of tamarind pulp and the water in which it was mashed. It should be strained to use. About 1 teaspoon of tamarind concentrate would equate with 1 tablespoon tamarind water.

Turmeric (Southeast Asia): This relative of ginger is the root which gives curries their characteristic yellow color. The fresh rhizome, strongly carrot-colored, with an earthy flavor, can sometimes be purchased at Asian greengrocers. It will keep for several weeks in the vegetable crisper. It can be added in a chunk, or grated directly into a dish. Powdered turmeric is more common, and is easy to obtain where spices are sold.

Vinegar, Rice (China/Japan): A mild, white vinegar akin to cider vinegar in flavor and strength. **Chinese black vinegar** is a dark, mild vinegar used in marinades and stir-fries; it is sold in Asian stores and it keeps for many months. **Red vinegar** is used primarily as a condiment.

Wasabi (Japan): Wasabi packs the punch of the hottest mustard with a flavor similar to horseradish. Made from a root indigenous to Japan, it is sold in ready-to-use squeeze-on tubes, or as a powder in small cans. Simply add water and mix to order.

Fire and Spice Chili Guide

Classifying chilies can be tricky. Certain chilies guarantee heat. Some of the more common varieties can subtly change in their flavor and heat levels in different climates and growing conditions. In general, small and slender chilies are hot. Green chilies are unripe, and turn red (orange, yellow or brown) when they ripen.

Anaheim: large, red or green; mild
Dutch: medium size, red, tapered; medium-hot
Fresno: short, squat, red; hot
Habanero: squat, rounded, all colors; very hot
Jalapeno: medium, wide-shouldered, red or green; medium-hot
Korean: slender, thin-fleshed, green; hot
New Mexico: large, red or green; mild-medium heat
Serrano: small, bullet-shaped, red or green; hot
Tabasco: small, yellow or red; very hot
Thai: small, elongated, red or green; medium-hot
Thai bird's eye: quite small, bullet-shaped, red or green; very hot

Chapter 2

First Flavors:
Soups and Salads

Soups

Thai Coconut Chicken Soup

Kim Chi (Chili-Pickled Cabbage) and Tofu Soup

Indian Vegetable Sambar

Seafood Dumplings in Chili Lime Soup

Black Pepper Soup

Seafood Soup Served over Crisp Rice Croutons

Sour and Hot Sichuan Soup

Thai Hot Shrimp Soup

Javanese Fish Soup

Salads

Warm Salad of Cuttlefish with Kaffir Lime

Crab and Coconut Salad

Seafood Salad in a Tangy Green Dressing (Yam Thalay)

Issan Chicken Salad

Kashmiri Chicken Chaat Salad

Thai Beef and Herb Salad

Pork and Peanut Salad

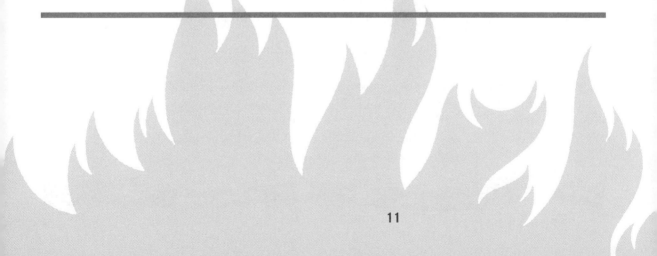

One Night in Bangkok

I was not prepared for Thailand on that first visit a quarter century ago. The press of people, the noise, the chaos of traffic that filled sticky, humid air with greasy clouds of black diesel fumes. The smells that invaded my small, dilapidated taxi were of frying oil, jasmine, putrid drains, spices, exhaust smoke and sweet exotic fruits. Speeding past a picket line of power poles entwined with purple flowering bougainvillea I caught my first glimpse of a Bangkok roadside kitchen. Impeccably polished aluminum pots in a precise row on a makeshift counter—what wonders lurked beneath their shining, flat lids? A teetering stack of bowls, an enameled wash-up tub adorned with red roses, a smiling attendant ladling creamy red sauce over plump ribbons of rice noodles. If only there was time to stop. The long taxi ride from the airport stretched into tedium. Will this teeming city's traffic problems ever be solved?

I was impatient to be on the streets with my first bowl of something hot and mysteriously spicy in front of me. Instead I was whisked to one of those protracted lunches well-intentioned tourist office executives put on for visiting VIPs and the media. The food was "safe," the kick boxing and swordplay exhibitions disturbing in the clammy afternoon heat, conversation was desultory, disinterested. The entertainment dragged on interminably to fixed smiles and dutiful applause.

For two full days I endured an exhausting program of too many visits to Bangkok's spectacular *wats* (temples), hotel facility tours and orchid farm inspections, classical dance presentations over touristy *kantoke* dinners, and river rides in one of those slender ferry boats that screech and splutter at breakneck speed along the sludgy Chao Praya River. And finally, oh blissful escape. Time on my own! I would browse through lamp-lit night markets in search of a bargain, then find an appealing little Thai restaurant tucked away in a side street to enjoy a real Thai dinner. Ha!! Foiled at every turn!! The taxi could no more comprehend my directions to the market than the waiter in the restaurant I finally selected understand my requests for "something typically local." He kept on parroting "fri ri, beef oster sor" (fried rice, beef in oyster sauce). Despairing, I walked into the kitchen, lifted the first lid I could reach and pointed to the curry within. "This, please," I said triumphantly to the distressed waiter who'd trailed me into the kitchen.

Have you ever had a dish so hot it hurts your brain? No tingling of the lips or beaded brow, this was just straight up there zapping the gray matter, dissolving neurons as fast as I could spoon it in. But having already "lost face" as much as I could bear in one evening, I was determined to regain

some of my battered dignity by showing them I could eat the lot. Net result. . . a few hours later, I was awoken by terrifying nightmares of my stomach being rent by razor-sharp bronze swords wielded by kick boxing champions dressed as Thai temple dancers. Diagnosis. . . extreme chili burn.

One of my unhappiest nights, yet one I often recall with nostalgia. That curry, whatever it was, was sensational! Chili is like a drug. Once it grips you, you don't want it to let go! It's kept me going back to Thailand at every invitation or contrived opportunity. On each visit I've traveled further and fared better than the last. Understanding the lifestyle a little more, discovering yet more exciting flavors and interesting dishes, learning just where to find perfect seafood, a searing jungle curry (page 142), an incomparable *nam prik kapi*. I've learned to slide excess "bird's eye" chilies from my plate into a napkin for later secret disposal, when I want to impress my hosts with an outstanding chili tolerance. I know not to mess my sauces through my rice, and pile several types of curry onto my plate at once. I dare to bite into a *Chiang Mai* sausage from a suspect-looking food stand anticipating its unique, fermented taste, and always eat my *kai yang* (page 194) with *som tam* (page 220).

Thai food is a symphony of flavors and textures, with a complex under-scoring of contrast and counterpoint. It is challenging, seductive, cleverly crafted, and never, never dull. It can be as bold and up front as a street walker, or as sophisticated and elegant as the royalty who have done so much to create and promote this unique cuisine. Thai is not food for the fainthearted, but that's exactly why we love it.

Thai Coconut Chicken Soup

Makes 6 servings

The classic Thai coconut chicken soup is usually quite mild and sparingly spiced. I prefer this deliciously creamy soup with a serious chili punch and plenty of citrus undertones.

2 chicken legs

2 cups water

2 stems lemon grass, trimmed and slit in half

3¹/₂ cups coconut milk or coconut cream

8 thin slices fresh galangal or young fresh ginger

4 to 6 medium-hot red chilies, seeded and stemmed

2 kaffir lime leaves, torn into strips

6 to 8 ounces chicken breast, cut into ¹/₂-inch cubes

¹/₃ cup canned straw mushrooms, oyster mushrooms or champignons, drained and sliced

2 scallions, white parts only, cut into ³/₄-inch pieces; finely slice the green tops to garnish the soup

3 to 4 tablespoons freshly squeezed lime juice

3 to 4 tablespoons fish sauce

Garnish

6 sprigs cilantro (fresh coriander)   Sliced scallion

● Place the chicken legs in a small saucepan and pour on the water. Add 1 stem of lemon grass slit in half lengthways. Bring to a boil and simmer for about 15 minutes, until the chicken is tender enough to fall off the bone.

● Remove chicken legs from the broth with tongs and when cool enough to handle, skin and debone the meat and break into small pieces. Set aside.

● Strain the broth into a large saucepan and add the coconut milk or cream, the remaining lemon grass, and the *galangal*, chilies and lime leaves. Bring barely to a boil, then reduce the heat and simmer for 2 to 3 minutes. Add the cooked and uncooked chicken and cook gently for 3 to 4 minutes.

● Add the mushrooms and scallions and cook a further 2 to 3 minutes. Season with the lime juice and fish sauce and a sprinkle of salt and pepper, if needed.

● Serve into bowls, add a sprig of cilantro and scatter on the scallions.

 Note: I like to leave the lemon grass, chili, galangal and lime leaves in the soup, but they can be removed before serving, if you prefer.

Kim Chi (Chili-Pickled Cabbage) and Tofu Soup

This vegetarian make-in-minutes soup is great for a winter menu. The kim chi gives it a peppery crunch that contrasts brilliantly with tender mouthfuls of tofu.

6 cups chicken stock, vegetable stock
   or water
4 ounces kim chi (page 269)
4 ounces fresh bean sprouts

8 ounces fresh tofu (bean curd)
4 scallions, greens only, cut into
   1-inch pieces
Salt

⊕ Bring the stock or water to a boil in a 3- to 4-quart saucepan.

⊕ Shred the *kim chi* finely, rinse the bean sprouts and cut the tofu into 3/4-inch cubes. Add them all to the saucepan and simmer for 5 minutes.

⊕ Add the scallions, check seasoning, adding salt to taste, and a small sprinkle of sugar if you feel it would improve the flavor (*kim chi* can be very tart).

⊕ Serve into deep bowls and offer chopsticks as well as a soup spoon.

Indian Vegetable Sambar

Makes 6 to 8 servings

Peppery sambars are an enticing prelude to an Indian meal, but there is no reason why this soup could not be served before a simple grill or roast. This vegetarian dish makes a great one-pot dinner for four, with a loaf of crusty bread, or thick cushions of Turkish-style flatbread.

1/2 cup red lentils
1/2 cup chopped onion
1 cup diced eggplant
1/2 cup diced carrot
1/2 cup diced zucchini or squash
1/2 cup diced potato, soaked in cold
    water

1/2 cup chopped red bell pepper
2 teaspoons salt
1 1/2 teaspoons black peppercorns,
    crushed
1 tablespoon besan (chickpea flour)
    or fine cornmeal
Sugar as required

Seasoning Paste

3 cloves garlic
6 shallots, peeled and coarsely
    chopped
3 to 6 medium-hot red chilies, seeded
    and coarsely chopped

1 1/2 tablespoons vegetable oil
1 teaspoon cumin seeds
2 teaspoons coriander seeds
1/2 teaspoon caraway seeds
1/3 cup shredded coconut

Fried Spices

1 teaspoon cumin seeds
1 teaspoon brown mustard seeds

6 to 7 curry leaves
1 tablespoon vegetable or coconut oil

Garnish

1/4 cup cilantro (fresh coriander)
    leaves, chopped

Lime or lemon wedges

Soak the lentils in cold water for 1 hour, drain well and return to the pan. Add 4 cups water and bring to a boil. Reduce heat and simmer for 15 minutes. Add the onion, eggplant and carrot and simmer another 15 minutes.

Sesame seeds can be toasted in a wok or frying pan, without oil over medium heat. Shake the pan and stir the seeds frequently so they cook evenly. Cook before using.

✦ In a small pan, cook the garlic, shallots and chilies from the seasoning paste ingredients in the oil, stirring, for a few minutes over medium heat. In a separate pan without oil and over medium heat, dry roast the cumin, coriander, and caraway seeds and the coconut until golden brown and aromatic (see sidebar). Transfer to a spice grinder, mortar or food processor fitted with the metal blade and grind to a powder, then add the sautéed ingredients and grind to a paste. Add a little water, if needed, to make a smooth mixture.

✦ Stir this into the vegetable pot and add the diced zucchini, potato, red bell pepper, salt and pepper.

✦ Bring back to a boil and simmer until the vegetables are tender, about 10 minutes. Stir in the *besan* and add about 4 cups of water to the soup.

✦ To complete the soup, fry the cumin and mustard seeds and curry leaves in the vegetable or coconut oil until very aromatic, about 1 minute. Serve the soup into bowls and scatter on chopped cilantro. Add the fried spices and serve at once with lime or lemon wedges.

Seafood Dumplings in Chili Lime Soup

Makes 6 servings

Tender seafood dumplings in a tangy soup.

Seafood Dumplings

4 ounces fresh shrimp meat

4 ounces boneless white fish

4 ounces cleaned squid

1½ teaspoons finely grated fresh
  ginger

¼ teaspoon salt

1 teaspoon fish sauce

¼ teaspoon ground white pepper

Cilantro (fresh coriander) leaves

Soup

6 cups fish stock, see sidebar

Salt

1 stalk lemon grass, trimmed and slit
  in half

3 cilantro (fresh coriander) roots

4 thick slices galangal or young fresh
  ginger

2 large mild red chilies, seeded and
  stemmed

3 kaffir lime leaves

¾ cup fresh oyster mushrooms, or
  small canned straw mushrooms,
  drained

3 tablespoons fish sauce

2 to 3 tablespoons freshly squeezed
  lime juice

Garnish

Cilantro (fresh coriander) leaves

Fine shreds of red chili

⊕ To make the seafood dumplings, place the seafood in a food processor fitted with the metal blade, add the ginger, salt, fish sauce and pepper and grind to a smooth paste.

⊕ Bring a pot of lightly salted water to a boil. Using a wet teaspoon, scoop up spoonfuls of the seafood mixture and press a cilantro leaf into the top of each one before sliding into the boiling water. Cook until they float to the surface, then remove with a slotted spoon and transfer to a bowl of cool water.

Fish stock

Most fishmongers will sell meaty fish carcasses and fish heads for stock. Chop them into chunks and place in a large saucepan, preferably nonaluminum, with a scallion and four or five slices of fresh ginger. Cover amply with water and place over medium-high heat until it comes to a boil. Reduce the heat enough to allow only the occasional bubble to rise to the surface. The stock will become cloudy and slightly bitter if the stock boils briskly. After about 10 minutes, strain through a fine nylon sieve into a storage container. The stock is ready to use immediately; otherwise refrigerate for no more than two days, or freeze.

✳ To make the soup, pour the stock into a stainless steel or other nonreactive saucepan. Add salt and bring to a boil. In the meantime, grind the lemon grass, cilantro roots, *galangal* or ginger, and chilies to a paste in a mortar, food processor or spice grinder. Stir into the soup and simmer for 5 minutes.

✳ Score the kaffir lime leaves lightly with the point of a knife. Add the mushrooms, kaffir lime leaves and the seafood dumplings to the soup and simmer for 1 minute. Season with the fish sauce, lime juice and salt and simmer briefly before serving into deep bowls, garnishing with the cilantro leaves and red chili shreds.

Do Ahead Note: You can make the dumplings in advance and keep refrigerated for several hours or overnight in cold water in a covered container.

Black Pepper Soup

Makes 6 servings

In the south of India they serve soups like this for breakfast, with dosas, huge rice and bean flour pancakes, or a couple of iddlys (steamed rice cakes).

6 cups water or vegetable stock

1/3 cup brown lentils*

2 tablespoons tamarind concentrate

1 to 1 1/2 tablespoons black peppercorns, crushed

1 teaspoon hot paprika

1 teaspoon chili paste

1/2 cup finely chopped onions

2 cloves garlic, chopped

2 tablespoons vegetable or coconut oil

1 1/2 teaspoons ground coriander

Salt

Garnish

Chopped cilantro (fresh coriander) leaves

Small wedges of fresh lime

Papadam Chips (see sidebar)

⊕ Combine the water and lentils in a saucepan with the tamarind, pepper, paprika and chili paste. Bring to a boil, reduce heat and simmer for 10 minutes, stirring occasionally.

⊕ In a separate pan, heat the oil on medium heat and cook the onions and garlic until translucent, then add to the soup. Sprinkle on the ground coriander and continue cooking until the lentils are so tender that one is easily mashed between two fingers. Season with salt to taste.

⊕ Serve into shallow soup bowls and garnish with chopped cilantro. Add the Papadam Chips immediately before serving, and offer lime wedges for squeezing.

* You can use other types of lentils, or cooked dried beans or chickpeas.

Papadam Chips

Strips of crisp-fried papadam make an attractive, crunchy garnish for thick soups or for peppery curries.

3 to 4 papadams, plain or seasoned

2 cups vegetable oil for deep frying

Use a sharp, heavy knife or Chinese cleaver to cut the papadams into 1/4-inch strips. In a wok or pan suitable for deep frying, heat the oil to very hot, then reduce the heat slightly. Add the papadam strips and immediately push them under the oil so they quickly expand and crisp. Remove before they become brown, and drain on a rack covered with paper towels.

Seafood Soup Served over Crisp Rice Croutons

Makes 6 servings

Crisped Rice

Chinese cooks use the layer of the rice that adheres to the inside of their rice cookers or saucepans. They allow it to dry in a warm oven, then crisp-fry it to serve as croutons in soups. If you cannot achieve this when you cook rice, press cooked white rice (short or long grain) into a greased oven tray and leave overnight in a very, very low oven. Cut or break into pieces and deep fry in very hot vegetable oil until lightly golden and crisp. Drain on paper towels for a few minutes before using.

This is a great dinner party dish. The crisped rice and the hot and peppery soup are taken to the table separately, so the soup can be served onto the rice with a sizzle and crackle, in front of your guests.

3 scallions (green and white parts), trimmed and chopped

2 cloves garlic, peeled and minced

3 teaspoons minced fresh ginger

2 teaspoons minced hot red chili

3 teaspoons finely minced sun-dried tomatoes

1 1/2 teaspoons tomato paste

5 cups water

1 teaspoon chili oil

1 1/3 teaspoons sesame oil

Salt and black pepper

4 ounces small unshelled fresh shrimp

4 ounces fresh white fish fillets, cut into 1/2-inch cubes

4 ounces cleaned fresh squid, cut into rings

4 ounces shelled mussels or clams

4 ounces crabmeat

3 ounces small straw mushrooms or champignons

2 ounces shredded bamboo shoots

2 tablespoons cornstarch mixed with 2 tablespoons of cold water

Garnish

Chopped cilantro (fresh coriander) or sliced scallion greens

To Serve

Crisped Rice (see sidebar)

⊕ Combine the scallions, garlic, ginger, chili, sun-dried tomatoes and tomato paste in a soup pot and pour on the water. Bring to a boil, stirring thoroughly, then reduce the heat and simmer for 5 to 6 minutes.

⊕ Add the chili and sesame oils, salt and pepper and the seafood. Simmer for 6 to 7 minutes, add the mushrooms, bamboo shoots and the cornstarch solution. Cook until the soup has thickened, then check seasonings, adding more chili oil if required.

⊕ To serve, place the warm Crisped Rice in a large bowl and take to the table with the soup in a separate pot. Pour soup over the rice at the table, garnish with cilantro or scallion greens and serve at once.

Sour and Hot Sichuan Soup

Makes 6 servings

The climate in Sichuan province, in central-western China, is challenging. Fiercely cold winters and suffocatingly humid summers require foods that warm or cool, but always stimulate the appetite. This is the one region in China where hot tastes are not just enjoyed, they're considered essential.

4 ounces pork leg meat, without skin or fat

2 teaspoons Chinese cooking (rice) wine, dry sherry or sake

2 teaspoons light soy sauce

Pinch of salt

4 ounces boneless chicken breast

2 teaspoons Chinese cooking (rice) wine, sake or dry sherry

1 teaspoon minced fresh ginger

Pinch of salt

1 ounce black fungus, or 6 large dried black mushrooms, soaked in cold water for 25 minutes and drained (trim stems of mushrooms or pare away the hard root section of fungus)

4 ounces firm fresh tofu (bean curd), cut into small strips

2 ounces sliced bamboo shoots, cut into fine shreds

2 ounces fresh bean sprouts

2 ounces fresh oyster mushrooms, cut into strips

3 to 4 Chinese cabbage (gai larn) leaves, shredded

3 large eggs, mixed with a pinch of salt and beaten lightly

Soup

7 cups water or chicken stock

2 to 3 tablespoons finely shredded fresh ginger

1 tablespoon chili oil

1 tablespoon dark soy sauce

2 tablespoons Chinese black vinegar, or malt vinegar

1/2 teaspoon white pepper

1/2 teaspoon crushed Sichuan peppercorns (optional)

2 tablespoons cornstarch mixed with 3 tablespoons of cold water

Crisp Wonton Skin Croutons

4 to 6 wonton skins

Vegetable oil for deep frying

Salt and crushed Chinese peppercorns (optional)

Cut the wonton skins into 1/3-inch-wide strips. Heat oil for deep frying and fry them until lightly golden and crisp. Remove from the oil and sprinkle with salt and pepper, or leave them plain. Lemon pepper or seasoned salt for fries could also be used to season these lightweight croutons.

Garnish

Small sprigs of cilantro (fresh coriander) and/or chopped garlic chives

To Serve

Crisp Wonton Skin Croutons (see sidebar)

Extra vinegar

Extra chili oil

⊕ Very thinly slice the pork, then stack the slices together and cut across them to make fine shreds. Place in a bowl and add the wine, soy sauce and salt, mix well and set aside for 20 minutes. Shred the chicken in the same way and marinate with wine, ginger and salt. Prepare the fungus or mushrooms, tofu and vegetables and set aside.

⊕ To make the soup, bring the water or chicken stock to a boil in a large soup pot. Add the ginger, chili oil, soy sauce and the shredded fungus or mushrooms and simmer for 2 minutes. Add the meat and vegetables and bring barely to a boil. Reduce heat slightly and simmer for 2 minutes.

⊕ Reduce heat a little more, then while stirring the soup very slowly in a circular motion, pour the eggs in a thin stream into the hot soup, so that it sets in threads. Add the vinegar, white and Sichuan peppercorns and the cornstarch solution and cook slowly, stirring frequently, until the soup thickens.

⊕ Transfer to a soup tureen and add the cilantro or garlic chives before serving with the croutons and additional vinegar and chili oil on the side.

Thai Hot Shrimp Soup

Makes 4 to 6 servings

Anyone who has eaten Thai food will know the joys of this searing soup with its fresh, sharp chili bite and myriad heavenly citrus flavors. My first bowl of Tom Yum Goong was the fiercest food I had ever tasted. It bubbled in a tabletop steamboat, an innocent-looking clear soup with a few floating lemon grass stems and lime leaves and with a couple of the biggest shrimp I had ever seen. Each mouthful was liquid fire that stunned me into a gasping silence and dampened my ardor for Thai food for several weeks. I take a more cautious approach with my soup, but it's still quite potent.

8 to 12 very large fresh shrimp in their shells

5 cups water

2 stems lemon grass, trimmed

4 green chilies, seeded and stemmed

4 shallots, peeled

4 cilantro (fresh coriander) roots

1 to 4 hot red Thai chilies, seeded and sliced

4 fresh kaffir lime leaves or 6 dried leaves soaked for 10 minutes in boiling water

2 scallions (white and green parts), trimmed and cut into 3/4-inch pieces

1/4 cup fish sauce

1/4 cup freshly squeezed lime juice

1/4 teaspoon white sugar

Garnish

1/3 cup cilantro (fresh coriander) leaves

● Place the shrimp in a large saucepan and pour on the water.

● Coarsely chop one lemon grass stem and green chilies, and place in a mortar or the small bowl of a food processor fitted with the metal blade, with the shallots and cilantro roots. Grind to a paste, then add to the saucepan. Bring to a boil and simmer for about 6 minutes.

● Remove shrimp from the broth with a wire strainer, peel them and return the shells to the broth. Boil for a further 5 minutes, then strain the broth into another pan or into a tabletop pot such as a fondue pot or Chinese steamboat.

● Add the reserved lemon grass stem, which has been slit in half lengthways, and add the red chilies, lime leaves, scallions, fish sauce, lime juice and sugar.

● Bring to a boil, reduce to a simmer and cook for 2 to 3 minutes only. At this point the soup is ready to take to the table to finish cooking in front of the guests, or it can be simmered for 3 to 4 more minutes in the kitchen.

● Return the shrimp to the soup, add the cilantro and serve into deep bowls.

Javanese Fish Soup

Makes 6 servings

1 large onion, sliced	³/₄ teaspoon ground turmeric
2 cloves garlic, minced	1¹/₂ teaspoons ground coriander
1 tablespoon vegetable oil	1 pound white fish fillets, skinned
5 cups fish stock or water	1 small bunch young spinach or
4 thin slices fresh ginger	arugula
1 green chili, seeded and sliced	Salt and freshly ground black pepper

To Serve

Crisp Fried Onions (page 279)   Sambal ulek or other chili
                                    paste/sauce

● In a wok or skillet, cook the onion and garlic in the oil over medium heat until they become translucent, about 6 minutes, stirring frequently. Transfer to a soup pot and add the stock or water, ginger, chili, turmeric and coriander. Bring to a boil, reduce heat slightly and simmer for 6 to 7 minutes.

● Cut the fish into ³/₄-inch pieces and add to the soup. Cook for about 5 minutes until the fish is barely tender.

● Thoroughly rinse the spinach or arugula, and pick off larger stems. Add to the soup, then check seasonings, adding salt and pepper to taste. Serve into deep bowls, scatter on the fried onions and offer *sambal ulek* or other chili paste.

Warm Salad of Cuttlefish with Kaffir Lime

Makes 4 to 6 servings

Squid or baby octopus could be used here. Before I planted my own kaffir lime tree, I used dried leaves soaked for 20 minutes in hot water. Other aromatic citrus leaves, such as Jamaican lime or tangerine, give fairly pleasing results.

2 pounds fresh cuttlefish (1¼ pounds cleaned weight)

1½-inch piece fresh ginger

4 kaffir lime or other citrus leaves

2 fresh mild red chilies

2 tablespoons vegetable oil

1½ teaspoons palm or soft brown sugar

2 tablespoons fish sauce

1 tablespoon freshly squeezed lime juice

Salt and freshly ground black pepper

To Serve

4 to 5 good-sized handfuls of mesclun, or your choice of small-leaf salad greens tossed with a few teaspoons of light olive oil

Fresh basil and/or dill

Lime wedges

⊕ Place the prepared cuttlefish in a flat dish.

⊕ Grate the ginger onto a piece of clean cloth and squeeze the juice over the cuttlefish. Leave for 20 minutes to marinate.

⊕ Very, very finely shred the lime or citrus leaves, discarding the central rib. Slit open the chilies, scrape out the seeds and any loose internal fibers, then cut the chilies into very fine shreds.

⊕ Assemble rinsed and dried salad greens on plates, and set aside.

⊕ Heat the oil in a wok or skillet until a haze of smoke rises over the pan. Put in the cuttlefish strips and stir-fry for about 30 seconds. Add the lime leaves and chili shreds, the palm sugar and fish sauce and stir-fry just long enough for the sugar to dissolve. Add lime juice, salt and pepper to taste and remove from the heat.

⊕ Pile the cuttlefish onto the salad and garnish with dill or other herbs. Serve with a wedge of fresh lime.

Cleaning Cuttlefish and Squid

If you have to clean the cuttlefish, do so in the sink under running cold water. First pull the heads away from the tube-like bodies—this should also draw out the gut. Next pull out the white cuttle-bone and discard. Peel off the pink-gray skin from the bodies, then turn inside out and scrape off any of the white gelatinous substance remaining. Rinse well. Cut the cuttlefish bodies into narrow strips. Cut off the heads just above the eyes and ensure the hard "beak" has been cut away too. The ring of tentacles can be used in most dishes, cut them into smaller pieces if too large.

Crab and Coconut Salad

This recipe works quite well with surimi crab; in fact, I would prefer that to canned or inferior frozen crabmeat.

Make an interesting variation on this recipe by substituting a crunchy vegetable for the coconut. Try jícama, Japanese pear, unripe papaya or unripe mango sliced into fine shavings with a vegetable parer.

14 ounces fresh crabmeat

1 large yellow onion, or red salad onion

2 whole scallions

1 fresh large red medium-hot chili, seeded

6 large basil leaves

1 cup very finely sliced fresh coconut *

Dressing

2 tablespoons fish sauce

2 tablespoons fresh lime juice

2¹/₂ teaspoons sugar

1 clove garlic, very finely chopped

¹/₂ teaspoon chili oil

2¹/₂ tablespoons coconut cream

To Serve

Crisp lettuce leaves

Lime wedges

Sweet basil sprigs

Pick over the crabmeat to separate out any bits of cartilage or shell. Break up larger pieces of crabmeat, and place them in a bowl.

Peel the onion and slice very thin. If using a yellow onion, it is best to reduce its pungency by steeping the sliced onion in boiling water for 1 minute. Drain, refresh in cold water and drain again very thoroughly. Wrap in a kitchen towel and squeeze to remove excess water. Very finely slice the scallions, discarding some of the green tops. Cut the chili and basil into fine shreds. Add the onions, chili, basil and the coconut to the crabmeat, and mix together lightly.

To make the dressing, whisk the fish sauce, lime juice, sugar, garlic, chili oil and coconut cream together in a small bowl. Pour over the salad and toss for a few moments until evenly distributed.

To serve, line cocktail glasses or salad plates with lettuce and present the salad in a high mound, garnished with a lime wedge and sprig of basil.

* If fresh coconut is not available, you can use shredded coconut moistened with water or coconut cream.

Seafood Salad in a Tangy Green Dressing (Yam Thalay)

Makes 6 servings (3 to 4 as a main course)

I have combined several types of fish, plus shrimp and squid in my recipe, but it's fine with any one of them on their own, whatever is freshest of the day. As an appealing appetizer, chop the seafood finely and serve in a hollowed cucumber boat, or wrap in a lettuce leaf Chinese style to eat from the fingers.

6 ounces sea bass or snapper fillets

6 ounces John Dory or other firm, flat fish

6 ounces shelled shrimp

4 ounces cleaned squid (see sidebar, page 26)

2 tablespoons shredded sweet basil leaves

2 small white onions, or red salad onions

Lime and Herb Dressing

3 to 4 small green chilies, minced (seeded, if preferred)

4 cloves garlic, finely minced

2 cilantro (fresh coriander) roots and stems, finely minced

2 scallions, white parts only, finely sliced

3 tablespoons fish sauce

1 tablespoon sugar

3 tablespoons freshly squeezed lime juice

To Serve

Thinly sliced cucumber, or washed lettuce leaves

Garnish

2¹/₂ tablespoons chopped roasted peanuts

1 fresh red chili, cut into fine shreds

⊕ Cut the fish into ¹/₂-inch cubes. Devein the shrimp and cut them in half. Cut squid in half, place on a board and score the squid in a close crosshatch pattern, cutting deeply, but not right through.

⊕ Bring a small pot of water to a boil and salt it lightly. Cook the squid for 20 seconds, remove with a wire strainer and set aside. In the same water cook the shrimp for 2 minutes, then retrieve with the wire strainer and set aside.

⊕ Reduce the heat and gently simmer the fish for about 3 minutes, not allowing the water to boil. Remove and place with the other seafood to drain and cool.

⊕ In a bowl combine the chili, garlic, cilantro, scallions, fish sauce, sugar and lime juice. Mix well, then add the cooled seafood and toss lightly. At this point the salad can be covered with plastic wrap and refrigerated for up to 4 hours before serving.

⊕ A few minutes before serving, add the basil leaves and onions, and toss again lightly. Serve onto small plates, over a lettuce leaf or thinly sliced cucumber, and scatter on the peanuts and chili.

Issan Chicken Salad

In the northeast of Thailand, a garnish of roasted and coarsely ground glutinous (sticky) rice is sprinkled over salads and fish dishes. It adds a pleasing nutty taste and an interesting grainy, crunchy texture. This salad is one of the better examples of that cooking style, which is also used in parts of Laos. If you prefer, however, you can use chopped roasted peanuts, pinenuts or toasted sesame seeds instead of preparing roasted rice.

2¹/₂ tablespoons raw long-grain glutinous white rice

1¹/₄ pounds boneless, skinless chicken breasts

¹/₃ cup finely sliced shallot or Spanish onion

¹/₄ cup cilantro (fresh coriander) leaves

¹/₄ cup small mint leaves

Dressing

5 tablespoons freshly squeezed lime juice

3 tablespoons Thai fish sauce, or to taste

2 to 3 teaspoons chili flakes

1 teaspoon sugar

Garnish

Sliced limes

Chili "flowers" (see sidebar, page 31)

⊕ Heat a nonstick wok or heavy skillet without oil over medium heat. Pour in the rice and cook, shaking and stirring, until the rice is evenly cooked to a light golden brown. Pour into a mortar, allow to cool briefly, then pound to fine granules—it should not be reduced to a powder.

⊕ Use a cleaver, or the metal blade in a food processor, to chop the chicken into very small dice. Wipe out the pan and then cook the chicken on medium-high heat stirring it constantly so that it does not stick. It should become white and firm, but not acquire any color during cooking. Transfer to a mixing bowl and when it has partially cooled, add the dressing ingredients, half the ground rice, the shallots and herbs. Toss well and serve onto a plate. Surround with lime slices and decorate with chili "flowers." Sprinkle on the remaining rice. Serve at room temperature.

Kashmiri Chicken Chaat Salad

Makes 4 servings

Chili Flowers are a decorative garnish that are quite easy to make. Select a small, very sharp knife. Hold the chili by the stem and run the point of the knife the length of the chili from just above the base to the tip. Cut through the flesh, but not through the inner seed pod. Do this at close intervals, until the chili is completely cut into strips, which remain attached to the base of the chili. Gently open the "petals" and use your knife again to scrape off any internal fibers that cling to them. Release the seed core from any "petals" still attached to it. When done, place the chili in a dish of iced water. It will take at least a half hour for the petals to curl outwards to form the flower, and then they can be kept in the refrigerator for several days.

These tart and tangy salads are often served with a curry meal in the northern part of India. In the state of Kashmir, where small crisp apples are grown, cooks slice them into a chaat salad with crunchy salad vegetables and firm fleshed pears. The chaat masala can be made in advance and stored with your spices.

8 ounces cooked chicken (a mixture
    of light and dark meat)

2 medium tomatoes

2 hard-boiled eggs

1 small cucumber

1 to 2 green chilies, seeded and
    shredded

2 tablespoons fresh lemon juice

Sugar to taste

1 recipe chaat masala (page 247)

To make the salad, tear the chicken into shreds and place in a salad or serving bowl. Cut the tomatoes and eggs into wedges, and slice the cucumber. Combine in the bowl and scatter on the chilies. Combine lemon juice and *chaat masala* and add sugar to taste. Pour over the salad and let stand for 10 minutes before serving.

Thai Beef and Herb Salad

Makes 4 to 6 servings

1 large clove garlic, mashed with
   ⅓ teaspoon salt

1 pound fillet or rump steak

2 tablespoons vegetable oil

2 yellow or red salad onions

1 cucumber

1 small green bell pepper, stem and
   seed core removed

4 red shallots

Dressing

2 to 4 cloves garlic

½ stem lemon grass, trimmed of
   outer tough leaves

1 to 2 hot red chilies, seeded and
   stemmed

1 small bunch fresh mint, stems
   removed

4 tablespoons fish sauce

5 tablespoons freshly squeezed lime
   juice

3 to 4 teaspoons sugar

½ teaspoon cracked black pepper

⊕ Rub the garlic and salt evenly over the steak. Heat a cast-iron pan over high heat. Sear the steak until well browned on both sides. It should remain quite rare internally. Remove and set aside on a plate.

⊕ Very finely mince the garlic, lemon grass and chilies with a sharp knife or Chinese cleaver, or chop finely in a food processor. In a small bowl, combine them with the mint leaves, fish sauce, lime juice, sugar and pepper. A good whisk of this dressing will help to release and amalgamate the flavors. Very thinly slice the beef and then cut it into strips about 2 inches long × ¾ inch wide. Pour the dressing over the beef and cover with plastic wrap. Chill for at least 20 minutes before assembling the salad to serve.

⊕ Peel the onions, trim the top and bottom flat, and use the point of a sharp knife to slice them into thin wedges. Separate them and set aside. Peel the cucumber and use a vegetable carving tool to score grooves along its length. Cut lengthways in half and scoop out the seeds, if you prefer, then cut into thin slices. Peel the shallots and slice very thin lengthways. Cut the pepper in half, then cut into matchstick pieces.

⊕ Mix the salad vegetables together and spread over a serving platter.

⊕ Arrange the marinated beef over the salad and serve at once.

Pork and Peanut Salad

Makes 6 servings

1¼ pounds ground (minced) lean
    pork

1 tablespoon fish sauce

½ teaspoon salt

2 tablespoons vegetable oil

6 ounces green beans or asparagus,
    diagonally sliced

1 to 2 fresh large mild red chilies,
    seeded and thinly sliced

2 medium salad onions, thinly sliced

6 to 8 thin slices tender fresh young
    ginger, cut into fine shreds *

12 large mint or basil leaves,
    shredded

12 sprigs cilantro (fresh coriander)

½ to 1 teaspoon chili flakes

2 tablespoons fish sauce

3 tablespoons freshly squeezed lime
    juice

Sugar

3 tablespoons chopped roasted
    peanuts

To Serve

Crisp lettuce leaves

Season the pork with fish sauce and salt. Heat the oil in a wok or skillet and stir-fry for about 4 minutes, until lightly cooked. Remove and spread on a plate to cool.

Bring a small pan of salted water to a boil and cook the beans or asparagus for 2 to 2½ minutes, until crisp-tender. Drain and refresh under running cold water, then drain well. Combine the pork and beans or asparagus in a mixing bowl with the chili, onions, shallots, ginger, the herbs, and the chili flakes.

In another bowl, combine the fish sauce and lime juice to make a dressing, adding sugar to taste. Pour over the salad. Allow to marinate for at least 20 minutes before mixing in the roast peanuts. To serve, place one or two lettuce leaves on each plate and mound the salad over them. Garnish with sprigs of fresh mint or basil and place a small wedge of lemon or lime on each plate.

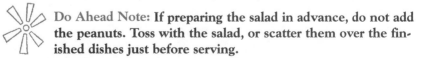 Do Ahead Note: **If preparing the salad in advance, do not add the peanuts. Toss with the salad, or scatter them over the finished dishes just before serving.**

* If you cannot buy young ginger, use only 2 to 3 slices, cut into very fine shreds.

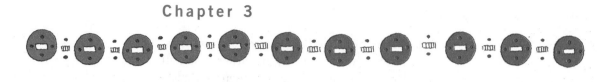

Chapter 3

Other First Flavors

Hot and Crunchy Fried Shrimp

Squid in Citrus Soy Sauce

Oyster Hot Shots

Cambodian Mussels

Panfried Sardines in Red Chili Sauce

Scallops on the Shell with Black Bean, Garlic
and Chili Oil Dressing

Malaysian Chili and Herb Omelet

Java Eggs

Sumatran Chicken Livers

Little Chicken Bites

"Bang Bang" Chicken

Peppered Duck Served over Pickled Vegetables

Pepper and Salt Pork

Golden Tofu with Spicy Peanut and Sweet
Chili Sauces

Chili—the Fruit of Fire

Chilies add zap and sparkle to dishes from almost every cuisine in Asia. They're mad about them, but it wasn't always that way. In earlier times, all they had for heat was pepper. When fifteenth-century Portuguese traders brought New World produce to the marketplaces of their protectorates spaced strategically throughout the Far East, it was chilies that led the onslaught, revolutionizing many of the cuisines of Asia. India appreciated this fiery new fruit, particularly in the vegetarian southern states where they like their food hot enough to blister the tongue. Even though the curries of the Punjab and the north are far less intense than southern Tamil fare, you'll still find strands of chilies drying in doorways and scarlet mounds of chili powder in every market, amongst a multicolored array of spices. Sri Lankans, true aficionados of the chili, think nothing of tossing thirty or so chilies into a single pot of curry. If you can still talk after eating one of these, you'll have to admit they know what they're doing when it comes to balancing heat with flavor. The effect is searing, yet supremely palatable.

The Chinese weren't entirely captivated by the chili. They went wild for it in Sichuan, making chili a favored seasoning after their own native pepper, but the Shanghainese retained a preference for white pepper. Cautious Cantonese prefer the chili's milder cousin, the bell pepper (capsicum), using just the occasional sprinkle of chili oil when they want to brighten up a dish. In China's far north, Mongolian cooks aren't adverse to a hint of chili, but would never take it to the extremes their Korean neighbors do. There, chili is a passion that warms the soul, and fires up the heart.

In Indonesia, they enjoy chili, but don't necessarily lavish it into their cooking. Theirs is the sensible approach, having chili on the side, to add to individual taste. This they do in the form of *sambals*, peppy relishes to spoon on beside the dish so you can incorporate a speck or a spoonful into every bite. Malaysians like their curries hot, and might use chili powder, a hot curry powder or paste, and fresh chilies, in a single dish. Thai cooks, similarly, add chilies with apparent abandon to achieve a heat factor bordering on the incendiary. The minuscule "bird's eye" or "bird" chili is the chili that distinguishes Thai dishes from those of her neighbors. These microscopic heat bombs have been affectionately dubbed "SCUDs," and can do to your palate the equivalent damage to what their military namesake might do an enemy encampment, with one quick and accurate hit. Several times in Thailand I've been served a dish in which chilies outweigh the other ingredients. You're not necessarily challenged to eat them all, but they'll be very impressed if you do (see my solution, page 13).

Singaporeans don't usually cook with chili, but they wouldn't serve a meal without it. The chili sauce bottle is a permanent fixture on the table, and dunking into a dip of fresh green chili sliced into soy sauce (page 255) is the only way to enjoy boiled shrimp. In Asia they eat chilies to warm the blood, stave off colds and flu, combat excesses of alcohol, but mostly they eat them because they make food taste sensational.

Fresh chilies, green and red, hot and mild, are added for color, heat and flavor. They can be simply plopped in whole, or minced, mashed, sliced or shredded as the recipe dictates. To decrease the heat factor, slit them open and scrape out the seeds and internal fibers. (Protect your hands with latex gloves before you begin, and when you remove them turn the gloves inside out to avoid contact with the potent oils they will have picked up.) Dried chilies acquire a subtle flavor change compared to fresh. Use them dry in curry powders, or rehydrate to use in curry pastes and other "wet" seasonings. Chop or slice them, or add them whole to slow-cooked dishes. Again, to decrease their potency, break them open and shake out the seeds. Chili flakes are coarsely ground dried chilies, together with their seeds. Chili pastes and chili sauces take many forms, varying from thick to thin, smooth to textured, and mild to potentially dangerous. This is a case of knowing what you're working with, and nothing beats a cautious taste (see also *sambal ulek* and Sichuan sauce, pages 8 and 254). Store chili pastes in the refrigerator, and to prolong life, smooth the top and cover with a film of oil to prevent oxidation. Chili oil is a favorite of the Chinese chef. It's the perfect way to add a hint of chili heat to a stir fry, and makes a perky dip for a *dim sum*. An infusion of vegetable oil with hot chili, it's sold in small shaker bottles. Roasted chili powder is a condiment used by Thai chefs bent on extending the chili experience to every level of the palate. They panroast finely ground dried chilies until they are dark and aromatic; it's easy enough to do. For added flavor dimensions, they may include salt and finely ground dried shrimp or shrimp paste. Incorporating a touch of garlic and vegetable oil to moisten makes roasted chili paste, which can be used as a powerful seasoning or a condiment to serve at the table.

The flavor intensity and heat factor of chilies varies markedly. Even two identical plants, grown under different soil and climatic conditions, will bear fruit of dissimilar taste and hotness. Ask your greengrocer for advice when purchasing. To keep it simple for the purpose of these recipes, I have specified chilies by heat and size, small to large, mild to hot. So be guided by your own taste preference. We have aimed for a high-heat tolerance, but if you need to play it safe use less, or if you want it hotter, simply add more! To make your choice easier, see my chili guide, page 10.

Hot and Crunchy Fried Shrimp

Makes 6 to 8 servings

Rice flour gives these spicy marinated shrimp a coating that emerges from the frying oil crunchy, crisp and golden. Serve them on lettuce leaves, with lime halves for squeezing and a choice of hot and sweet-hot sauces (pages 104 and 78) for dipping.

1½ pounds fresh shrimp in their shells

1 cup rice flour

3 to 4 cups oil for deep frying

Marinade

2 red shallots, peeled

1 large clove garlic, peeled

1-inch piece galangal or fresh ginger, peeled

1 to 2 fresh medium-hot red chilies, seeded and stemmed

1½ inches lemon grass

2 cilantro (fresh coriander) roots

4 to 5 sprigs cilantro (fresh coriander), stems discarded

1-inch piece kaffir lime rind, fresh or dried

1 teaspoon shrimp paste

1 teaspoon salt

½ teaspoon freshy ground white pepper

1 tablespoon freshly squeezed lime juice

3 tablespoons coconut cream

⊕ Shell the shrimp, leaving their tails intact if you like. Cut deeply along the center back of each shrimp and remove the dark vein. Rinse under running cold water and drain. Place in a flat dish.

⊕ To make the marinade, into the small bowl of a food processor fitted with the metal blade, or into a blender or spice grinder, place the shallots, garlic, *galangal* or ginger, chilies, lemon grass, cilantro roots and sprigs and lime rind and grind to a semi-fine paste. Add the shrimp paste, salt and pepper and grind briefly, then add the lime juice and coconut cream and process or grind just long enough to mix everything together, scraping the sides of the bowl. Pour the marinade over the shrimp and cover with plastic wrap. Refrigerate for at least 30 minutes.

⊕ Heat the deep frying oil in a wok or a deep pan suitable for frying, until the oil reaches medium-hot, 350°F.

⊕ Drain the shrimp well and coat with the rice flour. Place in the oil to fry until they are golden brown and the surface crisp. Turn once or twice during cooking, then remove and drain on paper towels. Serve within a few minutes.

Squid in Citrus Soy Sauce

Makes 4 to 6 servings

Flash-cooked squid is supremely tender. Plan your meal so this can go straight to the table!

6 large fresh cleaned squid, approximately 1¼ pounds

½ cup Japanese mirin (sweet rice wine)

2 tablespoons butter

2 tablespoons vegetable oil

½ cup Japanese dashi stock (pages 6–7)

1 to 1½ teaspoons chili flakes

1 tablespoon fresh lemon juice

2 tablespoons low-sodium soy sauce

1½ teaspoons sugar

1 to 2 bunches arugula, rinsed and drained (optional)

1 fresh medium-hot red chili, cut into very fine shreds

2 scallions (green parts only), cut into very fine shreds

1 carrot, cut into very fine shreds

Peel of 1 lemon, cut into very fine shreds

1 tablespoon pink preserved ginger

⊕ Cut the squid into ⅓-inch slices (rings), turn the rings inside out and rinse thoroughly. Dry thoroughly on paper towels.

⊕ In a small saucepan, boil the *mirin* until reduced almost by half.

⊕ Heat the butter and oil in a sauté pan over medium-high heat and cook the squid, stirring, for 15 seconds and not more. Remove from the pan and pour off half of the butter and oil. Add the reduced *mirin* and bring to a boil, stirring. Cook for 30 seconds, then add the stock and chili flakes, and boil another 30 seconds.

⊕ Add the lemon juice, soy sauce and sugar and simmer for a further 30 seconds. Return the squid and warm briefly in the sauce.

⊕ Arrange a few arugula leaves in the center of each warmed plate. Place the squid on top, mounding it high and cover with the shredded ingredients. Spoon over any sauce remaining in the pan and serve at once.

Oyster Hot Shots

Makes 12

Dedicated oyster and chili lovers will enjoy these potent oysters, served in shot glasses. When I'm doing a casual lunch in my garden, I offer just a single one of these, well iced, once all of my guests have assembled.

1 dozen fresh oysters

¼ teaspoon chili oil

⅓ teaspoon Tabasco

1 teaspoon dark soy sauce

1 teaspoon fish sauce

2 tablespoons iced vodka

1 tablespoon freshly squeezed lime juice

¼ cup well-chilled tomato or V8 juice

Remove the oysters from their shells, rinse briefly in cold water, and place each one in a small shot glass. In a glass bowl or jug combine the remaining ingredients. Pour over the oysters and serve at once.

Cambodian Mussels

Makes 6 servings

This is my interpretation of a cold dish I discovered in Cambodia, at a tiny street side food stall which sold nothing but these delicious mussels covered with chopped fresh herbs. Your guests are in for a special treat if you can find fresh or even frozen mussels in the shell to cook and serve this way. If you can't, shelled mussels make this a quick and easy dish that is just as impressive.

Mussels

36 fresh mussels in their shells

2 scallions (green and white parts)

1 thick slice fresh ginger

1 teaspoon salt

Dressing

3 cloves garlic, very finely minced

1 stem lemon grass, very finely minced

1 fresh hot red chili, seeded and very finely minced

3 thin slices galangal or fresh ginger, very finely minced

2 kaffir lime or other lime leaves, very finely shredded

2 teaspoons cilantro (fresh coriander) roots, very finely minced

3 teaspoons cilantro (fresh coriander) stems and leaves, very finely minced

1 3/4 tablespoons fish sauce

2 tablespoons freshly squeezed lime or lemon juice

1 teaspoon sugar

2 teaspoons Thai sweet chili sauce

Garnish

Finely shredded lettuce

2 tablespoons roasted peanuts, chopped

36 cilantro (fresh coriander) leaves, or small basil leaves

36 small strips of medium or mild red chili

36 small strips of lemon peel

⊕ If you are using mussels in their shells, place them in a large saucepan and add 1 cup of water, 1 teaspoon salt and the scallions and ginger. Cover and bring to a boil. Reduce heat and cook until the shells open, shaking the pan frequently to encourage opening and to expedite cooking.

⊕ Remove the pan from the heat and drain the mussels. To remove the top shell, hold in a cloth, twist off the the top shell and discard.

⊕ Slide the blade of a knife beneath each mussel to loosen it in its shell, then pull off the "beards" that attach to any of them. Allow them to cool. They will be served at room temperature, but you may chill them under plastic wrap in the refrigerator, if you prefer.

⊕ To make the dressing, prepare the ingredients and whisk together in a small bowl.

⊕ When ready to serve, arrange the mussels on side plates over shredded lettuce, six to a serving, or take to the center of the table on one large platter, decorated lavishly with chili "flowers" (page 31) and sprigs of cilantro. Cover each mussel with dressing. Decorate each mussel with a few chopped peanuts, a cilantro or small basil leaf and a strip each of chili and lemon peel.

Panfried Sardines in Red Chili Sauce

Fresh sardines, anchovies and fillets of fresh mackerel cut into finger-thick slices are all strongly flavored and oily enough to challenge this potent sauce.

Fish

18 to 24 small fresh sardines,
  cleaned

1 teaspoon salt

3 tablespoons all-purpose flour

1 cup vegetable oil

1 large onion, sliced

Sauce

1 cup coconut cream

6 dried red chilies, soaked in hot
  water for 20 minutes

4 cloves garlic

4 thin slices fresh ginger

1/2 teaspoon shrimp paste

1 stem lemon grass, trimmed and
  chopped

4 cilantro (fresh coriander) roots

2 to 3 teaspoons vegetable or
  coconut oil

1 teaspoon sweet paprika

2 teaspoons tomato paste

1/4 cup water

Garnish

Lemon wedges

Sprigs of cilantro (fresh coriander)

● Prepare the sauce before you cook the fish. Pour the coconut cream into a medium saucepan and simmer for about 15 minutes until it has reduced by about one-third and it has released a film of oil to float on the surface. Set aside.

● Drain the chilies and place in a blender, food processor fitted with the metal blade, or spice grinder with the garlic, ginger, shrimp paste, lemon grass and cilantro roots. Process to a coarse paste. Fry for 2 to 3 minutes in 2 to 3 teaspoons of the oil, stirring constantly, then add to the reduced coconut cream, adding also the paprika, tomato paste and water. Bring to a boil, then reduce to a simmer and cook for about 5 minutes, until thick and very aromatic. Keep the sauce warm while the fish is cooking.

Season the sardines with salt and coat lightly with flour. Heat the oil in a skillet or wok and fry the sliced onion until very well browned and beginning to crisp. Remove with a slotted spoon and drain on paper towels.

 Slip the sardines into the oil, cooking in two batches so the pan is not crowded. Cook over medium-high heat for about 2$\frac{1}{2}$ minutes, until golden and cooked through. Remove from the oil and drain briefly on paper towels.

 To serve, place three to four sardines on each plate, spoon over the sauce and scatter some of the fried onions over the top. Garnish with cilantro and serve with wedges of lemon.

Note: If you prefer, brush the sardines with oil, season sparingly with salt and pepper and cook on a barbecue or in a nonstick pan.

Scallops on the Shell with Black Bean, Garlic and Chili Oil Dressing

Makes 6 servings

If you can't buy scallops on the shell, use the tiny Chinese saucers or ramekins.

24 fresh scallops in the shell
8 thin slices fresh ginger
1 small bunch cilantro (fresh coriander)

1 tablespoon Chinese cooking (rice) wine or rice vinegar

Black Bean, Garlic and Chili Oil Dressing

3 teaspoons Chinese salted black beans
1 teaspoon finely chopped fresh ginger
1 teaspoon finely chopped garlic
1½ tablespoons very finely chopped red bell pepper

2 teaspoons very finely chopped seeded green or hot red chili
1 teaspoon light soy sauce
⅓ cup vegetable or light corn oil
Salt and freshly ground black pepper, to taste

Garnish

Sprigs of fresh herbs (basil, cilantro, dill, etc.)

⊕ Combine the dressing ingredients in a small saucepan and place over high heat. When the ingredients begin to simmer, remove from the heat and set aside to infuse for at least 20 minutes.

⊕ Scrub and rinse the scallops under running cold water. Place the ginger, cilantro and cooking wine or vinegar in the bottom of a large steamer and pour in several cups of water. Arrange the scallops on the steamer rack and set in place in the steamer. Cover and set over medium-high heat.

⊕ Cook until the shells have opened, then lift the scallops from the steamer. Remove and discard the top shells, drain liquid from the scallops and return them to the steamer rack. Place a spoonful of the sauce on each scallop and steam for 2 to 3 minutes, until the scallops are done. Serve on the shell onto large dinner plates, four to six scallops to a serving. Garnish the center of the plate with a small bunch of fresh herbs.

Malaysian Chili and Herb Omelet

Makes 4 servings

This is an easy start to a meal, and makes a tasty lunch or supper for two, supported by a salad and bread, or even rice. I sometimes make this for myself for breakfast, and if none of the family join me, save the leftovers to eat cold, sandwiched into a crusty roll for lunch.

6 large eggs

1 teaspoon sesame oil

1¹/₂ teaspoons vegetable oil

2 scallions (green and white parts), finely chopped

1 clove garlic, minced

1 large mild green chili, seeded and minced

1 tablespoon chopped cilantro (fresh coriander)

1 tablespoon chopped basil

1 tablespoon chopped celery leaves

¹/₃ teaspoon salt

2 teaspoons light soy sauce

¹/₄ teaspoon sugar

To Serve

Sprigs of fresh herbs

Hot chili sauce

⊕ Lightly beat the eggs in a bowl. Prepare all of the other ingredients and set aside.

⊕ Heat an omelet pan, or a medium nonstick pan and moisten with the sesame and vegetable oils. Cook the scallions and garlic, stirring, over medium-high heat for 1 minute. Add the remaining ingredients to the beaten egg, mix well, then pour into the pan, stirring to distribute the scallions evenly.

⊕ Cook over medium heat without stirring, until the underside is golden brown, then turn and cook the other side. To make this easier, cut the omelet in quarters before turning.

⊕ To serve, cut each quarter in half and serve on warmed plates, garnished with fresh herbs and with a spoonful of hot chili sauce on the side.

Java Eggs

Soften the pungency of this fiery sauce by serving over rice, or with a small salad of cucumber or pineapple with chopped mint. In Indonesia, potent dishes like this often accompany the main-course dishes. I think I first tasted this at a magnificent Rijstaffel banquet in Bali. Dishes from all over Indonesia were introduced in a huge menu of around 30 courses, presented by a line of sarong-clad waiters.

9 large eggs

1 large onion, finely chopped

2 cups vegetable oil

4 cloves garlic, minced

2 teaspoons minced fresh ginger

1 ounce dried shrimp, soaked in hot water for 20 minutes

5 dried red chilies, soaked in hot water for 20 minutes

1 tablespoon ground coriander

2 cardamom pods, lightly crushed

1 cinnamon stick

3/4 teaspoon ground turmeric

1/2 teaspoon freshly ground black pepper

1/3 teaspoon anise or caraway seeds, lightly crushed

2 medium tomatoes, peeled and seeded

1 1/3 cups coconut milk

Garnish

2 tablespoons Crisp-Fried Shallots or Garlic (see sidebar)

Sprigs of cilantro (fresh coriander)

Chili flakes

⊕ Place the eggs in a saucepan, cover with cold water and bring slowly to a boil. Cook for 8 minutes, then remove from the heat and place under running water to cool. When they are almost cold, peel them carefully and set aside.

⊕ Heat 2 tablespoons of the oil in a wok or skillet over medium heat and cook the onions, stirring, for 4 minutes, to a light golden brown. Add the garlic and ginger and cook another 1 minute, stirring frequently.

⊕ In the meantime, drain and dry the shrimp and chilies and grind to a paste in a mortar, blender, food processor fitted with the metal blade, or a spice grinder. Add to the pan and cook for 1 minute, again stirring frequently. Then add the spices and cook for about 20 seconds.

Crisp-Fried Shallots and Garlic

Crunchy slivers of golden-brown fried shallots or garlic are featured as a dressing on dishes in several Southeast Asian cuisines. They are simple to make, though require close attention to prevent burning in the final few minutes of cooking.

Peel shallots, garlic cloves or small onions. Slice them finely, preferably lengthways. Heat a pan of oil for deep frying, and fry them until they have turned a rich golden brown. You will need to keep them moving in the oil, so they cook evenly. When done, drain on paper towels until cold. They should become very crisp and dry. Store in an airtight jar until needed; they will keep for several weeks.

❀ Next add the tomatoes and increase the heat slightly. Cook for 2 minutes, while stirring and mashing the tomatoes with a wooden spoon to break them up. Pour in the coconut milk and continue to cook, without allowing it to come to a boil, until the sauce is thick and very aromatic, about 10 minutes.

❀ The eggs are deep fried before simmering in the sauce. Heat the remaining oil to reasonably hot in a wok or a pan suited to deep frying. Ensure the eggs are dry on the surface, and carefully place in the oil to fry until their surface is golden and bubbly. Remove with a slotted spoon and drain.

❀ Cut the eggs in half lengthways, or into wedges, and heat gently in the sauce for a few minutes. If necessary, moisten the sauce with a little warm water.

❀ To serve, place two or three pieces of egg on a plate, sprinkle with crisp-fried onion or garlic and garnish with herbs.

Sumatran Chicken Livers

Makes 6 servings

1 pound chicken livers

1 tablespoon light soy sauce

1 large onion, minced

3 cloves garlic, minced

3 thin slices fresh ginger, minced

3 tablespoons vegetable oil

1 stem lemon grass, very finely chopped

2 fresh medium-hot red chilies, seeded and chopped

3/4 teaspoon shrimp paste

1/2 teaspoon ground turmeric

1 tablespoon ground coriander

1 1/2 tablespoons sweet soy sauce (kecap manis)

1/2 teaspoon palm or soft brown sugar

1 to 2 teaspoons sambal ulek or other chili paste/sauce

1/4 cup chopped roasted peanuts

To Serve

1 large cucumber, seeded and very thinly sliced

Small wedges of flatbread, crisped in the oven

Cut the livers into bite-sized pieces and place in a shallow dish. Sprinkle on the soy sauce and set aside for 7 to 8 minutes. Heat a wok or skillet over medium-high heat and add the vegetables and oil.

Stir-fry the onion, garlic, ginger and lemon grass for about 1 1/2 minutes. Increase the heat, add the chicken livers and stir-fry until they are lightly browned, about 1 1/2 minutes.

Add the chilies, shrimp paste and spices and stir-fry on the same high heat for about 1 minute, before adding the sweet soy sauce, sugar and *sambal ulek*. Stir-fry for a further 40 seconds, then add most of the peanuts and heat through, stirring continually.

Serve the hot livers over a bed of cucumbers sliced paper thin or cut into julienne. Or serve with wedges of flatbread crisped in the oven, brushed with sesame oil and seasoned with salt. Scatter the remaining peanuts over the top.

Little Chicken Bites

Makes 24 servings

8 ounces boneless and skinless
    chicken meat

2 scallions (white part only), finely
    minced

1 clove garlic, minced

1 teaspoon grated fresh ginger

1/2 hot green chili, seeded and minced

2 ounces water chestnuts or jicama,
    minced

2 teaspoons light soy sauce

1/3 teaspoon salt

1/3 teaspoon white pepper

6 small green beans

1 1/2 cups vegetable oil

1 teaspoon sesame oil (optional)

⊕ Cut the chicken into cubes. Place in a food processor fitted with the metal blade. Process, using the pulse control, until the chicken is reduced to a smooth paste. Add the other ingredients, except the beans and oils and process just long enough to mix together. Use a very sharp knife to cut the beans into paper-thin slices. Fold into the chicken mixture.

⊕ Heat the vegetable oil in a wide skillet or pan over medium heat. Add the sesame oil, if using. With oiled hands form the mixture into walnut-sized balls, flattening them slightly. Cook about twelve at a time (so as not to crowd the pan) until golden brown underneath, then turn and cook the other side. They will need to cook for at least 3 minutes to ensure they are cooked right through.

⊕ Remove from the oil and set on paper towels for a few minutes to drain. As a canape, serve little chicken bites on toothpicks with a spicy chili sauce for dipping; as a first course, serve four to a plate, with a portion of marinated cucumber (page 130) and a little hot chili sauce, or with a fresh tomato sauce spiced up with chili.

"Bang Bang" Chicken

Makes 6 servings as a first course, 4 as a main with other shared dishes

This classic Chinese banquet "small dish" is particularly enjoyed in Sichuan province, where their appreciation of hot and spicy foods is legendary.

The name came from the Chinese technique of 'banging' the cooked chicken with a wooden stick to soften the fibers.

14 ounces steamed or roasted
     chicken breast meat*

Sauce Dip

1 tablespoon minced scallion greens

2 tablespoons sesame paste (tahini)

1 1/2 tablespoons light soy sauce

1 teaspoon sugar

1/2 to 1 1/2 teaspoons chili oil

1 teaspoon sesame oil

1/2 teaspoon Chinese black vinegar

2 tablespoons water

Salt to taste

Large pinch of Sichuan pepper
     (ground Sichuan peppercorns)

Garnish

Sprigs of cilantro (fresh coriander)

1 1/2 cups finely sliced cucumber

1 1/2 cups finely shredded or grated
     daikon (giant white/icicle radish)

⊕ Remove the skin from the chicken breast, then beat it with a meat mallet, rolling pin or piece of dowel to flatten and tenderize it, before tearing it into strips with the fingers.

⊕ Pile the shredded chicken onto a small plate and decorate it with the cilantro, cucumber and radish. Cover and chill for a few minutes.

⊕ Combine the sauce dip ingredients and mix thoroughly. Add a little extra water, if ncessary, to make a creamy sauce. Spoon the sauce evenly over the chicken just before serving, or serve it in small dishes for dipping.

For this dish to be very good, the chicken must be moist. A Chinese cook would poach or steam it after brushing with oil and a squeeze of ginger juice.

Peppered Duck Served over Pickled Vegetables

Makes 4 to 6 servings

A crisp and spicy duck dish from Sichuan province in China was the inspiration for what has become a favorite dish in our household. I usually buy two whole ducks, and use the breasts for this dish, freezing the remainder for use when I want to make the Red Duck Curry with Lychees on page 133.

Duck

4 portions duck breast, each about 4 ounces

1 tablespoon light soy sauce

1 tablespoon Chinese cooking (rice) wine, sake or 2 teaspoons brandy

2 teaspoons grated fresh ginger

2 teaspoons Chinese five-spice powder

³/₄ teaspoon Sichuan pepper (ground Sichuan peppercorns)

1¹/₂ teaspoon freshly ground black pepper

1 teaspoon salt

Pickled Vegetables

4 ounces pickled shallots

2 to 3 ounces sweet pickled garlic

2 to 3 ounces pink pickled ginger

1 small bunch cilantro (fresh coriander)

2 to 3 scallions (green and white parts)

Lettuce or small salad leaves

Dressing

1 tablespoon vegetable oil

1 tablespoon sesame oil

1 tablespoon dark soy sauce

2 teaspoons very finely minced seeded medium-hot red chili

1 teaspoon sugar

⊕ Trim the duck breasts to remove as much fat as possible. Leave the skin on for better flavor, or remove if guilt intervenes. Rub with the soy sauce, wine or brandy and the juice obtained by squeezing the grated ginger in a clean cloth. Set aside for 20 minutes to marinate.

⊕ Preheat the oven to 450°F. Pat the duck breasts with paper towels to remove excess moisture.

⊕ Combine the three kinds of pepper and the salt and sprinkle evenly over the duck breasts, then place them in the oven tray, skin side up.

⊕ Roast for 20 minutes. When done, they should ideally be quite rare, but allow extra cooking time if preferred. Remove from the oven and set aside to cool and firm.

⊕ Slice the pickled shallots and garlic lengthways. Rinse the cilantro and cut the stems short. Cut the scallions into 2-inch lengths, then shred them finely lengthways.

⊕ Spread the cilantro and scallions on plates over the salad leaves, then pile the pickled vegetables, including the ginger, in the center. Cut the duck breasts into very thin slices and fan over the vegetables.

⊕ Whisk the dressing ingredients together and pour over the duck just before serving.

 Note: **Peppered duck is wonderful served Peking Duck style, wrapped in thin crepes with hoisin sauce and scallions.**

Pepper and Salt Pork

Makes 6 to 8 servings

This crunchy pork is a favorite on many Chinese menus. It can be made from small pork chops or pork ribs with a generous layer of meat.

2 pounds pork chops or meaty pork ribs

2 tablespoons light soy sauce

1 large clove garlic, mashed

1½ cups cornstarch

4 to 5 cups vegetable or peanut oil

2 large hot red chilies, seeded and chopped

3 scallions, trimmed and chopped

2 cloves garlic, chopped

Spiced Salt

2½ tablespoons kosher or fine salt

2½ teaspoons Chinese five-spice
    powder

1 teaspoon Sichuan peppercorns,
    ground

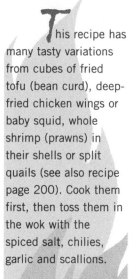

This recipe has many tasty variations from cubes of fried tofu (bean curd), deep-fried chicken wings or baby squid, whole shrimp (prawns) in their shells or split quails (see also recipe page 200). Cook them first, then toss them in the wok with the spiced salt, chilies, garlic and scallions.

To Serve

Finely shredded lettuce, or crisp-fried
    rice vermicelli

Sprigs of cilanto (fresh coriander)

⊕ Use a Chinese cleaver or heavy knife to cut the chops or ribs into 1½-inch pieces. Place in a single layer in a wide, shallow dish.

⊕ Combine the soy sauce and garlic, spread over the ribs, stir with a wooden spoon to mix in evenly, then set aside for 1 hour, turning several times. Remove from the dish and pat with paper towels to absorb moisture.

⊕ In a wok or deep pan, heat deep frying oil to very hot. Divide the pork into three batches. Place one batch in a strong plastic or paper bag with the cornstarch. Shake the bag vigorously, holding it tightly closed, to lightly and evenly coat the pork. Pour into a colander and shake to remove excess cornstarch. Return the cornstarch to the bag and coat the other batches.

⊕ Put one batch of the pork into the hot oil to fry for about 6 minutes. Cook the remaining pork in the same way. Pour the oil from the wok or pan. Rinse the pan and dry thoroughly before returning to the heat. Pour in the salt and when it is well heated, add the spice powder and Sichuan pepper and mix well. Immediately remove the pan from the heat, then after a few seconds, pour the spiced salt into a bowl to cool.

⊕ Add 2 to 3 tablespoons of the oil to the wok and fry the chilies, scallions and garlic until crisp, about 2½ minutes. Return the pork and stir with the chilies until it is well warmed. Add one-third of the spiced salt and stir to distribute it evenly.

⊕ Pile the pork ribs onto a warmed serving plate over shredded lettuce or crisp-fried noodles. Serve the remaining salt separately, for dipping.

Golden Tofu with Spicy Peanut and Sweet Chili Sauces

Makes 6 servings

Golden batons of fried tofu, with a dressing of creamy peanut supplemented by Thai sweet chili sauce, make a great platter of finger food for a party. As a first course, serve them with a crunchy Asian-style salad, recipe below, or a stir-fry of Napa cabbage, green beans and sliced carrot. Enjoy them also as a vegetarian main course.

14 ounces fresh tofu (bean curd)*	**1 recipe Peanut Sauce (page 252)**
3 cups vegetable oil	**1/4 to 1/3 cup Thai sweet chili sauce**

Salad

1 small bunch baby bok choy leaves	**2 whole scallions, shredded**
2 small bunches young arugula leaves	**2 teaspoons fresh lime juice**
1 1/2 cups fresh bean sprouts, blanched, drained and refreshed in cold water	**1 1/2 teaspoons sesame oil**
	Salt and freshly ground black pepper

⊕ Combine the salad ingredients in a bowl and set aside. Prepare the peanut sauce, allowing time for it to cool before serving. It should be the consistency of cream; thin with extra water or coconut cream if necessary.

⊕ Cut the tofu into batons about 1/2-inch thick, 1-inch wide and 1 1/2-inches long. Sit them on paper towels to drain while the oil is heating in a wok or large pan.

⊕ Carefully slide the tofu into the oil to fry for about 3 minutes, turning several times. The surface should be crisp and golden. Remove to a rack covered with paper towels to drain.

⊕ To serve as finger food, cover a platter with paper napkins or finely shredded lettuce. Set small bowls of the peanut and sweet chili sauce on the platter and pile the tofu beside them. As a first course, mound the salad (or stir-fried vegetables) in the center of salad plates and arrange the tofu over it. Spoon the peanut sauce over the tofu, and drizzle on the sweet chili sauce.

* When buying the tofu, select one with a slightly firm texture.

Chapter 4

More First Flavors And Great Party Foods

Versatile Small Eats that are Wrapped, Battered, Stuffed, Skewered and Dipped

Sizzling in Sichuan

You need an iron-clad digestive system to survive a lengthy stay in China's Sichuan province. It's not only the chilies which they lavish into just about everything, but also the intricate layering of powerful flavors. Sichuan cooking is structured on a seven-flavor principle. Chili for heat, bean pastes and sauces for intensity, garlic for pungency, ginger for brightness, black vinegar for depth, sugar and richly nutty sesame to smooth and bind everything together. And the magic ingredient? Pass the pepper shaker please! Sichuan peppercorn (more on pages 180–81) is not as hot as common pepper, but has a subtle pepperiness with a hint of lemon and anise. It's the astringency that catches out the unwary, leaving them numb-lipped and gasping. Its effect on a dish is sensational. Chefs love it so much they are not content to merely cook with it, but must crust the surface of a dish with powdered pepper, for good measure. You learn to deal with it, after a few excess-induced near disasters render you speechless and panicking about throat constriction. You learn to never be first to help yourself from the communal plate, and thus end up with most of it in your bowl. You learn to stir the contents of your bowl, dispersing it evenly before you begin eating. And you learn to resist the urge to add more, if pepper is offered at the table.

To travel and eat in Sichuan is to challenge all of your senses. It's exhilarating, challenging, exhausting, invigorating. I've never tried to do more than five days at a stretch, and I know from my last visit there that I won't return in midsummer, unless I'm going high into the mountains where the air is cooler—and where exotic mushrooms and game beasts dominate the cuisine.

Sichuan is a natural basin bounded in the north and west by towering ranges, and looped to south and east by the raging Yangtze River. Her tributaries dissect the Red Basin making it one of the richest farming lands of China.

A rural province, Sichuan remains largely untouched by development, which means less ostentatious hotel accommodations, but which rewards visitors with the genuine food of the area—if they can take it!

To say that our group, on that last trip, had to endure a series of banquets is to mislead. As one of the first serious gourmet tours to the region, we were feted, sated by lunch and dinner banquets each day, and rarely less than thirty courses. I do not exaggerate, my stained and spotted notebook lists them all! If Sichuan were not a major contributor to the cuisine of China, I would say that we tasted every single local dish in five days. But I know that we only scratched the surface. For centuries, Sichuan has been the training ground for many of China's best chefs. Both Chengdu and Chongqing have important hospitality training schools, whose graduates are in demand by leading restaurants all over China.

The *yin-yang* hotpot on the final evening of my last visit brought our group to our knees. It was 52°C, 112°F outside, thirty of us compacted into a too-small restaurant, with a ventilation system that might have made it almost too cozy in the depths of a Chengdu winter. The Sichuan hotpot is a communal, fondue-style affair where diners cook skewered foods in a wok inset in a table, over a wood or gas fire. The woks are divided into two sections by a curved baffle in the interlocking teardrop shape that symbolizes *yin* and *yang*. One section is filled with a light clear stock (*yin*), the other with a potent brew red with chili, hot with Sichuan peppercorns and seething in its intensity (*yang*).

Massive piles of skewered foods were brought to the tables, adding to the congestion and confusion that already threatened the success of the meal. The bamboo slivers held amber oyster mushrooms and ears of wood fungus, peppers, small local cabbages, tiny freshwater eels, small whole fish, cubes of river turtle. No ceremony here, everyone grabbed and stabbed, splashed, munched and gasped. Calling for more water, more beer. . .more chili!! This was winter food, in midsummer. Madness, but we wouldn't have wanted to be anywhere else on that night. We were drenched, besplattered, overheated, euphoric! We'd had too much wine, too much food, too many chilies. We went too far, we should not have ordered the snake!

Green Chili Dip

Makes 1³/₄ to 2 cups, or 4 to 12 servings

Serve this peppy cream dip with vegetable sticks, crisply fried seafood or cold shrimp.

2 to 3 large green chilies

2 scallions (green and white parts)

1¹/₂ tablespoons minced basil or cilantro (fresh coriander) leaves

¹/₃ teaspoon salt

1 teaspoon ground coriander

¹/₄ teaspoon cumin or caraway seeds, lightly crushed

¹/₄ teaspoon freshly ground black pepper

1 cup soft cream cheese

¹/₄ cup sour cream

1 to 1¹/₂ tablespoons freshly squeezed lime juice

Very finely mince the chilies and scallions and place in a bowl. Add the remaining ingredients, except the lime juice and beat until smooth and creamy. Add lime juice to taste.

Pork Dip with Rice Crisps

or   if using bought rice crisps

Makes 6 to 8 servings

I don't think my daughter, Isobel, has ever eaten at a Thai restaurant without beginning with this totally delicious little dip. It is best eaten with the traditional chunks of crisped rice, but it can be tricky to get it just right. In a pinch, resort to purchased rice crisps or cakes.

Rice Crisps

3 cups cooked long grain white rice (1¹/₃ cups uncooked rice)

Oil for deep frying

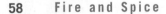

Pork Dip

1/2 cup coconut cream

3/4 cup coconut milk

1 1/2 teaspoons minced fresh ginger

1 1/4 tablespoons Thai Red Curry Paste (page 248)

2 tablespoons fish sauce, or to taste

2 1/2 tablespoons palm sugar, or soft brown sugar lightly packed

1 tablespoon dried shrimp, rinsed and dried

6 ounces lean pork, finely ground

1/3 cup roasted peanuts, ground to crumbs*

White pepper to taste

Very finely chopped cilantro (fresh coriander)

⊕ To make the rice crisps, brush a cookie sheet or oven tray with oil, and heat the oven to 90°F. Press the rice lightly onto the tray in an even layer of no more than 1/3 inch. It should be compacted enough that the grains will stick together, but not so firmly that it will result in a thick, heavy crisp. Dry in the oven for at least 8 hours, but preferably overnight.

⊕ Remove from the oven and set aside to dry for a further 1 to 2 days. Ensure the rice is not subjected to moisture or humidity as this can cause a bloom of mold to cultivate on the rice. You may have best results by covering with grease-proof paper and storing in the refrigerator. Break the dried rice into pieces, and if doing ahead, store in an airtight container until needed.

⊕ Heat oil to 385°F, over high heat, then reduce the heat to medium. Slide the pieces of rice into the oil to fry for just a few seconds. Do not overcook; they should not be allowed to turn more than a very light golden color. The rice grains should explode in the same way as popcorn, making the crisps light and dry. Remove and drain, then allow to cool before serving.

⊕ To make the pork dip, in a small saucepan boil the coconut cream slowly until it becomes oily and well reduced, about 25 minutes. Grind the dried shrimp in a food processor then add the coconut milk, salt, ginger, curry paste, fish sauce and sugar and grind to a smooth paste. Pour into the saucepan with the reduced coconut cream, add the pork and cook for 10 minutes over medium heat. If the mixture is lumpy, return to the food processor and grind smooth before adding the peanuts. Continue to cook until the dip has thickened. Check seasonings—it should have both sweet and salty flavors.

⊕ Add pepper to taste, and stir in chopped cilantro or sprinkle it over the finished dip before you serve.

*If using salted peanuts, rinse off excess salt first.

Thai Shrimp Paste Dip

Makes 3/4 to 1 cup, or 6 to 12 servings

Dip

2 dried red chilies, soaked in hot
    water for 20 minutes

4 fresh small hot Thai chilies

2 tablespoons dried shrimp, soaked
    in hot water for 20 minutes

2 to 3 shallots, peeled

1 to 2 cloves garlic, peeled

1 lemon grass stem or 1½ teaspoons
    ground dried lemon grass

3 thin slices fresh young ginger
    (or 2 slices older ginger)

1 tablespoon soft shrimp paste

2 teaspoons vegetable or peanut oil

2 tablespoons fish sauce

1 to 2 tablespoons palm sugar, or
    dark brown sugar, lightly packed

1½ cups coconut cream

Vegetable/Salad Platter

6 small, round white Thai eggplants
    (or 12 fresh button mushrooms)

1 medium carrot

3 small cucumbers

3 thin, dark-green Asian snake
    beans (long beans)

6 scallions (green and white parts)

1 red bell pepper

Lettuce leaves

To make the dip, drain the chilies and cut open, scrape out and discard the seeds. Deseed the small chilies as well. Coarsely chop the drained and dried shrimp, chilies, shallots, garlic and lemon grass. Place in a mortar, blender, food processor fitted with the metal blade, or a spice grinder. Add the ginger and grind to a thick smooth paste. Add just enough of the coconut cream to keep the processor or blender running smoothly.

Place the shrimp paste and vegetable oil in a small nonstick saucepan and cook for 1 minute, stirring continually. Add the prepared paste and cook over medium-high heat for 1 minute, still stirring continually. Add the fish sauce and sugar and the balance of the coconut cream and simmer for about 20 minutes until the mixture has thickened and is very aromatic.

To prepare the vegetables and salad ingredients, begin with the eggplant or mushrooms, cutting a deep cross in the top of each with a sharp knife.

Note: The metal of some kitchen knives has a chemical reaction with the juices of raw eggplant, causing the cut surface to darken.

 Peel the carrot and cut at an extreme angle into slices, then use a vegetable carving tool to trace designs on the surface of each slice to resemble leaves or flowers. Cut each cucumber lengthways into quarters, then trim away the seeds and at least half of the flesh, so you have mostly skin remaining. Cut in half and use a small sharp knife to pare into leaf shapes, then repeat the tracing of designs on the skin. Cut the beans into 4-inch lengths and tie in figure eight knots. Trim the scallions, discarding most of the green tops. Shred the white ends and place them in iced water so they curl. The pepper can be cut into bite-sized pieces. Cover a serving platter with lettuce, and arrange the prepared vegetables attractively on the platter.

The dip may be served in the carved skin of a small, hollowed pumpkin or squash, a bell pepper or in a small melon half.

Note: Unused shrimp paste dip can be stored in the refrigerator in a covered glass jar for many weeks.

Tangy Avocado Cream

For casual entertaining, serve this dip with a mass of crisply chilled vegetable sticks or two bite-size points of toasted flatbread. For more formal occasions spread it thickly onto croutons of toast or crackers, or pipe into canape shells. Add small shelled shrimp, diced avocado or diced tomato and serve it in a lettuce cup as an appetizer. This tangy avocado cream also makes a good sauce for grilled fish or chicken breast, see recipe page 192.

2 large ripe avocados

2 scallions, white part only, finely minced

1/2 clove garlic, finely minced

3 to 5 teaspoons sweet chili sauce, to taste

1/2 teaspoon chili oil or hot chili sauce

2 teaspoons finely minced sweet basil leaves

2 tablespoons mayonnaise

Salt and freshly ground black pepper

Freshly squeezed lime juice

If you need to prepare avocado dips or sauces in advance, reserve the stones and press them into the top of the dip then cover with plastic wrap and refrigerate. The stone helps to prevent natural oxidation, which turns the avocado brown.

Cut the avocados in half and remove their stones. Use a spoon to scoop the flesh into a mixing bowl. Reserve two half shells for serving. Mash with a fork and add the remaining ingredients. It's worth the small effort to mash the avocado by hand as pureeing it in a food processor can produce an unpleasant bitter aftertaste. Add salt and pepper, and freshly squeezed lime juice to taste, mixing in well.

Spoon the dip back into the avocado shells and set them on platters, using finely shredded lettuce to support them. Surround with the prepared sticks of chilled vegetables or crackers.

Red Hot Chili Shrimp in Lettuce Parcels

Makes 6 servings

1 pound peeled and precooked small shrimp

3 teaspoons light soy sauce

3 teaspoons Chinese cooking (rice) wine or sake

3 tablespoons skinned raw peanuts, chopped

1 cup vegetable oil

1 teaspoon sesame oil

1/4 teaspoon chili oil

3 scallions, green and white parts, chopped

3 cloves garlic, chopped

1 tablespoon Sichuan chili sauce

2 tablespoons pink preserved ginger, finely chopped, or 2 teaspoons grated fresh ginger and 1 teaspoon white vinegar

2 tablespoons finely chopped celery, chayote or Chinese squash

2 tablespoons finely chopped bamboo shoots

2 tablespoons finely chopped straw mushrooms, or black fungus, soaked and drained

1 fresh hot red chili, finely chopped

1/3 teaspoon sugar

Salt to taste

To Serve

Small lettuce cups

Mint or cilantro leaves

Rinse and thoroughly drain the shrimp and place in a dish. Sprinkle on the soy sauce and wine and set aside. In a large skillet, heat the vegetable and sesame oils, and cook the peanuts and scallions, stirring over medium heat until the peanuts are golden and the scallions soft and translucent. Add garlic, chili sauce, pickled ginger, diced celery (or chayote or Chinese squash) and the bamboo shoots. Stir-fry for 1 minute, then add the shrimp and stir-fry another 1 1/2 to 2 minutes. Season to taste with sugar and salt. Serve into small lettuce cups and garnish each with mint or cilantro leaves. Roll up to eat.

Crisp-Fried Shrimp Rolls

Makes 12

12 large raw shrimp

3 ounces shrimp meat, minced

Pinch of salt and pepper

1 scallion, white part only, minced

1 teaspoon grated fresh ginger

3 teaspoons Chinese cooking (rice) wine or dry sherry

1/4 teaspoon sugar

1/4 teaspoon salt

12 wonton skins (wrappers)

1 large fresh mild red chili, seeded

4 garlic chives or Chinese chives

12 sprigs cilantro (fresh coriander)

1 egg white, lightly beaten

3 to 4 cups vegetable oil

To Serve

1 to 2 ounces rice vermicelli

Sprigs of cilantro (fresh coriander)

Soy and chili dip, or sweet chili sauce

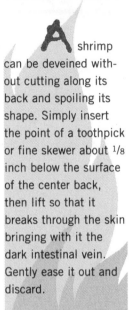

A shrimp can be deveined without cutting along its back and spoiling its shape. Simply insert the point of a toothpick or fine skewer about 1/8 inch below the surface of the center back, then lift so that it breaks through the skin bringing with it the dark intestinal vein. Gently ease it out and discard.

Shell each shrimp leaving just the last section and the tail in place. Use a toothpick to devein the shrimp (see sidebar). Then cut a deep pocket on the underside of each. Mash the shrimp meat to a paste and combine with the salt and pepper, scallions and half the ginger. Press a portion of this mixture into the cavity made in each shrimp and reshape the shrimp around it. Place the shrimp in a shallow dish. Combine the remaining ginger with the wine, sugar and salt. Spread over the shrimp and cover with plastic wrap. Set aside for 20 minutes.

Thaw the wonton skins, if necessary. Cut the chili into 12 long, narrow strips. Cut the chives into 2-inch pieces. Place a shrimp on each wonton skin allowing the tail to protrude past the edge. To each add a piece of chili, chive and cilantro. Roll up the wrapper. To seal, brush the outer edge of the wonton skin with beaten egg white and pinch the base.

In a deep pan suitable for deep frying, heat the oil to medium hot (375°F). Put in the wrapped shrimp to fry for about 2 minutes until the pastry is golden and the shrimp cooked right through. Remove to a strainer lined with paper towels to drain. Increase the heat, and after a minute, add the rice vermicelli to fry for just a few seconds until expanded and snowy white. Remove quickly with a slotted spoon and turn off the heat under the oil.

Crumble the vermicelli on a platter, arrange the shrimp rolls over it and decorate with the cilantro. Serve immediately, with the dip of your choice.

Spicy Fried Oysters

Makes 4 servings

24 large fresh oysters, about
 1½ pounds with shells
5 teaspoons light soy sauce
6 teaspoons hoisin sauce
1½ teaspoons hot chili sauce
2 teaspoons minced fresh ginger

2 teaspoons minced scallion whites
2 teaspoons rice wine, sake or very
 dry sherry
⅓ teaspoon freshly ground black
 pepper
Oil for deep frying

Batter

½ cup rice flour (nonglutinous)
½ cup cornstarch
¼ cup water
3 egg whites

½ teaspoon salt
1 to 2 teaspoons very finely minced
 cilantro (fresh coriander) or
 sweet basil leaves

To Serve

Spiced Salt or Pepper-Salt
 (page 246)

Sweet or hot chili sauce

⊕ If the oysters have not been freshly opened, rinse quickly in a bowl of cold water, drain on absorbent paper for a few minutes, then place in a flat dish.

⊕ Combine the sauces, ginger, scallion, wine and pepper and pour evenly over the oysters. Marinate for 20 minutes, then drain on absorbent paper. Serve the marinade as a dip. (If you're worried about the risk of bacteria, just prepare double the amount of marinade and use the second batch for dipping.)

⊕ In a mixing bowl, combine the rice flour, cornstarch and water. Whip the egg whites with salt to snowy soft peaks, then fold into the flour mixture, adding the minced herbs.

⊕ Heat the deep frying oil to medium-hot (375°F). Dip the oysters one by one into the batter, coating them reasonably thickly. I do this with a thin satay skewer. Carefully place in the oil to fry until they float to the surface, then flip and briefly cook the other side until they are puffy and golden. Drain on paper towels. To serve as finger food, pierce each one with a toothpick and arrange on a platter lined with paper napkins or an attractive leaf. Serve the spiced or pepper salt and the sauces in small dishes, for dipping.

Scallop Skewers with Wasabi Cream

Makes 6 servings

18 large fresh sea scallops

1/4 teaspoon salt

3 teaspoons Chinese cooking (rice) wine, or sake

1/2 teaspoon sugar

2 teaspoons ginger juice (see sidebar, page 96)

4 to 6 scallions, white parts only

6 thin bamboo skewers, soaked in cold water for 1 hour

2 tablespoons vegetable oil

Wasabi Cream

1/2 cup light cream

2 1/2 teaspoons wasabi paste or powder

1 teaspoon horseradish cream, or 1/2 teaspoon pure grated horseradish

1 large egg

Salt to taste

To Serve

2 cups hot white rice, preferably short grain

1/2 sheet nori (compressed seaweed)*

1 small carrot

Sprigs of Japanese mitsuba herb, or arugula leaves

⊕ Prepare and heat an electric, gas or coal-fired barbecue, and when heated, place an iron griddle or cooking plate over it.

⊕ Place the scallops in a dish and sprinkle on the salt, wine, sugar and ginger juice. Mix gently with a wooden spoon to evenly distribute the seasonings, then cover with plastic wrap and set aside for 15 minutes. Cut the scallions into 1 1/3-inch pieces. Thread three scallops and two pieces of scallion onto each skewer and brush evenly with the oil.

⊕ Place the skewers on the hot griddle to cook for about 4 minutes in all, turning several times.

⊕ In the meantime, to make the wasabi cream, pour the cream into a small saucepan and add the wasabi and horseradish cream or horseradish. Bring to a

*If nori is unobtainable, omit it or use finely chopped mint or parsley.

boil, stirring to dissolve the wasabi. In a metal bowl beat the egg thoroughly. Place the bowl over a pan of gently simmering water and pour in the hot cream. Whisk continually while the sauce cooks for a few moments only. Season with salt.

 To prepare the rice, warm the nori over a flame or electric burner until it is bright green and crisp. Then cut into very small flakes. Finely grate the carrot. Stir the nori and carrot into the rice and press into an oiled cake pan, preferably triangular shaped.

 Unmold the rice and cut into slices, wiping the blade of the knife with a wet cloth between each slice. Place a slice or two on each plate and position a skewer on top. Spoon on the sauce and garnish the dish with a few sprigs of mitsuba or arugula.

Note: Wasabi Cream is a superb sauce for grilled salmon steaks or smoked salmon which has been gently warmed in a microwave oven, and served over a bed of boiled new potatoes.

Scallop and Cilantro Dumplings in a Lemon Grass Cream Sauce

Makes 4 servings

If you cannot find really plump fresh scallops, you may have to put two smaller ones in each dumpling. Fresh salmon is a superb alternative to scallops. I cut it into bite-sized chunks, one per dumpling.

Dough

1 cup all-purpose flour

1/2 teaspoon salt

3 eggs

2 tablespoons finely chopped cilantro (fresh coriander) leaves

Filling

1 large bunch fresh spinach, or 4 ounces frozen chopped spinach, thawed

1 to 2 cloves garlic, mashed with 1/2 teaspoon salt

2 tablespoons heavy cream

1 1/2 teaspoons ground coriander

1 1/4 teaspoons seeded and finely minced red chili

Salt and 1/3 teaspoon freshly ground black pepper

1 1/2 tablespoons butter or light olive oil

24 large fresh bay scallops, about 14 ounces

Lemon Grass Cream Sauce

2 cups coconut cream

1 stem lemon grass, coarsely chopped

2 kaffir lime leaves, torn

1 small hot red chili, seeded and sliced

1/2 teaspoon fish sauce

Salt and freshly ground black pepper

1 kaffir lime leaf, cut into fine threads

⊕ To make the dumpling dough, sift the flour and salt into a mound on a work-top and make a well in the center. Break the eggs into the well, then slowly work them into the flour with the fingertips. When it is well mixed and beginning to form into a dough this is the time to add a little tepid water if the dough is dry, or a sprinkle of extra flour, if moist. Add the chopped cilantro and begin kneading vigorously. To obtain an excellent, glossy dough, work the dough for at least 10 minutes. Wrap in plastic wrap and set aside for 1 hour.

To make the filling, thoroughly rinse the fresh spinach and place it in a sauté pan with the garlic to cook, stirring over medium-high heat for 5 to 6 minutes. Cook frozen spinach in the same way. Chop very finely, then return to the pan with the cream, coriander, chili, and salt and pepper. Cook gently for about 1 minute, to a cohesive mass. Sear the scallops in the butter or oil over a well-heated hotplate for no more than 30 seconds. (Salmon can be cooked in the same way.)

Make the sauce by simmering the coconut cream with the lemon grass, torn lime leaves and chili in a saucepan over medium heat, until the coconut cream has thickened and is very aromatic. Check seasonings, adding fish sauce, plus salt and pepper. Strain before using and stir in the shredded lime leaves.

Bring a large pan of salted water to a boil.

To make the dumplings, cut the dough in half and pass the pieces separately through a pasta machine, decreasing the setting until you have two sheets of thin dough or roll out the dough very thinly on a lightly floured board; cut in half. Place one piece on a worktop and set the other aside under a cloth.

Space teaspoons of the spinach filling evenly over the sheet of dough, and place a scallop on each, then cover with another teaspoon of the filling. Lightly beat the extra egg and use to moisten the dough between each portion of filling. Cover with the other sheet of dough, pressing firmly between each mound of filling. Use a sharp knife or a pasta dough cutter to cut between each dumpling.

Drop the dumplings gently into the boiling water and cook them in batches of about 8, for around 4 minutes each. They should float to the top after a few minutes. Leave one more minute, then remove with a slotted spoon.

Divide the cooked dumplings evenly between four shallow bowls. Cover with the sauce and serve at once.

Nori Maki of Tuna with Wasabi and Chili Pepper Soy

Makes 4 to 6 servings

1 cup rice, preferably short-grain

1 tablespoon rice vinegar

1/2 teaspoon salt

1 teaspoon sugar

4 sheets nori (compressed seaweed)

1 tablespoon Japanese shichimi seasoning

8 ounces fresh tuna

3 teaspoons wasabi powder or paste

Wasabi and Chili Pepper Soy

1 1/2 teaspoons wasabi powder or paste

1/2 teaspoon very finely minced red chili

1 teaspoon very finely minced preserved or 1 1/2 teaspoons minced fresh ginger

1/4 cup low sodium or light soy sauce

⊕ Cook the rice by the absorption method, adding 1 1/3 cups of water. Cover, bring to a boil, then reduce heat to the lowest possible setting and cook for about 16 minutes until the rice has absorbed all of the water and is plump and fluffy.

⊕ Combine the vinegar, salt and sugar and while the rice is still hot, stir it in a teaspoon at a time, taking care that the rice is not mashed and made sticky in the process.

⊕ Hold each sheet of nori over a flame for a few seconds until it crisps and turns a brighter green. Place on a kitchen towel or a Japanese sushi mat and spread with a 1/3-inch layer of rice, allowing a 1-inch border along one edge. Sprinkle the rice evenly with the Japanese seasoning. Cut the fish into 1/2-inch sticks and place end to end across each sheet of nori parallel with the border, positioning them in the center of the rice. Smear the tuna with a little wasabi paste or powder moistened to a paste with water. Roll up beginning with the rice covered edge and ending with the uncovered edge. Moisten this with a little water and stick down to secure the roll. Wrap the rolls together in several sheets of paper towel, then in plastic wrap and refrigerate for several hours.

⊕ Use a sharp knife, moistened in water, to cut the rolls into pieces about 1 1/2 inches long. Stand them on end side by side on serving plates.

⊕ To prepare the sauce, combine the ingredients and stir until thoroughly mixed. Serve into several small bowls, for dipping.

Pepper-Crusted Tuna Skewers

Makes 6 to 8 servings, 4 as a main course

1¼ pounds tuna steaks

3 tablespoons olive or vegetable oil

3 cloves garlic, mashed

1 teaspoon crushed dried basil

1 teaspoon salt

1 teaspoon chili oil (optional)

2 teaspoons cracked black peppercorns

2 teaspoons chili flakes

1 teaspoon sweet paprika

1 teaspoon crushed coriander seeds

24 thin bamboo skewers

To Serve

1 medium carrot

1 daikon (giant white/Japanese radish)

1 to 2 scallions, green and white parts, cut into long shreds

1½ tablespoons fish sauce

3 tablespoons fresh lime juice

⅓ teaspoon salt

2 teaspoons white sugar

Lime or lemon wedges, fresh herbs

Cut the tuna into ¾-inch cubes. Place in a dish. Combine the olive or vegetable oil, garlic, basil and salt, plus the chili oil if using, and pour over the fish. Stir the fish with the fingers until each piece is evenly coated with the oil. Cover with plastic wrap and set aside for 30 minutes.

Prepare the vegetables next. Use a vegetable shredder or parer to cut the carrot and radish into long, fine strips. Combine the vegetables in a bowl. Whisk the fish sauce and lime juice together and season with salt and sugar, continuing to whisk until the sugar has dissolved. Pour over the vegetables and set aside for at least 15 minutes.

Combine the pepper, chili, paprika and coriander. Thread the fish cubes onto the skewers, then sprinkle the pepper mix evenly over, and leave another 10 minutes.

Heat a cast-iron skillet or hotplate to very hot and rub the surface with a balled up piece of paper towel dipped in oil. This helps make the surface as smooth and nonstick as possible. Place the skewers on the hotplate and cook the fish just long enough to sear the surface, ideally no longer than ½ minute on each side. The fish should remain tender and practically raw inside. Remove from the heat and arrange several sticks on each plate. Add a portion of the salad and garnish with a lime or lemon wedge and a few sprigs of fresh herbs.

Indonesian Coconut Fish Parcels

Makes 12 servings

Banana leaf is used to wrap bite-sized parcels of fish coated with a fiery seasoning of chili and coconut. In Indonesia, they are usually of incendiary heat; these are more subdued. Roasting over charcoal makes them irresistible, but they can be cooked indoors in a heavy pan.

10 ounces fish fillets (sea bass or
    mahi mahi)

1 cup finely grated fresh coconut or
    shredded coconut (unsweetened)

³/4 cup coconut cream (plus an extra
    ¹/4 cup if using shredded
    coconut)

1 medium onion

2 cloves garlic, mashed

2 teaspoons finely grated fresh ginger

³/4 teaspoon ground turmeric

¹/2 teaspoon galangal (laos) powder
    (optional)

2 teaspoons sambal ulek or
    chili powder

1 teaspoon salt

¹/2 teaspoon ground white pepper

1¹/2 teaspoons ground coriander

Fine threads of red chili and sweet
    basil leaves

Fresh or frozen banana leaves, or
    aluminum foil

A little vegetable or coconut oil

◈ Prepare and light a charcoal barbecue, about 35 minutes before you plan to start cooking to allow the fire to reduce to glowing coals.

◈ Cut the fish into ¹/3-inch-thick slices approximately 4 inches × 1 inch.

◈ Moisten the coconut with the coconut cream. Grate the onion, and squeeze out excess water. Combine the coconut, onion, garlic, ginger and the spices and mix well.

◈ Cut twelve 8-inch squares of banana leaf avoiding the hard central rib, or if unavoidable, pare it flat with a small knife. Hold each square of leaf over a flame until it has softened, then brush the face of each leaf with vegetable oil. (If using aluminum foil, fold a double thickness and brush one side with vegetable oil.)

◈ Spread a thin layer of the coconut seasoning along the center of each prepared wrapper, shaping it roughly the size of the fish pieces. Place a piece of fish over it and add a few shreds of chili and basil leaf to each. Spread on more of the coconut seasoning, completely covering the fish, then fold the banana leaf around the fish like an envelope, securing each parcel with toothpicks. (To wrap foil parcels, bring the edges of the foil together over the top and fold twice to seal, then fold in the two ends, and pinch firmly to ensure they are sealed.)

Cook over the heated coals for about 3 minutes on each side. If cooking in the kitchen, broil or cook on top of the stove on medium-high heat in a heavy pan, turning frequently. The banana leaf may char slightly, and this will add interesting flavor to the dish.

 Serve the parcels as soon as they are cooked, to be unwrapped at the table.

Do Ahead Note: Coconut Fish Parcels can be prepared in advance for cooking the following day. They can be frozen, uncooked, and thawed slowly in the refrigerator before cooking.

Thai-Style Stuffed Chicken Wings

Makes 6 servings

These are a bit tricky to do, but taste sensational enough to make the effort worthwhile. They can be prepared well ahead of time, even frozen uncooked. A whole large wing makes a generous first course, and could be served as a main course, with accompanying spicy vegetables and rice.

6 large chicken wings, at least 4 ounces each (see note)

2 to 3 teaspoons fish sauce

Salt and freshly ground black pepper

3 to 4 cups oil for deep frying

2 tablespoons sesame oil (optional)

Stuffing

4 ounces finely ground (minced) chicken or pork

2 tablespoons minced water chestnuts

3 scallions, white part only, minced

1½ teaspoons grated fresh ginger

½ teaspoon minced garlic

1 teaspoon minced red chili

1½ teaspoons minced lemon grass

3 teaspoons minced cilantro (fresh coriander) leaves

2 teaspoons fish sauce

⅓ teaspoon white pepper

⅓ teaspoon salt

To Coat

½ cup all-purpose flour

To Serve

2 scallions, green and white parts, chopped

3 to 4 tablespoons sweet chili sauce

1 tablespoon finely chopped roasted peanuts

⊕ Debone the upper and central joints of the wings, taking care the skin is not pierced. Using a small knife with a sharp thin blade, cut around the bones, then scrape the meat back until the bones are exposed to the joint nearest the tip. Twist them and pull them away. The wingtip remains unboned. Combine the stuffing ingredients, mixing thoroughly. Stuff into the prepared wings, filling them

loosely. If too full, the skin may burst during cooking. Secure the top opening with toothpicks, then gently squeeze the wings into their original shape. They can be stored in the refrigerator, or frozen, at this stage.

❀ Season the wings first with fish sauce, then with salt and pepper.

❀ Heat the deep frying oil to 375°F, medium hot in a wok or large pan and add the sesame oil. Make a thin batter with the flour and cold water, stirring it until barely mixed. Dip the chicken into the batter, then place in the oil to cook for about 6 minutes, or until the skin is a rich golden brown, and the chicken cooked right through. You may need to cook in several batches. Remove them from the pan and place on a rack lined with paper towels to drain.

❀ Transfer about 1¹/₂ tablespoons of the oil to another pan and fry the scallions until crisp. Remove from the pan with a slotted spoon and pour off the oil. Return the onions to the pan, adding the sweet chili sauce to gently heat. Cut each chicken into several thick slices, and arrange on individual plates or on one serving plate. Spoon on the sauce, or serve in small dishes for dipping. Scatter on chopped peanuts and serve at once.

 Note: If you can't purchase large chicken wings, use chicken drumsticks instead. Scrape the meat from the bone down to the last 1 inch. Use a heavy knife or cleaver to chop through the bone, then press the prepared stuffing into the cavity, reshape the drumstick, and secure the opening with the wooden skewers.

Beef and Lentil Samosas

Makes 24 samosas; 6 to 8 servings

Pastry

2 cups fine whole wheat flour, sifted

1 teaspoon salt

1 teaspoon garam masala, or mild curry powder

1/2 teaspoon sweet paprika

1 tablespoon finely minced cilantro (fresh coriander) leaves

1 1/2 tablespoons softened ghee (clarified butter) or vegetable oil

Tepid water

Beef and Lentil Filling

2 ounces red lentils

1 large onion, finely chopped

8 ounces lean ground or minced beef

1 tablespoon ghee (clarified butter) or vegetable oil

1/3 teaspoon asafoetida (optional)

1 1/2 teaspoons finely grated fresh ginger

3/4 teaspoon crushed garlic

2 teaspoons garam masala, or mild curry powder

1 teaspoon chili powder

1/2 teaspoon turmeric

1/2 teaspoon ajwain or aniseed

1/2 teaspoon salt

1/4 teaspoon black pepper

2 ounces frozen green peas, thawed

2 tablespoons chopped cilantro (fresh coriander) leaves

1 tablespoon lemon or lime juice

5 to 6 cups ghee (clarified butter) or oil for deep frying

To Serve

Mint Yogurt Sauce (page 256)

Sour Cream and Chili Chutney (page 257)

Sweet Chili Sauce (page 253)

⊕ Combine the dry ingredients for the pastry in a mixing bowl and make a well in the center. Add the chopped herbs, oil and a half cup of water and begin to mix in, then slowly add more water, as needed, until you have a firm dough. Turn out and knead for 5 minutes, adjusting water or flour to give a smooth and pliable dough. Wrap in plastic wrap and set aside while the filling is prepared.

In a small saucepan combine the lentils, chopped onion and 1 cup water. Bring to a boil, reduce heat and simmer for about 12 minutes. The lentils should be not quite tender enough to crush between two fingers. Pour into a colander to drain off excess water.

Cook the beef in the *ghee* or oil, stirring, over medium-high heat until lightly browned, about 3 to 4 minutes. Add the *asafoetida* and cook briefly, then add the ginger and garlic and cook, stirring, for 2 to 3 minutes. Add the lentils and onion, the spices and salt and pepper and the thawed peas, cover the pan and cook for about 6 minutes. Stir in the chopped cilantro and lemon juice, then spread on a plate to cool.

Roll out the pastry, pressing firmly, until it is very thin. Cut into 3^1/$_2$-inch squares. Place a portion of filling in the center of the pastry, moisten two edges with water and bring them together to form a triangle. Decorate and seal the edges by pressing the points of a fork around the edge.

Heat the *ghee* or oil in a wok or other pan suitable for deep frying. When it is medium hot, test with a small scrap of pastry. It should immediately begin to bubble, but not brown too quickly. Fry the samosas, about 6 at a time, until golden brown. Drain on paper towels before serving with the chutney or a sauce.

Beef Satay with Pineapple and Sweet Soy Sauce

Makes 6 to 8 servings

1³/₄ pounds lean beef steak

18 to 24 bamboo skewers, soaked in cold water for 1 hour

¹/₂ large fresh pineapple, cubed

2 tablespoons desiccated or finely shredded coconut, toasted (optional), or chopped fresh mint

Marinade

1 tablespoon ground coriander

1¹/₂ teaspoons finely minced lemon grass, or 1 teaspoon grated lemon peel

1¹/₂ tablespoons dark soy sauce

2 teaspoons palm or soft brown sugar

¹/₂ teaspoon freshly ground black pepper

¹/₂ teaspoon chili powder or hot chili sauce

1 tablespoon lemon juice

2 tablespoons vegetable oil

Sweet Hot Sauce

1 cup sweet soy sauce (kecap manis)

1 tablespoon palm or soft brown sugar, or to taste

¹/₂ cup pineapple juice

8 red shallots, or 1 medium red salad (Spanish) onion, minced

2 cloves garlic, minced

1 large fresh red chili, seeded and minced

3 "bird's eye" chilies, minced (unseeded), optional

Salt

⊕ Cut the meat into ²/₃-inch cubes and place in a bowl. Add the marinade ingredients, mix well and cover. Refrigerate for 2 to 3 hours, or overnight.

⊕ Make the sauce at least one hour before the satays are cooked, to allow time for the flavors to develop. Combine the soy sauce, sugar and pineapple juice in a bowl and stir until the sugar has dissolved, then add the remaining ingredients. Spoon into several shallow dishes suitable for dipping the satays. Set aside, covered.

⊕ Prepare and light a small bed of coals in a barbecue suitable for cooking the satays. Allow the heat to subside, until the coals are glowing a dull red. In the

meantime, put on rubber gloves and thread the marinated meat onto the soaked skewers, to make 18 to 24 skewers. Place them over the charcoal to grill, and turn them frequently. In Indonesia, the cook will gently fan the coals as the satays grill, which imparts a delicious smokiness to the meat.

Serve the cooked skewers onto a platter, perhaps lined with a piece of washed banana leaf or another large, decorative leaf, and surround with the cubed pineapple. Scatter on the coconut or mint, and serve with the prepared sauce.

Sichuan Dumplings in Hot Sauce

Makes 30 dumplings; 6 servings

Dumplings

6 ounces lean pork, coarsely ground

2 garlic chives, finely chopped, or
1 scallion, green and white
parts, and 1 large clove garlic,
minced

1½ teaspoons grated fresh ginger

¼ cup finely chopped bamboo shoots

3 tablespoons chopped cilantro (fresh
coriander), leaves and stems

Salt and freshly ground white pepper

30 wonton skins/wrappers
(see sidebar)

Sauce

1 tablespoon sesame oil

1 teaspoon chili oil

1 tablespoon vegetable oil

1 tablespoon soy sauce

1 tablespoon hoisin sauce

2 to 3 teaspoons hot Sichuan bean
paste or sambal ulek

½ teaspoon minced garlic

⅓ teaspoon grated fresh ginger

2 tablespoons minced scallion
(green and white parts)

½ teaspoon Sichuan peppercorns,
ground

4 to 5 tablespoons chicken stock

1 teaspoon sugar

If you buy frozen wonton skins, wrap them loosely in a cloth and set aside for at least a half hour to thaw. When working with them, keep the stack of skins covered to prevent them from drying out. Unused fresh or thawed skins should be wrapped in several layers of plastic wrap, or placed in a snaplock bag and returned to the freezer where they can be kept for several months. Wonton skins make an interesting, crunchy garnish for a soup, see page 22.

❀ To make the dumplings, mix the pork with the garlic chives, garlic, ginger, bamboo shoots and 2 tablespoons of the cilantro (reserve the remainder for garnish) and season with salt and white pepper.

❀ Place a rounded teaspoon of the mixture in the center of each wonton skin and fold over. Pinch the edges together to seal, after moistening them with cold water.

❀ Bring a large pan of lightly salted water or chicken stock to a boil. Put in the wontons, preferably in two batches to avoid overcrowding the pan. After they float to the surface, reduce heat and cook gently for another 3 minutes. Retrieve with a wire ladle and distribute between six bowls.

❀ To make the sauce, combine all ingredients in a small nonstick saucepan and heat gently, without allowing it to boil. Spoon the sauce evenly over the wontons and serve at once, garnished with the remaining cilantro.

Vegetarian Rice Rolls with Chili Lime Mayonnaise

Makes 12 rolls; 4 to 6 servings

Twelve 6-inch Vietnamese rice wrappers (banh trang)

6 large dried black mushrooms, soaked for 25 minutes in warm water

12 small lettuce leaves

1 small carrot

1 rib of celery

1 red onion

2 scallions (green and white parts)

4 ounces fresh bean sprouts

3 ounces snow pea sprouts, or julienned snow peas

12 sweet basil leaves

Chili Lime Mayonnaise

2 tablespoons sweet chili sauce

2 teaspoons fresh lime juice

3 1/2 tablespoons mayonnaise

1 1/2 teaspoons chopped sweet basil

Fill a bowl with cold water, and have ready several clean kitchen towels. Dip the rice wrappers one by one into the cold water, leaving them immersed long enough to soften and turn white. Place them side by side on the towel.

Drain the mushrooms, use a sharp knife to trim off the hard stems, then shred the caps finely. Rinse and dry the lettuce leaves. Cut the carrot, celery, onion and scallions into fine julienne.

To assemble the rolls, place a piece of lettuce on the upper side of each wrapper, with the end overlapping the curved top of the wrapper. On this place a few pieces of each of the vegetables, allowing them to protrude past the curved side, but not extend past the center of the wrapper. Fold the lower portion of the wrapper over, then fold in the sides around the vegetable filling, leaving the salad protruding from the top.

Combine the mayonnaise ingredients in a small bowl. To serve, place two rolls on each plate. Garnish with sprigs of fresh herbs and tiny salad tomatoes if you like. Spoon over some of the mayonnaise, or serve it in small dishes, for dipping.

Stuffed Chilies

Makes 12 stuffed chilies; 4 to 6 servings

Any of the larger, rounder chilies are suitable for stuffing. Use a hot variety, if you prefer.

12 large fresh mild chilies (Anaheim
    or banana)

4 ounces finely ground (minced) pork

1 small onion, minced

1 clove garlic, minced

1 tablespoon vegetable oil

1 tablespoon chopped cilantro (fresh
    coriander) or basil leaves

1 teaspoon ground coriander

1/4 to 1/2 teaspoon chili powder

1/4 teaspoon freshly ground black
    pepper

1/2 teaspoon salt

All-purpose flour

To Fry

1/2 cup all-purpose flour

2 egg yolks

Ice water

4 cups vegetable oil

To prepare fresh chilies for stuffing, arrange them side by side on a cookie sheet or oven tray and place in a hot oven (425°F) for about 12 minutes. Remove from the oven and transfer the chilies to a plastic bag for 5 minutes. The steam trapped inside the closed bag helps to lift off the skin. Peel them, then use a small, sharp knife to slit them open, and without disturbing the stem or piercing through the flesh of the chili, scrape out the central seed core and fibers.

To prepare the filling, heat a small skillet or saute pan and cook the pork, stirring, in the vegetable oil with the onions and garlic over medium-high heat for about 3 minutes. Add the cilantro, ground coriander, chili powder, pepper and salt.

Use a teaspoon to spoon the mixture into the chilies and squeeze each gently to spread the filling evenly inside the chilies. Coat them very lightly with flour and place in the refrigerator for 10 minutes.

Heat the oil for deep frying to 375°F.

To make the tempura-style batter, sift the flour into a bowl and add the egg yolks and a little ice water. Stir lightly, continuing to add water until the mixture is the consistency of thin cream. Do not beat the batter; it is ready when it has achieved the right thickness, even if some of the flour has not been stirred in.

✤ Dip the chilies into the batter, coating evenly. Lower carefully into the hot oil to fry until golden, turning several times during cooking. Remove and drain before serving immediately. You may want to offer the Sweet Chili Sauce on page 253 for dipping.

Cauliflower Pakoras

Makes 6 to 8 servings

A great finger food. Serve on folded napkins on a big platter, with toothpicks and dunking sauce, such as the Sweet Chili Sauce (page 253).

1 whole head of cauliflower, about
    2 pounds

1 large egg, beaten

1 cup all-purpose flour

3/4 teaspoon baking powder

1 tablespoon ground coriander

1/2 teaspoon cracked black pepper

2 teaspoons chili flakes

1/3 teaspoon ground turmeric

2 tablespoons minced cilantro
    (fresh coriander)

11/2 teaspoons salt

4 to 5 cups oil for deep frying

Chili Tomato Sauce

Makes 1 1/2 cups

8 fresh red chilies, seeded and
    chopped

2 tablespoons vegetable oil

1 teaspoon minced garlic

1 medium onion, finely chopped

1 pound very ripe tomatoes

3 tablespoons sugar

3 tablespoons distilled white vinegar

1/3 teaspoon celery or anise seeds

Salt and freshly ground black pepper

◈ To make the sauce, cook the chilies, stirring, in the oil over medium-high heat for 2 minutes. Add the garlic and onion and cook, stirring, until softened, 2 to 3 minutes. In the meantime, bring a pan of water to a boil. Put in the tomatoes and remove with a slotted spoon after 10 seconds. Peel off the skin. Cut the tomatoes in half, squeeze out the seeds and chop the flesh finely. Add the tomatoes to the saucepan, with the sugar and vinegar and simmer gently until the mixture is reduced to a thick paste. Press through a sieve, or process to a puree in a food processor or blender, then pass through a sieve. Add the celery or anise seeds and season to taste with salt and pepper, and if needed, simmer a little longer to reduce.

◈ To prepare the *pakoras*, divide the cauliflower into flowerets. Bring a pan of salted water to a boil, and put in the flowerets to cook for about 5 minutes, until crisp-tender, but retaining their shape. Drain well.

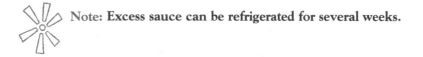 In a bowl combine the beaten egg and flour with the baking powder, coriander, pepper, chili flakes, turmeric, cilantro and salt to taste. Add cold water to make a creamy batter.

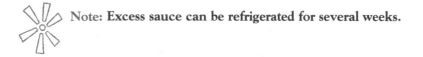 Heat the oil in a wok or large, deep pan until it shimmers, about 395°F, then reduce heat slightly. Dip the flowerets into the batter, allowing excess to drip, then place in the oil to fry until golden and crisp, about 1 minute. Retrieve from the oil with a wire ladle and drain on paper towels spread over a rack, before serving hot with the sauce in bowls for dipping.

Note: **Excess sauce can be refrigerated for several weeks.**

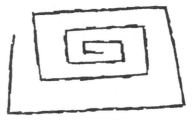

Vegetable Pakoras

Makes 6 to 8 servings as a first course

Another great party dish.

Batter

1 cup besan (chickpea flour) or fine
   cornmeal

1/3 cup all-purpose flour

1 1/2 teaspoons salt

1 1/2 teaspoons baking powder

1 1/2 teaspoons ground coriander

1 1/2 teaspoons garam masala, or mild
   curry powder

1/3 teaspoon turmeric

1 1/2 cups tepid water

Pakoras

2 medium potatoes, peeled and
   halved

1 1/4 cups chopped cauliflower or
   broccoli

3 medium-sized golden zucchini, cut
   into pea-sized dice

2 slender Asian eggplants, cut into
   pea-sized dice*

1/2 cup frozen peas, thawed

4 to 5 fresh spinach, or Chinese
   green vegetable, leaves

2 green chilies, seeded

1 tablespoon fresh lemon juice

4 to 6 cups vegetable oil for deep
   frying

⊕ Cook the potatoes in boiling, lightly salted water for about 15 minutes, until cooked but holding their shape.

⊕ While the potatoes are cooking, sift the dry ingredients for the batter into a bowl large enough to hold the vegetables. Make a well in the center and add three-quarters of the water. Stir to a thick paste, then add the remaining water and stir to a smooth batter.

⊕ Set aside for at least 20 minutes.

⊕ When the potatoes are barely cooked through, remove and set aside for a minute to drain, then cut into pea-sized dice. Prepare the other vegetables, chopping the spinach or other greens and the chilies finely. Mix the vegetables together in a bowl and sprinkle on the lemon juice.

⊕ In a wok or other pan suitable for deep frying, heat the oil to 375°F. Add the vegetables to the batter and mix thoroughly. Test the oil with a teaspoon of the

You may replace the eggplant with parcooked pumpkin, cut into pea-sized dice.

batter. If it bubbles and floats immediately to the surface in a halo of fine bubbles, it is ready. Add the battered vegetables a tablespoon at a time to the oil, allowing them to float to the surface before each addition so they do not mass together beneath the surface of the oil.

⊕ Cook to golden brown, turning several times with a slotted spoon or wire ladle.

⊕ Remove *pakoras* from the pan and place on a rack lined with paper towels to drain for a few minutes. As a first course, serve the *pakoras* in shallow bowls or piled on small plates. For a party arrange them on a big platter with toothpicks, and pass around with the Tamarind Sauce from page 268, Sweet Chili Sauce from page 253, or the Mint Yogurt Sauce from page 256 for dipping.

Indonesian Sweet Corn and Chili Fritters

Makes 6 to 8 servings

11 ounces whole kernel corn (do not use creamed corn)

1/2 cup finely chopped shallots

1/4 cup finely chopped celery

2 cloves garlic, finely chopped

1 fresh red chili, seeded and finely chopped

2 eggs, lightly beaten

3 tablespoons all-purpose flour

1³/4 teaspoons baking powder

Salt and freshly ground black pepper

3 ounces small peeled precooked shrimp (optional)

Deep frying oil

⊕ Place the corn, shallots, celery, garlic and chili in a food processor fitted with the metal blade and grind *very briefly*, so the ingredients are partially bound together, but *not* pureed. This could be done in a mortar, crushing the ingredients lightly with the pestle. Add the eggs, flour and baking powder, with salt and pepper and process again briefly. The mixture should be reasonably thick, but not too firm; if it is too thick, mix in a little cold water. Set aside for 15 minutes to allow time for the baking powder to activate. Stir in the shrimp if you are using them.

⊕ In a wok or a large, deep pan suitable for deep frying, heat the deep frying oil to 375°F.

⊕ When the oil is ready, slide piled teaspoons of the batter into the oil to cook until golden brown, turning several times. It is best to test a few first to check the consistency of the batter. If they fly apart in the oil, thicken the batter by adding a little extra flour, or perhaps an extra egg. Lightness is the requirement here, so allow for a certain amount of airiness in the fritters. When cooked, retrieve from the oil with a wire ladle and drain on paper towels spread over a rack.

⊕ Serve into shallow bowls or warmed plates as a first course. For a party, serve on folded napkins on a platter with toothpicks and a sweet chili sauce for dipping.

Onion Bhajias

Makes approximately 36 bhajias; 6 to 8 servings

4 large onions

3 cloves garlic, finely minced

1 tablespoon ground coriander

1½ teaspoons ground cumin

1 tablespoon minced green chili

2 tablespoons minced cilantro (fresh coriander) leaves

1½ teaspoons salt

2 large eggs (optional, or substitute ¼ cup milk)

1½ cups besan (chickpea flour), or fine cornmeal

2½ cups vegetable oil

Accompaniment

Tamarind Sauce (page 268)

Sweet Chili Sauce (page 253)

Tomato ketchup fired up with hot chili sauce

⊕ Peel the onions and cut in half. Slice very thinly and separate the layers, place in a bowl and pour on boiling water to cover and leave for 3 minutes. Drain and spread on a kitchen towel to dry off excess water. Return to the bowl and add finely minced garlic, the spices, chili, cilantro leaves and salt. Combine the ingredients thoroughly, then stir in the beaten eggs and the *besan* and mix well. Moisten with extra milk or cold water, if needed.

⊕ Heat the oil in a wok or large, not too deep pan to 385°F. Place rounded table-spoons of the batter in the oil to fry until golden brown on the underside. Turn and cook until the other side is golden brown. Remove them from the pan and place on a rack lined with paper towels to drain. Keep warm while the remaining *bhajias* are cooked. As a first course, place several *bhajias* on each warmed plate, with a sprig of fresh herb and a slice of lemon to garnish, before serving with one or two of the suggested sauces.

⊕ For a party, place the sauce in the center of a platter, and stack the *bhajias* around, and serve with toothpicks.

Do Ahead Note: For convenience, bhajias can be prepared and cooked in advance and reheated in the oven or microwave.

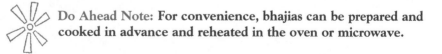

Chapter 5

Flavors of the Sea

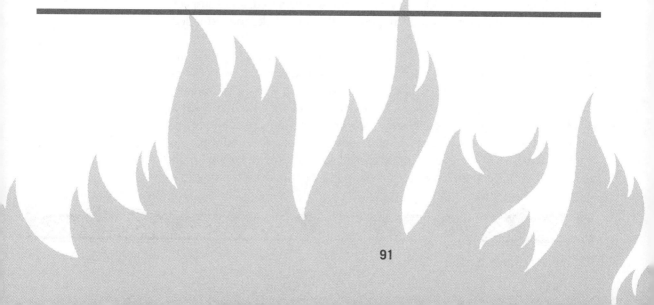

Balinese Beginnings

Indonesia to me is Bali. My part-time home for several years sat high above a valley, terraced with tiers of rice paddies in a patchwork of greens from the palest to rich, deep jade. To reach it, I flew into Denpasar, and hired a motorcycle or risked the local bus to Ubud, bumping along an unmade road past cane and banana farms, up into the mountains. No roads took me on the final leg. First a walk the length of the village, which always set off a cacophony of dog barking—could they smell my foreignness?—and at a certain point I turned left and headed out through the rice fields, trying to stay on the narrow walkways along the banks of the paddies. The house was a typical Balinese structure of stitched coconut-frond walls, flap-out woven cane windows, with coconut thatching above. You had to make it home before sunset, as an impenetrable, inky blackness falls over Bali at night, and—I was informed in awe by a villager—the spirits come out! Tourism had not yet discovered Ubud, though it was already a mecca for local artists, and I usually left with an order for paints and supplies to bring on my return. A hewn-stone terrace with carved temple gates for dance presentations sat in the center of this charming village, and behind an elaborately carved and decorated royal retreat that was to become a hotel in later years.

A local family cared for me at my Bali home, even insisting their two teenage sons sleep on either doorstop to protect me from "things in the night." I was less concerned about possible mystical manifestations than about their very real human male presence, but I did appreciate the gesture. My laundry was carried to the stream below for washing, spread over bushes to dry in minutes in searing tropical sunshine. At mealtimes, mother brought up my meal set out on a small wooden table, which she balanced on her head cushioned by a rolled sarong cloth. She'd invariably be trailed by several children, her own and hangers on, who would crowd into the house to watch and giggle as I ate. She was bemused, and I suspect more than a little flattered, by my request to learn to cook, and extended an open invitation to her kitchen.

So my Indonesian cooking lessons began at grass roots, in a tiny bamboo pole-and-coconut thatch lean-to on a hard, dirt floor. Water was brought up from the river, the clay stove burnt coconut husks and we had little more equipment than two pots, a few coconut shell spoons, a grinding stone for spices and a single well-worn knife. Within the limits of her meager assets, she was a passionate cook, and a patient, informative teacher. We'd work for several hours each day, cooking the family lunch and preparing for dinner. Everything was done by hand, even husking rice

from their own crop. Unlike the Javanese who follow Muslim dietary laws, the Balinese eat pork, and a favorite is *babi kecap* (page 160) slow cooked with the local thick sweet soy sauce. Roasted in the Cantonese way with crunchy, bubbling crackling over succulent pink meat, suckling pig is special-occasion food, traditionally served on a banana leaf cone filled with rice, and topped with a dollop of fiery *sambal ulek*. Balinese villages are usually overrun by families of piglets squealing and snuffling around the kitchens, competing for vegetable scraps with large and aggressive ducks. Her kitchen was typical, with livestock and children providing constant, noisy diversion.

She showed me how to pound chilies with salt to make *sambal ulek*, how to grate coconut with a curved, serrated blade. We gathered *kangkung* water vegetable from the banks of paddies to cook with shrimp paste and chilies. We killed a duck to stuff with cassava leaves and cook in a pit of charcoal as *bebek betutu*. We threaded satays onto slivers of bamboo carved by her husband, and ground chilies, garlic, cilantro (fresh coriander), shrimp paste, peanuts, and freshly harvested ginger for the sauce. We picked banana blossoms to slice into salads, and wove the leaves into little parcels around minced pork to grill over a tiny charcoal stove. My contribution to her housekeeping budget allowed her some rare extravagances on the family menu, so I think we all benefited from our time together.

Thai Fried Fish with Hot Sauce

Makes 6 servings

1¹/₃ pounds fish fillets of hake, cod, sea bass, or snapper

¹/₂ cup cornstarch

1¹/₂ cups corn or vegetable oil

1 small bunch fresh basil

1 large mild fresh red chili, seeded and thinly sliced

Chili Paste

8 shallots, peeled

8 medium dried red chilies, seeded and soaked in hot water for 20 minutes

2 thin slices fresh ginger

2 cilantro (fresh coriander) roots, washed

2 large cloves garlic, peeled

1 stem lemon grass, coarsely chopped

1 tablespoon dried shrimp or 1¹/₄ teaspoons shrimp paste

2 tablespoons vegetable or peanut oil

Sauce

1 tablespoon white sugar

1¹/₂ tablespoons fish sauce

¹/₂ teaspoon soft fresh shrimp paste

¹/₄ cup water

Place the ingredients for the chili paste in a blender or mortar, or in the small bowl of a food processor fitted with the metal blade, or a spice grinder, and grind to a smooth paste. Fry in a nonstick saucepan for 3 to 4 minutes over medium heat, stirring continually. Add the sugar, fish sauce, shrimp paste and water and simmer until thick and paste-like.

Cut the fish into 1-inch fingers and coat lightly with cornstarch. Heat the oil in a wide nonstick skillet or pan over medium-high heat and fry the fish to a golden brown on both sides for about 2 minutes on each side. Remove and drain well. Pour off the oil and return the fish. Spread the chili sauce over the fish, cover and simmer for a few minutes on gentle heat, then serve.

Braised Fish with Garlic and Chili

Serve with steamed white rice and stir-fried vegetables or sautéed spinach with garlic and dried shrimp.

1¼ pounds fish fillets (sea bass, cod, etc.), about 1 inch thick

⅓ cup cornstarch

2 cups vegetable or light olive oil

12 cloves garlic

3 medium-hot fresh red chilies, seeded

1½ tablespoons light soy sauce

1½ tablespoons hoisin sauce

1 tablespoon Chinese cooking (rice) wine or sake

½ to 1 teaspoon chili oil

1½ teaspoons sugar

Salt and freshly ground black pepper

⅓ cup water or fish stock

1½ teaspoons cornstarch

2 tablespoons finely sliced scallion greens

Holding the knife at a 45° angle, cut the fish into ⅓-inch slices and coat lightly with the cornstarch. Heat the oil in a wok or large skillet over high heat until the surface of the oil begins to shimmer. Add the garlic cloves and the chilies and fry for about 1½ minutes, lowering the heat slightly. Retrieve them with a slotted spoon and set aside. Add the fish pieces, one at a time, and fry for about 3 minutes until very well cooked and crisped on the surface. Remove them from the pan and place on a rack lined with paper towels to drain.

Pour off all but 2 tablespoons of the oil and reheat. Slice the garlic cloves and chop the chilies. Return to the oil and fry for 30 seconds over medium-high heat, then add the sauces, wine, chili oil, sugar and salt and pepper and stir-fry for about 30 seconds.

In a small bowl, combine the cornstarch with the water or stock and pour into the pan. Cook, stirring slowly and continually, until the sauce thickens. Return the fish slices and warm in the sauce turning each slice carefully to evenly glaze them with the sauce. Serve onto an oval plate and scatter the scallion greens over.

Sichuan "Fragrant" Fish

Makes 6 servings

1¹/₃ pounds fish fillets (cod, sea bass, etc.), about ³/₄-inch thick

2 teaspoons ginger juice or wine (see sidebar)

¹/₃ teaspoon white pepper

2 to 4 tablespoons cornstarch

2 cups vegetable or light olive oil

Sauce

¹/₂ cup minced scallion greens

1 tablespooon minced garlic

1 tablespoon minced fresh ginger

2 tablespoons light soy sauce

1 tablespoon dark soy sauce

1 tablespoon hoisin sauce

1 tablespoon Chinese chili bean paste, or use 1 tablespoon Japanese red miso paste and 1 teaspoon chili sauce

1 tablespoon Chinese black vinegar or balsamic vinegar

1 tablespoon sugar

¹/₂ teaspoon ground Sichuan peppercorns

³/₄ cup water

Ginger juice or wine adds subtle, peppery flavors to marinades and sauces. Make it by grating 1 tablespoon fresh ginger onto a piece of clean fine cloth. Squeeze the liquid and use the pure juice, or to make ginger wine, mix into ¹/₄ cup Chinese yellow rice wine (cooking wine) or dry sherry.

⊕ Holding the knife at a 45° angle, cut the fish into ¹/₃-inch slices and place in a dish. Sprinkle on the ginger juice and pepper and set aside for 10 minutes, then coat with the cornstarch. Heat the oil in a wok or skillet over high heat until a haze appears over the surface. Add the fish and fry for about 1¹/₂ minutes, cooking in several batches so you do not overcrowd the pan. Remove them from the pan with a slotted spoon and place on a rack lined with paper towels to drain.

⊕ Pour off the oil. Rinse, dry, and reheat the pan over high heat. Add the scallion, garlic and ginger and stir-fry for 20 seconds. Then add the sauces, bean paste, vinegar, sugar and pepper and stir until the sauce is very aromatic. Add the water and mix well. Lower the heat and simmer until the sauce is smooth, then return the fish and turn carefully in the sauce to coat each slice evenly. Simmer gently for 2 to 3 minutes. Serve onto a warmed plate.

Mackerel in Golden Chili Sauce

Makes 4 servings

Pickled Vegetables

Peel and slice 1 carrot and 1/3 Japanese daikon. Cut 1 small cucumber in half and scoop out the seeds; slice thinly. Peel and slice a medium onion and place in a bowl. Cover with boiling water and let stand for 5 minutes, then drain. Combine 1/2 cup white vinegar with 2 table-spoons white sugar and 2 teaspoons salt, stir to dissolve. Pour over the vegetables and set aside for 1 hour. Drain to serve.

8 small fresh mackerel fillets or steaks, skin on (approximately 1 1/4 pounds total)

2 tablespoons peanut or vegetable oil

1/2 cup minced shallots

1 teaspoon minced garlic

2 teaspoons grated fresh galangal or 1/2 teaspoon powdered laos, or 1 extra teaspoon grated fresh ginger

1 1/2 teaspoons grated fresh ginger

2 1/2 teaspoons grated fresh turmeric root, or 1 teaspoon ground turmeric

1 tablespoon finely minced red chili

1 1/2 cups coconut cream

Salt and freshly ground black pepper to taste

Marinade

1 tablespoon fresh lime juice

1 tablespoon vegetable oil

1/2 teaspoon salt

1/4 teaspoon white pepper

◈ Place the mackerel fillets in a flat dish. Combine the marinade ingredients and brush evenly over top. Cover with plastic wrap and refrigerate for 25 minutes.

◈ In the meantime, heat the oil in a medium saucepan over medium heat and cook the shallots, garlic, *galangal*, ginger, fresh turmeric and chili for 3 to 4 minutes, stirring constantly.

◈ Pour in the coconut milk (if using powdered *laos* and ground turmeric, add them at this point) and bring to a boil. Reduce heat and simmer, stirring with a wooden spoon, for about 12 minutes until the sauce has reduced and thickened, and the flavors are well developed.

◈ Heat a broiler or ridged hotplate and brush with oil. Cook the fish over high heat, skin side down, for about 2 minutes. Brush the top with oil, turn and cook until done and the surface crisped. Invert onto warmed plates and cover with the sauce.

A Fish Curry from Goa

Makes 6 servings

Goa is the home of the fiery vindaloo, one of India's hottest curries. This fish curry, in its potent scarlet sauce, packs the same chili punch. Serve with white rice, a sweet fruit chutney, and the cabbage dish on page 223 or 230.

1 1/2 pounds skinless fish fillets (cod, sea bass, etc.) about 3/4 inch thick

1 tablespoon freshly squeezed lime or lemon juice

3/4 teaspoon ground turmeric

1 teaspoon salt

2 tablespoons vegetable oil

2 1/2 cups water

1/3 cup canned crushed tomatoes

1 teaspoon tomato paste

Salt, freshly ground black pepper and sugar

A few small, hot green chilies, sliced (optional)

Cilantro (fresh coriander) or mint leaves

Curry Paste

10 large fresh hot red chilies, seeded

1 1/2 teaspoons paprika

3/4 cup grated fresh coconut (or 1/3 cup shredded coconut moistened with coconut cream)

1 onion

2 teaspoons crushed garlic

1 teaspoon grated fresh ginger

1 teaspoon tamarind concentrate

1 tablespoon coriander seeds

1 teaspoon cumin seeds

⊕ Cut the fish into pieces about 2 1/2 × 1 inch and marinate in a mixture of the lime or lemon juice, plus half the turmeric and salt, for about 25 minutes.

⊕ To make the curry paste, soak the chilies in hot water for 20 minutes, strain and reserve the water. In a blender or mortar or the small bowl of a food processor fitted with a metal blade, or a spice grinder, grind them to a paste with the paprika, coconut, half the onion finely chopped, the garlic, ginger, half the tamarind and the remaining turmeric and salt. Toast the coriander and cumin seeds in a small dry pan over high heat until they begin to pop and are very aromatic. Grind them finely and add to the curry paste. Add some of the reserved chili water, if needed, to ensure the curry paste is pureed smoothly.

⊕ Mix the remaining tamarind with 1 tablespoon of the chili water and set aside. Finely slice the remaining half onion. Cook it in a large skillet, stirring over

medium heat in 2 tablespoons oil until lightly colored and tender, about 4 minutes. Add the spice paste and cook, stirring, for a few minutes. Add the water, the tomatoes, the tomato paste and the green chilies and bring to a boil. Reduce the heat and simmer until the sauce is fragrant and has partially thickened. Stir from time to time. Add the tamarind and fish and cook for just a few minutes, until the fish is tender. Check seasonings, adding salt, pepper and sugar, as needed. Transfer to a serving dish and garnish with chilies and cilantro.

Javanese Fish

Makes 6 servings

Serve with yellow (turmeric) coconut rice, or steamed white rice and an assortment of vegetables simmered in coconut milk.

1 whole fish like red snapper, sea bass or bream, approximately 2¼ pounds total

1 teaspoon tamarind concentrate, or ⅔ tablespoon lemon juice

1 teaspoon salt

1 tablespoon coconut, peanut or vegetable oil

Sauce

2 medium onions

1 cup vegetable or peanut oil

¾ teaspoon galangal or powdered laos or 2 teaspoons grated fresh ginger

½ teaspoon shrimp paste

2 teaspoons ground coriander

½ teaspoon ground cumin

1 tablespoon ground candlenuts, raw cashews or macadamias

1 to 3 teaspoons minced medium-hot red chili

1 cup coconut cream

Garnish

1 tablespoon kecap manis (thick sweet soy sauce) (optional)

Lime wedges

Small tomato wedges

Cilantro (fresh coriander) or dill sprigs

⊕ Prepare and light the coals for a barbecue, or heat an electric or gas barbecue or broiler (grill).

⊕ Clean the fish and score it diagonally on both sides at ¾-inch intervals. Dilute the tamarind with 2 teaspoons water and add the salt. Rub into the fish on its surface and in the cavity, and set aside for 10 minutes.

⊕ Peel the onions and cut each in half. Very finely slice one onion and brown it in a small skillet or sauté pan with the oil over medium-high heat, stirring frequently, until it is very well colored and crisp, about 10 minutes. Remove with a slotted spoon and set aside. Drain off all but 2 tablespoons of the oil.

⊕ Very finely chop the remaining onion and brown in the smaller amount of oil over medium heat, until well colored, about 4 minutes. Add the shrimp paste and spices and stir briefly over high heat. Add the ground nuts and chili and the coconut milk and bring to a boil. Lower the heat and simmer, stirring frequently, until the sauce is thick and creamy, about 8 minutes.

⊕ In the meantime, brush the fish with oil and place on the well-heated barbecue or broiler to cook. Turn it frequently to ensure it cooks evenly.

⊕ Lift onto a serving platter. Test by piercing the fish at its thickest part with the point of a knife. It should flake easily. If you prefer, before serving, carefully lift and remove the skin, then spoon the sauce evenly over the fish. Scatter on the fried onions and then drizzle the *kecap manis* in fine lines over the sauce. Garnish the platter with lime and tomato wedges and sprigs of herbs.

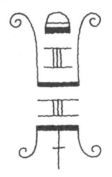

Crisp Coral Trout with Sweet Chili Sauce and Basil

Makes 4 servings

This is a spectacular dish as the centerpiece of a meal. Serve this to six very impressed guests, followed perhaps by a creamy Thai curry such as Red Duck Curry with Lychees, page 133, Thai Vegetables and Tofu Curry, page 240, and white rice.

1 coral trout or other reef fish (or sea bass or snapper), approximately 1³/₄ pounds

1 large stem lemon grass

6 thin slices fresh ginger

³/₄ cup water

1 teaspoon salt

¹/₂ cup cornstarch

1 bunch sweet basil leaves

6 to 8 cups vegetable or light olive oil

Sweet Chili Sauce

6 fresh red chilies

3 tablespoons vegetable or light olive oil

¹/₃ cup rice vinegar

¹/₂ cup sugar

1 tablespoon minced garlic

³/₄ cup water

¹/₂ teaspoon cracked or coarsely ground black pepper

3 teaspoons cornstarch combined with 2 tablespoons cold water

Clean and scale the fish and rinse thoroughy. Wipe dry and make deep diagonal slits across each side, cutting to the bone. Place lemon grass and ginger in a food processor or blender and chop finely. Add the water and salt and blend thoroughly. Strain this liquid over the fish and discard the solids. Set the fish aside for 25 minutes to marinate.

To make the sauce, cut the chilies in half lengthways and trim away stem and scrape out the central seed core and fibers. Mince 4 of the chilies and set aside.

Heat the 3 tablespoons oil in a wok or medium-sized nonstick, nonreactive saucepan over medium heat. Add the minced chili and fry for about 40 seconds, stirring constantly. Add the vinegar, sugar and garlic and boil until well reduced. Add the water and the halved chilies and bring to a boil, lower the heat and simmer for about 5 minutes, or until syrupy. Add the pepper, stir in the cornstarch solution, simmer until thickened, then set aside.

Heat the 6 to 8 cups oil over high heat to about 375°F in a large wok or pan suitable for deep frying the whole fish. Drain the fish and pat dry with paper towels. Coat lightly with the cornstarch. Carefully lower the fish into the oil to cook until crisp. Use a large spoon to carefully ladle the hot oil over the fish as it cooks. (You may want to protect your hand by wearing a close-fitting oven mitt.) When thoroughly crisped on the surface, carefully lift it out, using large tongs or two slotted spoons. Drain on paper towels, and stand it on a platter, by spreading the cavity open so the fish can stand upright, making the meat on both sides accessible.

While the oil is still hot, add the basil leaves to fry for about 25 seconds, or until crisp. Remove and drain on paper towels. Pour the sauce over and around the fish and surround with basil leaves.

Whole Fried Fish in a Hot Chili Sauce

Makes 2 servings

Serve with Thai-style fried rice noodles or fried rice.

2 small whole fish, approximately
    1 pound each

4 cups vegetable oil

Hot Chili Sauce

1 medium onion, very finely chopped

1 tablespoon minced garlic

1 tablespoon minced fresh ginger

2 tablespoons minced red chili

1 to 2 teaspoons chili oil

1 1/2 tablespoons dried shrimp, ground
    to fine threads in a food proces-
    sor or blender

1 1/2 tablespoons smoothly ground
    roasted peanuts or 2 tablespoons
    peanut butter

3/4 cup coconut milk

Salt and freshly ground black pepper

Garnish

Lime wedges

Cilantro (fresh coriander) sprigs

Rinse and dry the cleaned and scaled fish. Heat the oil in a wok or pan over high heat until very hot. Carefully slide in the fish and reduce the heat slighty. Fry for about 3 minutes, turning several times. Remove them from the pan and place on a rack lined with paper towels to drain.

Transfer 2 to 3 tablespoons of the oil to another pan and cook the onion, stirring over medium heat until well cooked, about 3 1/2 minutes. Add the garlic, ginger and chili and stir-fry for 1 minute, then add the chili oil, dried shrimp and peanuts or peanut butter and cook briefly. Add the coconut milk and bring to a boil. Reduce heat to low and simmer until the sauce is very thick and reduced, about 12 minutes. Season to taste with salt and pepper. If preferred, puree the sauce smooth in a blender.

Reheat the oil and fry the fish a second time until well crisped on the surface. Drain and place them on a serving plate. Spoon the sauce over the fish and serve garnished with lime wedges and sprigs of cilantro and dill.

Salt and Chili Shrimp on Sautéed Spinach

Makes 4 to 6 servings

Serve with the Balinese Coconut Chicken Legs on page 128 or Indonesian Beef Rendang on page 169, and rice vermicelli or steamed jasmine rice.

24 medium shrimp (about 1¼ pounds), peeled

1 tablespoon Five-Spice Salt (page 246)

One large bunch fresh spinach

1 to 2 cloves garlic, finely chopped (optional)

3 cups vegetable oil for deep frying

Salt and freshly ground black pepper

1 cup cornstarch

2 teaspoons sesame oil

1 to 2 fresh mild red chilies, seeded and minced

2 scallions (green and white parts), minced

2 tablespoons minced cilantro (fresh coriander) leaves

Devein the shrimp, cutting deeply into the backs, and press the shrimp open. Rinse in cold water, drain and dry. Place them in a dish, sprinkle the spiced salt over them evenly and set aside for 10 minutes.

Thoroughly rinse the spinach and drain well. Place in a steamer over simmering water to steam until barely wilted, about 3 minutes, or stir-fry with the garlic in 1 to 2 tablespoons of the oil until tender, about 4 minutes over medium heat. Season lightly with salt and pepper and set aside.

Heat the oil to about 395° F over high heat in a wok or deep pan suitable for deep frying. The oil is ready when the surface shimmers. Coat the shrimp evenly and lightly with the cornstarch, shaking off excess. Deep-fry the shrimp until they are cooked and crisped on the surface, about 1¼ minutes. Remove them from the pan with a slotted spoon and place on a rack lined with paper towels to drain.

Pour off the oil, rinse and drain the pan then reheat and add the sesame oil, chilies, scallions and cilantro. Cook over high heat, stirring continually, for about 40 seconds, then return the shrimp and toss in the oil for a further 30 to 40 seconds.

Mound the spinach on warmed plates and arrange the shrimp on top. Garnish, if you like, with shreds of red chili.

Crisp-Fried Shrimp with Four Peppers

Makes 4 servings

The Chinese love these crisp and peppery shrimp. They achieve their best flavor when fried in their shells, so for ease of shelling at the table, cut them deeply down the back, so the shell can be peeled off with the flick of a chopstick.

Complete a menu with Chengtu Chicken, page 124, or the Fiery Shredded Pork with Mushrooms and Bamboo Shoots on page 154.

1 1/2 pounds medium shrimp in their shells

2 tablespoons ginger wine (see sidebar, page 96)

1/2 teaspoon white pepper

1 1/4 teaspoons salt

2 cups vegetable or light olive oil

1/2 teaspoon ground Sichuan peppercorns

1/2 teaspoon coarsely ground black pepper

1 teaspoon red pepper flakes

2 tablespoons very finely chopped scallion greens

Rinse the shrimp. Without removing the shells, use a sharp knife to cut deeply down the back of each shrimp. Remove the dark vein. Use kitchen shears to trim off the legs. Place the shrimp in a shallow dish.

Season the shrimp with the ginger wine, white pepper and salt. Set aside for 25 minutes.

Heat the oil over high heat in a wok or deep skillet to about 375°F. Drain and dry the shrimp on paper towels. Slide into the oil to fry for about 1 1/2 minutes on high heat. Remove and set aside. Pour off the oil and return the unrinsed pan to medium heat. Return the shrimp to the pan, and sprinkle on the peppers, red pepper flakes and scallion greens and stir-fry over high heat for about 45 seconds, until the shrimp are evenly coated with the peppers. Serve onto a warmed plate and have finger bowls of warm water for rinsing the fingers, and extra bowls for the shells ready.

Beijing Shrimp in Wine and Chili Sauce

Makes 4 servings, or more if sharing several dishes

Serve with plain white rice and perhaps Chinese Country-Style Shredded Beef and Peppers, page 162.

1¼ to 1½ pounds medium shrimp, shelled but with tails intact

1 tablespoon salt

2 tablespoons cornstarch

2 cups vegetable oil

5 cloves garlic, peeled and finely sliced

2 fresh red chilies, seeded and sliced

⅓ cup Chinese cooking (rice) wine or sake

1 tablespoon cognac or extra rice wine

2½ teaspoons sugar

1 cup chicken stock

1 teaspoon chili oil

Salt and freshly ground black pepper

⊕ "Butterfly" the shrimp by cutting deeply down their backs. Remove the dark vein. Place shrimp in a colander, sprinkle on the salt, and place under running cold water, rubbing lightly with the fingers. Rinse thoroughly and dry by patting between double layers of paper towel. Coat lightly with cornstarch, reserving about 2 teaspoons. Heat the oil in a wok or large skillet to 375°F. Add the garlic and fry for about 30 seconds, then add the chili and fry another 30 seconds. Remove with a slotted spoon and set aside.

⊕ Increase the heat to high and add the shrimp. Fry until they turn pink and are firm and almost cooked, about 1½ minutes. Remove with a slotted spoon, set aside, and pour off the oil. Return the pan, unrinsed, reheat and add the garlic and chili and the rice wine, cognac and sugar. Bring to a boil, stirring.

⊕ Combine the stock with the reserved cornstarch and pour into the sauce. Add the chili oil and salt and black pepper, and cook, stirring, until the sauce thickens and becomes translucent. Return the shrimp and warm in the sauce, then transfer to a serving dish.

Tamarind Shrimp on Pickled Vegetables

Makes 4 servings

In Malaysia, where this is a popular dish, they leave the heads and tails on the shrimp, removing just the central part of the shell. An equally attractive presentation is this Chinese method of "curling" shrimp. Butterfly the shrimp by cutting very deeply down the back, then make an incision in the center, through which the tail is pushed.

1 tablespoon tamarind concentrate

1 cup tepid water

2 teaspoons chili sauce

1 tablespoon sugar

Salt and freshly ground black pepper

1¼ pounds medium shrimp, shelled and deveined

3 tablespoons vegetable oil

2 tablespoons sliced pickled ginger

1 recipe Pickled Vegetables (see sidebar, page 97)

⊕ Mix the tamarind and water with the chili sauce, sugar, salt and pepper. Stir until the sugar dissolves, then add the shrimp and mix in well. Set aside to marinate for 20 minutes. Remove the shrimp with a slotted spoon and reserve the marinade to use in the sauce.

⊕ Heat the wok or a large skillet on high and add the oil. When it is well heated and the pan smoky, put in the shrimp and stir-fry for about 1½ minutes until they have turned pink and are cooked—they should remain crisp in texture.

⊕ Remove from the pan and keep warm. Increase the heat, pour in the reserved marinade and bring to a boil. Reduce heat and simmer until the sauce is well reduced. Return the shrimp and reheat gently in the sauce, then stir in the pickled ginger.

⊕ To serve, mound the pickled vegetables in the center of a platter and surround with the shrimp.

Shanghai Shrimp in Chili Tomato Sauce

Makes 3 to 4 servings

In Shanghai where this is one of their most popular banquet dishes, they leave the heads on the shrimp and arrange them on a big platter in the shape of a fan. Serve with white rice, or steamed Chinese bread.

12 very large shrimp in their shells

2 tablespoons finely shredded fresh ginger

1/4 cup vegetable oil

1 teaspoon sesame oil

1/4 cup chopped scallions (green and white parts)

Chili Tomato Sauce

1 tablespoon Chinese cooking (rice) wine or dry sherry

1 1/2 teaspoons rice vinegar

3 tablespoons tomato ketchup

2 teaspoons sugar

1 tablespoon light soy sauce

1/2 to 1 tablespoon chili bean sauce or sambal ulek/Sichuan chili sauce, to taste

Salt and freshly ground black pepper

2 teaspoons cornstarch

1/2 cup chicken or fish stock, or water

⊕ Leaving the shrimp unshelled, use a sharp knife to cut down the center back of each shrimp, then remove the dark vein. Rinse and thoroughly dry the shrimp, then use kitchen shears to trim off the legs, close to the body.

⊕ Combine the sauce ingredients, except the cornstarch and stock. Heat a wok or large skillet with the oil and sesame oil over high heat. Stir-fry the shrimp and ginger for 2 to 3 minutes until the shells turn red and the meat begins to firm up.

⊕ Add the sauce mixture to the pan and stir-fry for 1 to 2 minutes, until the dish is very aromatic and each shrimp is cooked and evenly glazed with the sauce. Use tongs to lift each shrimp from the pan onto a serving plate. Stir the cornstarch into the stock or water and pour into the pan. Cook over medium-high heat, stirring constantly, until the sauce thickens. Add the scallions and pour over the prawns.

Lobster and Shrimp Curry

Makes 4 servings

This is my version of a superb dish created by Thai master chef Chalie Amatyakul for the legendary The Oriental Bangkok Hotel. It needs no more accompaniment than Thai jasmine rice.

2 large lobster tails, approximately 1¼ pounds in the shell

4 large tiger prawns or other shrimp

2 tablespoons butter

2 tablespoons vegetable oil

1 large fresh mild red chili, seeded and finely sliced

1 tablespoon finely shredded fresh ginger

2 to 3 tablespoons Thai Red Curry Paste (page 248)

1⅓ cups coconut cream

½ cup water

½ cup Chinese jujube fruit (red dates), seeded, or use large white grapes or cherry tomatoes

1½ tablespoons fish sauce

2 teaspoons sugar

⅓ cup loosely packed fresh Thai or sweet basil leaves

Remove the lobster tail meat from the shells and cut into thick slices. Shell the shrimp and cut in half lengthways, removing the dark vein in the process.

Heat the butter and oil in a wok over high heat. Add the seafood, stir-fry for about 2 minutes, remove and set aside. Add the chili, ginger and curry paste and stir-fry for 1½ minutes, stirring continuously. Pour in the coconut milk and water and bring to a boil. Add the dates (add grapes, cherry tomatoes later), fish sauce and sugar, reduce heat and simmer for 6 to 7 minutes, uncovered.

Return the seafood to the sauce (add grapes or cherry tomatoes at this point) and cook until tender, about 4 minutes. Stir in the basil leaves just before serving.

Peppered Crab

Serve with rice, or rice noodles fried Thai style with bean sprouts.

2 large crabs

1 large fresh hot red chili, seeded

8 cloves garlic, peeled

6 shallots, peeled

6 thin slices fresh ginger

2 tablespoons butter

1 1/2 tablespoons vegetable oil

2 tablespoons fish sauce

2 1/2 tablespoons cracked, coarsely
   ground black pepper

3 teaspoons fine white sugar

1 1/2 teaspoons Chinese black vinegar
   or balsamic vinegar

Salt to taste

2 to 3 tablespoons chopped cilantro
   (fresh coriander)

Garnish

Sliced lemon

Fresh herbs (Thai or sweet basil,
   dill, Vietnamese mint)

To prepare the crabs, lift off the shell, then remove and discard the inedible parts. Cut the crab bodies into four pieces. Crack the claws at the joints and use a Chinese cleaver or heavy knife to chop the claws in half diagonally.

Place the chili, garlic, ginger and shallots in a blender or the small bowl of a food processor fitted with the metal blade and chop finely.

Heat the butter and oil in a wok or large skillet over medium-high heat. Put in the crab pieces and cook, stirring, until the shells have turned bright red, and the flesh feels firm, about 4 minutes. Remove from the pan and set aside. Add the chopped ingredients and cook, tossing and stir-frying, on medium-high heat for 1 1/2 minutes. Add the fish sauce, pepper, sugar and vinegar and return the crab. Stir-fry over high heat for about 1 1/2 minutes, or until done. Add salt to taste and the chopped cilantro, mix well, and transfer the crab to a serving plate. Surround with sliced lemon and sprigs of fresh herbs.

Singapore Chili Crab

Makes 2 to 4 servings

Red hot and absolutely sensational. In Singapore this is a plastic tablecloth affair, with plenty of napkins and finger bowls.

1 large or several small crabs, approximately 3 pounds total

3 cups vegetable oil

1 tablespoon sesame oil

1 medium onion, peeled

5 to 6 cloves garlic, minced

1/4 cup minced fresh ginger

2 large fresh mild red chilies, seeded and minced

1 to 2 tablespoons hot chili sauce

1 tablespoon tomato ketchup

2 teaspoons sweet paprika

1 1/2 tablespoons light soy sauce

1 1/2 tablespoons cornstarch

1 1/4 cups chicken or fish stock, or water

2 large eggs, beaten (optional)

Salt and freshly ground black pepper

1/4 cup chopped scallions (green and white parts)

To prepare the crab, lift off the shell and remove the inedible parts. Scoop the creamy orange-yellow tomalley into a small bowl and set aside. Using a Chinese cleaver or heavy knife, chop the body of the crab into portions, each piece with a leg attached. Cut the claws into pieces, chopping diagonally through the shell.

Heat the oil and sesame oil in a wok or large skillet over high heat to 395°F, until the oil shimmers. Put in the crabs and deep fry for about 2 minutes, until the shells are bright red and the meat is partially cooked. Remove the crabs to a plate and pour off all but 1 tablespoon of the oil. The oil can be saved to cook other seafood dishes.

Cut the onion into small wedges and separate the layers. Reheat the oil and stir-fry the onion for about 1 1/4 minutes to soften. Add the garlic, ginger and chili and stir-fry for 1 minute, then add the chili sauce, tomato ketchup, paprika and soy sauce and stir-fry briefly.

Stir the cornstarch into the stock or water and pour into the pan. When it is boiling, return the crabs. Cook, stirring continually, until the sauce thickens and coats the crab. Pour in the eggs, if using, and add the reserved crab tomalley. Stir gently and slowly so they set in the hot sauce. Add salt and pepper to taste and stir in the chopped scallions. Serve onto a large platter.

Hot Sauce Clams

Makes 4 servings

To convert this potent clam sauté into a chowder you'll never forget, simply add more fish stock and thickening, adjusting the seasonings to taste. Serve with plain white rice.

3/4 pounds fresh clams in their shells

3 tablespoons vegetable oil

1 medium onion, chopped

4 cloves garlic, sliced

2 tablespoons julienned fresh ginger

2 fresh hot green chilies, seeded and sliced

1 tablespoon fish sauce

1 to 3 tablespoons Thai sriracha hot chili sauce

2 kaffir lime leaves, scored with the point of a knife or 1 teaspoon grated lime/lemon zest

1 1/2 cups fish stock or water

Salt and freshly ground black pepper, to taste

1 1/3 tablespoons cornstarch

1/2 cup cold water

1/2 cup chopped cilantro (fresh coriander) leaves

Freshly squeezed lime juice, to taste

⊕ Soak the clams overnight in cold water to ensure no sand remains within the shells. Drain the clams well and set aside.

⊕ Heat the oil over medium heat in a saucepan or a wok and cook the onion, stirring, for 1 1/2 minutes. Add the garlic, ginger and green chili and cook, stirring, for 30 seconds. Add the drained clams and stir in the oil for 30 seconds, then pour on the stock or water and add the fish sauce, chili sauce and lime leaves or zest. Cover the pan and cook over medium heat until the clams open, about 7 minutes.

⊕ Shake the pan from time to time to encourage opening, and discard any clams that do not open. Remove the clams to a serving dish. Stir cornstarch into the 1/2 cup of water and pour into the pan. Add salt and pepper and stir over high heat until the sauce thickens. Remove and discard the lime leaves. Add the cilantro and lime juice. Pour over the clams.

Chili Squid

Makes 4 servings, or more if sharing several dishes

Larger fresh or frozen squid (up to 7 inches) or cuttlefish is best here. Serve with steamed rice or thai noodles, and stir-fried vegetables.

1 pound fresh squid

4 thin slices fresh ginger

6 shallots, peeled

3 cloves garlic, peeled

3 fresh hot red chilies, seeded and stemmed

2¹/₂ tablespoons vegetable oil

1¹/₂ tablespoons fish sauce

¹/₂ teaspoon sesame oil

¹/₂ teaspoon shrimp paste

1 teaspoon oyster sauce

1 tablespoon rice wine, sake or dry sherry

¹/₂ cup water reserved from boiling squid

2 teaspoons cornstarch

Salt and pepper

1 scallion (green part only), chopped

1 tablespoon chopped cilantro (fresh coriander) leaves

⊕ The squid, including the tentacles, must be cut into strips, scored and parboiled to tenderize it before frying.

⊕ Clean, skin and rinse the squid (see sidebar, page 26), and cut into strips of ¹/₂ × 1¹/₂ inches. The tentacles can be used as well. Place in small saucepan with the ginger slices and cover with water. Bring to the boil, reduce heat to medium-low, and simmer for 5 to 6 minutes. Drain thoroughly, reserving ¹/₂ cup of the liquid.

⊕ Slice the shallots on a diagonal, into ³/₄-inch pieces. Finely chop the garlic, and finely slice the chilies. In a wok or skillet, cook the shallots and garlic in the oil over medium heat, stirring, for 1¹/₂ minutes. Add the chilies and cook briefly, stirring, then increase the heat to high. Add the squid and stir-fry for about 45 seconds, then add the fish sauce, shrimp paste, sesame oil, oyster sauce and wine and stir-fry briefly.

⊕ Stir cornstarch into the reserved cooking liquid and pour into the pan to make the sauce. Cook over medium heat, stirring continuously, until the sauce thickens. Season with salt and pepper and stir in the scallion and cilantro, reserving a little for garnish.

Chapter 6

Main Flavors: Chicken and Other Birds

On the Spice Trail

Part of the joy of being in Asia is its wondrous food aromas. Wandering down a side street in Shanghai, you might catch the tantalizing toasty fragrance of onion cakes browning in a pan somewhere nearby. Bussing northwards to Chiang Mai, you can't miss the roasty-smoky smell of *kai yang* (barbecued chicken) drifting from a roadside cookhouse. Entering a marketplace in Malaysia you're met with a kaleidoscope of fragrances from sweet-putrid *durian* and earthy turmeric to delicate ginger blossoms. In Indonesia, the nutty smell of coconut pervades; in India, it's pungent cumin, and maple-smelling fenugreek, and the divinely rich caramel aromas of *barfi* and a plethora of other delightful creamy sweetmeats. There's the smoky lure of *tandooris* baking plump cushions of *naan* bread, and char-grills crackling the glossy red skin of a suckling pig. There are explosive flashes of pure olfactory delight from woks sizzling ginger, and garlic, and shellfish, and sesame oil. Thailand and Vietnam counterbalance their pungent and offensive fish sauces and shrimp pastes with heavenly scents of fresh herbs and a proliferation of titillating citrus aromas. But the most intoxicating smells of all are those of the spice markets. Subtle, woody cinnamon; heady, overpowering cloves; delicately scented cardamom; deep and pervasive cumin; lemony coriander. There are aromas of licorice and citrus, nasal-assaulting pepper and chili; there are earthy, vegetative fragrances, and the unmistakable elegance of saffron.

Spices transform the ordinary into the sensational. That many of the world's most exciting spices are indigenous to southeast Asia has obviously been an influential factor in making them an integral part of the cuisines of those countries. But Asian cooks are not merely making the most of local produce. They have developed the use of spices into an art form. Nowhere are spices more important than in Indian cooking, where the *masala* (spice mix) dictates the style of the dish. *Garam masala* literally means "hot spice," though the hot aspect comes mostly from peppercorns. The other elements of a *garam masala* mix (see page 247) indicate a distinct regionality of flavor, which is directly reflected in the food. An all-purpose mix may contain black cardamom, cinnamon, cloves, cumin, black peppercorns and nutmeg. In southern states they would prefer green cardamom, and add coriander. In Kashmir they use locally harvested black cumin and add aniseed or fennel, while the *moglai* or royal style of cuisine, praised for its richness and subtlety, eschews the "common" spices cumin and coriander in favor of the sweet spices cardamom, cinnamon, nutmeg and cloves—with peppercorns for heat. Curry powders contain a proliferation of spices, but also chili, hot spices like mustard and fenugreek, and often turmeric, the root spice that gives curries their characteristic golden color.

Curry pastes are complex combinations of both spices and fresh seasonings like ginger and garlic, with the moistening agents of oil, water or vinegar dictating the final style of the paste. Prepared curry pastes retain their flavor and aroma constituents longer than dry powder mixes, especially if kept in the refrigerator in warmer climates.

Even when a commercial curry powder or paste is used in southeast Asia, the cook may choose to exercise individuality by adding whole or freshly ground spices as well. Seed spices can be "dry roasted" in the oven or in a pan without oil, which serves several purposes simultaneously. Firstly, it freshens the flavors and brightens aromas. Next, it darkens the color of the resultant *masala* which means a browner, more-appetizing looking curry with a deeper, more intensified and slightly smoky flavor; and lastly, it makes spices easier to grind.

Spices can of course, be used whole, where their effect will be minimalized in dishes that cook quickly, but fully extracted and utilized in a dish that cooks slowly and gently. Their best attributes emerge only after cooking, so the smart curry cook never simply throws in curry paste, powder, *garam masala*, or spices, but ensures that they are gently cooked in the oil or *ghee* until their full fragrance emerges.

For optimum freshness it is wisest to purchase whole spices and grind them as needed. Seed and ground spices should be stored in well-sealed spice jars away from damp and heat. The common spices specified in these recipes include cinnamon, coriander, cloves, cumin and fennel, plus the elegant, intensely aromatic star-shaped star anise, loved by Chinese cooks, but also used in Indian and Malaysian dishes. Some less-known spices are also used. *Ajwain* or *carom* is a seed spice related to cumin and has a flavor similar to the herb thyme. It can be omitted, or replaced by aniseed or celery seeds in a recipe. Aniseed is a small seed spice with a distinct licorice flavor. Fennel and dill seeds are similar to aniseed, and have a particular affinity with seafood. Cardamom is a smooth pale green or coarse-textured dull brown seed pod containing numerous highly aromatic black seeds. Purchase whole pods in preference to seeds or ground spice. Fenugreek has amber-colored, irregular-shaped seeds which smell of maple syrup. This spice is relatively easy to obtain. Wild onion seed or *nigella* is often erroneously called "black cumin." Although the taste is similar it is not related, but cumin can be substituted in a dish.

Possibly the best words of advice I ever received in my many years of studying and researching food all over Asia were from a very old Indian lady in New Delhi, over whose curry pot I leaned for several days. "If you want to be a great cook, never be mean with spices. But you must first understand them to use them properly."

Main Flavors: Chicken and Other Birds   117

Thai Sauté Chicken with Basil

Makes 4 servings, or more if sharing several dishes

When you want to add a dish that provides a fiery highlight in a curry meal, this is the one! Serve with steamed white rice; perhaps molded by pressing into a small bowl and inverting onto the plate.

1 pound boneless, skinless chicken breasts

1/4 cup peanut or vegetable oil

4 scallions (green and white parts), chopped

1/2 red bell pepper, very thinly sliced

11/2 to 3 tablespoons Thai "bird's eye" (small, hot) chilies

1/4 cup fish sauce

1 teaspoon crushed palm sugar or soft brown sugar

Freshly ground black pepper, to taste

1 to 11/2 cups loosely packed sweet basil leaves

⊕ Cut the chicken into very small dice. Heat a wok or skillet over high heat and add the oil. When it has heated sufficiently to create a light smoke haze in the pan, add the chicken and stir-fry until it is very lightly browned, about 1 minute. Remove the chicken with a slotted spoon and set aside.

⊕ Add the scallions, pepper and chilies to the pan and stir-fry over high heat for about 11/2 minutes. Drain the oil, leaving about 2 teaspoons in the pan.

⊕ Return the chicken, add the fish sauce, sugar and pepper and stir-fry for about 30 seconds. Stir in the basil leaves, then serve it quickly onto a slightly warmed serving plate and take to the table. If the basil leaves are overheated, their flavor may dominate the dish, so ensure this final step is done immediately before serving.

Hoisin Chicken

Makes 2 to 3 servings

A light and spicy dish that takes less than 10 minutes from start to table. Great for a speedy mid-week dinner, with rice and some quick-poached spinach or Chinese greens. Serve with white rice or boiled noodles, and perhaps stir-fried bean sprouts or snow peas.

12 ounces boneless, skinless chicken breasts

2 tablespoons vegetable oil

1 large onion, chopped

2 cloves garlic, minced

3 to 4 slices fresh ginger, minced

3 ounces canned shredded or sliced bamboo shoots, drained

1/4 cup hoisin sauce

2 teaspoons light soy sauce

Salt and freshly ground black pepper

⊕ Cut the chicken into 1/2-inch cubes. Heat the oil in a wok or heavy skillet over medium heat and cook the onion, garlic and ginger, stirring, for about 1 1/2 minutes, until limp and translucent.

⊕ Increase the heat to high. Add the cubed chicken and stir-fry using a wide, flat spatula to stir and turn the chicken constantly in the Chinese way, for almost 2 minutes, until cooked.

⊕ Add the bamboo shoots, *hoisin* and soy sauces and stir until each piece of chicken is coated. Check for seasoning, adding salt and pepper, as needed.

Sichuan Piquant Chicken

Makes 4 to 6 servings

In China's central-western province of Sichuan they are passionate about intensely strong and often explosively hot flavors. This dish is typical. Serve it with plenty of white rice or with rice noodles, and some crunchy sweet-pickled vegetables like those on page 272, or stir-fried Chinese cabbage or greens.

14 ounces boneless, skinless chicken
    breasts
1 tablespoon grated fresh ginger
1 large onion
1 tablespoon cornstarch
1 egg white, lightly beaten
1/4 cup vegetable oil

1/2 cup diced green pepper
1/2 cup sliced straw mushrooms or
    champignons
1/2 cup sliced bamboo shoots
1/4 to 1/2 teaspoon ground Sichuan
    peppercorns or black pepper

Piquant Sauce

3 teaspoons minced garlic
2 teaspoons minced fresh ginger
1 to 3 teaspoons minced red chili
2 tablespoons minced scallion greens
1 tablespoon light soy sauce
1 1/2 teaspoons dark soy sauce
2 to 3 teaspoons chili-bean sauce

1/2 teaspoon chili oil
2 teaspoons Chinese black vinegar,
    or 1 teaspoon balsamic vinegar
2 teaspoons sugar
2 teaspoons sesame oil
2 teaspoons sesame paste (tahini)

⊕ Cut the chicken into small cubes and place in a bowl. Put the grated ginger into a small piece of clean cloth and squeeze the juice over the chicken. Mix the chicken up well, then set aside for 10 minutes.

⊕ Peel the onion and cut into small squares. In a small bowl, combine the cornstarch, beaten egg white and enough water to make a thin paste. Pour over the chicken and stir up with your hands to evenly and thinly coat each piece of chicken.

⊕ Heat the oil in a wok or large, heavy skillet over high heat. Add the chicken and stir-fry until it is lightly golden and beginning to firm up, about $1^{1}/4$ minutes. Remove and set aside.

⊕ Add the onions and stir-fry over high heat until well cooked about $2^{1}/2$ minutes. Add the green pepper and cook about 45 seconds. Add the mushrooms and bamboo shoots, and return the chicken. Stir and toss the ingredients until well mixed.

⊕ Add the sauce ingredients beginning first with the garlic, ginger, chili and scallions. Stir-fry for 30 seconds, then add the remaining ingredients, and stir-fry until the ingredients are well mixed and the chicken is cooked. The dish should be very aromatic. Serve onto a plate and sprinkle on the pepper.

⊕ At the table, stir up the dish with chopsticks to mix in the pepper before serving.

Chicken in Chili and Sesame Oil Sauce

Makes 4 servings, or more if sharing several dishes

This peppy dish is best served as part of a Chinese-style menu of shared dishes. A crisp-fried fish or shrimp deep fried in their shells with pepper-salt, Chinese greens with oyster sauce, and a pork or beef stir-fry with white rice would be a nicely balanced meal.

1¼ pounds boneless, skinless chicken breasts

2 teaspoons Chinese cooking (rice) wine or sake

¾ teaspoon sugar

2 teaspoons cornstarch

4 stems garlic chives

1½ tablespoons corn or other vegetable oil

1 rib celery, julienned

Chili and Sesame Oil Sauce

1 tablespoon sesame oil

3 red chilies, chopped (unseeded)

2 to 3 teaspoons chili oil

½ to 1 teaspoon sugar

Cut the chicken into ¾-inch cubes, and place in a dish with the wine, sugar and cornstarch. Mix well and set aside for 20 minutes. Cut the garlic chives into 2-inch pieces.

Heat the oil in a wok or skillet over medium-high heat and stir-fry the celery until softened. Remove from the pan and set aside. Add the chicken and cook until it has firmed, and is barely cooked through, about 2½ minutes. Remove from the pan and set aside. Rinse the pan and reheat.

To make the sauce, add the sesame oil and cook the chilies, stirring, for 2 to 3 minutes over medium-high heat. Add the chili oil and sugar and return the chicken. Cook until the chicken is evenly coated with the oils, then stir in the garlic chives and celery and heat through. Transfer to a serving plate.

Note: To soften the heat of the dish, add a handful of bean sprouts in the last stages of cooking.

Butter Chicken

🌶 or ⊙ if Tandoori Chicken Tikka was prepared in advance

Makes 4 to 6 servings

If you don't want to spend the time making the tandoori chicken required for this recipe, simply use boneless chicken breasts rubbed with some purchased tandoori paste, and pan-fried or grilled until cooked through. Serve with white rice flavored with a crushed cardamom pod.

1 recipe Tandoori Chicken Tikka (page 191)	1 to 2 fresh red chilies, seeded and finely sliced
1¹/₄ pounds soft red tomatoes	1¹/₄ ounces raw cashews, ground to a paste
4 to 6 ounces (1 to 1¹/₂ sticks) unsalted butter	Salt and freshly ground black pepper
1 tablespoon minced fresh ginger	¹/₄ to ¹/₂ cup thick cream* (optional)
2 to 3 teaspoons minced garlic	¹/₄ cup chopped cilantro (fresh coriander) leaves
1 teaspoon sweet paprika	

⊕ Cook the Tandoori Chicken Tikka and set aside to cool.

⊕ To skin the tomatoes, bring a pan of water to a boil, add the tomatoes and remove after about 8 seconds. Slit the skin with a sharp knife and peel off. Cut the tomatoes in half and gently squeeze out and discard the seeds. Chop the tomatoes finely.

⊕ Melt the butter in a heavy saucepan or a medium-size skillet or saute pan over medium heat. Gently cook the ginger and garlic for 2 minutes. Add the tomatoes and continue to cook over medium heat, stirring frequently, until they are reduced to a soft pulp, about 15 minutes. Add a small amount of cold water if the mixture begins to dry out.

⊕ Force the tomato through a sieve, or puree in a blender and then strain. Return to the saucepan and add the paprika, chilies and ground cashews. Cook for 3 to 4 minutes, then season with salt and pepper, add the cream and half the cilantro.

⊕ Cut tandoori or grilled chicken into bite-sized pieces and put them in the sauce. Cook on low heat just long enough for the chicken to warm through. Serve into a shallow serving bowl and scatter on the remaining cilantro.

The added cream gives a thick, rich sauce.

Chengtu Chicken

Vegetarians can enjoy this tasty dish by substituting firm tofu (bean curd).

1¼ pounds boneless, skinless
   chicken breasts (or firm tofu)
½ cup vegetable oil
½ cup raw, skinned peanuts
3 whole scallions, sliced diagonally
   into 1-inch pieces

2 cloves garlic, sliced
1 tablespoon shredded fresh ginger
1 green chili, seeded and sliced
1 fresh red chili, seeded and sliced
1 yellow chili, seeded and sliced
   (optional)

Seasoning for Chicken

1 teaspoon sesame oil
2 teaspoons light soy sauce

2 teaspoons Chinese cooking (rice)
   wine or sake

Sauce

1 tablespoon light soy sauce
¼ to ½ teaspoon chili oil
2 teaspoons Chinese cooking (rice)
   wine or sake, or ¾ teaspoon
   brandy

½ cup chicken stock
2 teaspoons cornstarch
Freshly ground black pepper, to taste

Garnish

Reserved sliced chili or chili "flowers"
   (page 31)

⊕ Cut the chicken (or tofu) into ½-inch cubes and place in a dish. Sprinkle on the seasoning ingredients, mix well and let marinate for 15 minutes.

⊕ Heat the oil over medium-high heat in a wok or skillet and fry the peanuts until golden, about 1½ minutes. Remove the pan and set aside. Pour off half the oil. Add the chicken (or tofu) to the pan and stir-fry over high heat until it turns a light golden brown, about 2 minutes. Remove from the pan and set aside.

Reheat the pan briefly over medium-high heat, add the scallions, garlic, ginger and most of the chilies, reserving a few slices for garnish. Stir-fry for 1½ minutes. Return the chicken (or tofu) and add the soy, chili oil and wine. Stir briefly.

 Combine the chicken stock and cornstarch, pour into the pan and cook, stirring, until the sauce thickens and becomes translucent. Add pepper to taste and, finally, stir in the peanuts.

 Serve onto a plate and garnish with the reserved sliced chili, or chili "flowers."

Note: To make a milder dish, stir 2 teaspoons of sesame paste (*tahini*) and a little extra stock or water into the sauce.

Thai Braised Chili Chicken

Makes 6 servings

Cook up a stir-fry of napa cabbage, carrot and broccoli, or serve with the Chili Coconut Cabbage on page 223, to complete a simple family style menu.

2¹/₂ pounds chicken parts

2 stems lemon grass, slit in half lengthways

4 kaffir lime leaves, scored on the surface

6 slices galangal or fresh ginger

2 tablespoons fish sauce

¹/₂ teaspoon salt

1 teaspoon sugar

³/₄ cup small straw mushrooms, or champignons

Chili Paste

6 to 12 dried red chilies, soaked for 15 minutes in warm water

1¹/₂ tablespoons dried shrimp, soaked for 15 minutes in warm water, or 1¹/₄ teaspoons shrimp paste, or 2 tablespoons mashed anchovies

1 medium onion, roughly chopped

4 cloves garlic, peeled

2 to 3 slices fresh galangal, or ¹/₂ teaspoon laos powder, or 6 thin slices fresh ginger

2 cilantro (fresh coriander) sprigs, with stems and roots, coarsely chopped

¹/₂ teaspoon ground turmeric

⊕ Use a Chinese cleaver or large, heavy knife to chop the chicken into bite-sized pieces, cutting through the bones. Place in a saucepan with water to cover, and the lemon grass, lime leaves and *galangal*. Bring to a boil, reduce heat and simmer for 10 minutes.

⊕ In the meantime, drain the chilies and slit open so the seeds can be scraped out. Place chilies and the other chili paste ingredients into a mortar, blender, the small bowl of a food processor fitted with the metal blade, or a spice grinder. Grind to a smooth paste, then stir into the cooking liquid and continue to simmer, until the chicken is tender and the sauce reduced, stirring occasionally, about 25 minutes.

⊕ Add the fish sauce, salt and sugar, adjusting the seasonings to taste, if necessary. Add the mushrooms and simmer for about 2 minutes.

⊕ Serve in a deep dish, with steamed long grain rice or with steamed "sticky" rice (glutinous white rice) in the tradition of northern Thailand.

Burmese Caramelized Chicken

Makes 6 servings

The original Chinese formula for "sweet and sour" was sugar caramelized to an amber brown in a pan with a little oil, then thinned and acidulated with vinegar. In this dish from Burma, a similar principle is used, but the chicken is first marinated with ginger and one of their favorite seasonings, turmeric, which grows abundantly there. It is modestly hot, in this version, but feel free to indulge in extra chili. Serve with steamed white rice and a simple salad.

2½ pounds chicken parts

1⅓ teaspoons salt

1¼ teaspoons ground turmeric

¾ to 1 teaspoon chili powder

¾ teaspoon fine white pepper

2 teaspoons mashed garlic

2 teaspoons finely grated fresh ginger

3 tablespoons vegetable oil

¾ cup cornstarch

¾ cup all-purpose flour

4 to 6 cups vegetable oil for deep frying

Caramel Glaze

¾ cup soft brown sugar

3 teaspoons minced garlic

5 teaspoons chopped cilantro (fresh coriander) leaves

1½ to 2 teaspoons cracked or coarsely ground black pepper

1½ teaspoons chili flakes

⅓ to ½ cup rice vinegar

⊕ Rinse the chicken parts, drain and dry. Combine the salt, turmeric, chili powder, white pepper, garlic, ginger and vegetable oil in a large bowl and add the chicken. Mix until the chicken is evenly coated, then cover with plastic wrap and refrigerate for 2 to 3 hours.

⊕ Heat the oil in a wok or large, deep pan suitable for deep frying to medium, 360°F. Combine the cornstarch and flour on a flat plate. Coat each piece of chicken lightly and evenly with the flour, and shake off any excess. Fry 5 to 6 pieces at a time, for 12 to 15 minutes, until well cooked and golden brown. Remove and drain. When all of the chicken is done, set aside, keeping warm.

⊕ In a clean wok or large nonstick pan, heat the sugar until it melts. Add the remaining glaze ingredients and mix well. Simmer for 2 to 3 minutes over medium heat until the mixture begins to caramelize.

⊕ Add the chicken pieces a few at a time, turning them in the caramel to coat evenly. Pile them onto a platter and serve.

Balinese Coconut Chicken Legs

Makes 4 servings, or more if sharing several dishes

Nothing could be easier to do than chicken legs baked in a coconut sauce. It makes a great family meal, served with rice or noodles, and you can pep them up by serving a fiery sambal or chili sauce. Serve with Nasi Goreng (page 277) or with plain white rice and the Indonesian Fruit and Vegetable Salad on page 218.

**12 small chicken legs, about
  1¹/4 pounds**

**1 stem lemon grass, slit in half
  lengthways**

**¹/2 teaspoon soft shrimp paste, or
  3 teaspoons fish sauce**

**1 hot, green chili, slit in half length-
  ways (seeded, if preferred)**

**2 small ripe tomatoes, cut into
  wedges**

1¹/2 cups coconut cream

³/4 teaspoon salt

³/4 cup water

**2 to 3 teaspoons chopped fresh basil
  or scallions**

Preheat the oven to 350°F.

In a casserole or ovenproof dish, warm the lemon grass, shrimp paste or fish sauce, chili, tomatoes, coconut milk, salt and water over low heat for about 6 minutes.

Add the chicken and place, uncovered, in the oven. Bake for about 35 minutes or until the chicken is tender, turning several times, and basting with the sauce. Stir in chopped basil or scallions just before serving.

Malay Curried Chicken

Makes 6 servings

This chicken dish, along with steamed white or brown rice, and the Indian Spiced Cauliflower or the Hot and Aromatic Okra on pages 227 and 228, would make an ideal menu for an informal meal.

2 pounds chicken parts or chicken legs

1 medium onion, chopped

2 tablespoons peanut or vegetable oil, or ghee (clarified butter)

3/4 cup coconut cream

4 small new potatoes, halved

1 cup green peas, fresh or frozen

2 tablespoons chopped cilantro (fresh coriander) or sweet basil leaves

Curry Sauce

3 to 6 dried red chilies

2 tablespoons coriander seeds

1 teaspoon cumin seeds

4 red or golden shallots, minced

2 to 3 cloves garlic, minced

1 inch piece fresh ginger, grated

1 teaspoon ground turmeric

1 cinnamon stick

3 whole cloves

1/2 teaspoon ground mace or nutmeg

1/3 teaspoon fenugreek seeds

1/4 teaspoon aniseed or fennel, lightly crushed

1 1/2 teaspoons salt

3/4 teaspoon white peppercorns

✺ Rinse the chicken in cold water and drain. Place in a saucepan with water to barely cover and bring to a boil. Reduce the heat and let chicken simmer.

✺ To prepare the curry sauce, heat a medium saucepan or wok without oil and roast the chilies and coriander and cumin seeds over medium-high heat until very aromatic and the seeds begin to pop and jump about in the pan, about 2 1/2 minutes. Shake the pan and stir frequently so the seeds color evenly. Break open the chilies and shake out and discard the seeds, then place the chilies in a spice grinder or mortar with the coriander and cumin and grind to a powder. Remove and set aside, then grind the shallots, garlic and ginger to a paste.

✺ Heat the oil in a sauté pan or wok and fry the onions over medium heat until well browned, about 12 minutes, then remove. In the same pan cook the shallots, garlic and ginger for 1 minute. Add the ground spices, fennel and remaining whole spices and fry briefly.

✺ Add the coconut cream and a large spoonful of liquid from the chicken and bring to a boil, simmering until the spices are well blended. Pour into the chicken pot, add the fried onions and the potatoes (and fresh peas, if using.) Simmer until the chicken and potatoes are tender. Add frozen peas, and half the cilantro and check the seasoning.

✺ The sauce is fairly thin, but can be thickened with a dilution of cornstarch in cold water, if preferred. Serve into a deep bowl and sprinkle on remaining cilantro.

Note: **Hard-boiled eggs, cut into wedges, are an excellent addition to this curry.**

Aromatic Crisp Skinned Chicken with Sweet Chili Sauce

Makes 6 servings

This is an easy dish to do, but you will need to plan ahead. You will obtain a crisper skin using a large chicken. As an alternative to the sweet chili sauce given with this recipe, try the Sichuan Sauce Dip on page 254. Serve with fried rice, and the Stir-fried Bean Sprouts with Chinese Sausage and Chili Shreds, on page 225, as an accompaniment.

1 large fresh chicken (about 4 pounds), or 3 small fresh chickens (each 1 to 1¼ pounds)

3 tablespoons honey

2½ teaspoons Chinese five-spice powder

2½ teaspoons salt

¾ teaspoon ground Sichuan peppercorns or white pepper

Garnish

Cilantro (fresh coriander) sprigs

Pickled Cucumber (see sidebar)

Sweet Chili Sauce

4 fresh red chilies, chopped finely

3 cloves garlic, minced

1 tablespoon minced or grated fresh ginger

2 tablespoons vegetable oil

¾ cup water

⅓ cup white vinegar

½ cup sugar

Few drops of red food coloring

4 teaspoons cornstarch

1 tablespoon very finely chopped scallion greens

⊕ Rinse the chicken(s) in cold water and drain well. Bring a large kettle of water to a boil. Hold the chickens with tongs over the sink and slowly pour the boiling water over the skin. Place it/them on a rack over a large drip bowl and set aside for about 30 minutes to drip, then place uncovered in the refrigerator for at least 4 hours, to dry the skin.

⊕ Heat the oven to 400°F. Dilute 3 teaspoons of the honey with 1½ tablespoons boiling water and brush evenly over the chicken(s). Combine the five-spice powder, salt and pepper and rub into the chicken skin. Sprinkle any remaining

Pickled Cucumber

Small cucumbers, no more than 4 inches long, fresh-pickled in salt, sugar and vinegar, are a perfect accompaniment to crisp fried or roasted chicken. You will need about four for this recipe. Slit them in half, then slice finely and place in a glass or stainless steel bowl. Sprinkle 2½ teaspoons of salt evenly over them and leave for 10 minutes, then squeeze and knead them gently with your fingers to work in the salt and help soften them. Next, rinse them briefly in cold water and drain well. In a small saucepan heat ½ cup of white vinegar with ½ cup of water and 1 to 2 tablespoons of fine white sugar, just until the sugar dissolves. Pour it over the cucumbers and let steep at least 20 minutes before removing from the marinade with tongs.

seasonings inside the chicken cavity. Place the chicken(s) on a rack in a baking pan and place in the oven for 15 minutes.

⊕ Dilute the remaining honey with 3 tablespoons of boiling water. Use a brush to paint the chickens with honey solution. Reduce the heat to 350°F, and continue to roast until the chicken(s) are done—about 50 minutes for a large chicken, 25 for smaller chickens—basting occasionally with the honey solution.

⊕ To make the sweet chili sauce, cook the chilies, garlic and ginger in the oil in a small, nonstick saucepan over medium heat for 2 to 3 minutes, until softened. Mix the cornstarch with 2 tablespoons of cold water and set aside. Add the water, vinegar, sugar and red food coloring to the saucepan. Boil for 2 minutes, then add the cornstarch solution and cook, stirring, until thickened. Stir in the scallions.

⊕ Cut the chickens into serving portions and arrange on a platter over a bed of pickled cucumber, garnish with cilantro and serve the sauce separately.

Sri Lankan Chicken Curry

Serve in a deep bowl with rice and a vegetable dish such as the Pumpkin Fugarth on page 232, or make a complete Sri Lankan meal by cooking the eggplant dish on page 234.

2½ pounds chicken parts

3 tablespoons vegetable oil

1 medium onion, finely sliced

1 large onion, chopped

1 small bunch amaranth or spinach

½ cup raw cashews, fried in vegetable oil to golden

Salt, freshly ground black pepper, and sugar

Curry Sauce

10 dried red chilies

2 teaspoons black peppercorns

2 tablespoons coriander seeds

1 teaspoon cumin seeds

1 teaspoon brown mustard seeds

1 cinnamon stick

4 cloves garlic, minced

1 cup coconut cream

1½ teaspoons tamarind concentrate

⊕ Brown the chicken parts in two batches in the oil over medium-high heat for about 4 minutes. Set aside, keeping warm. Pour off all but 2 tablespoons of oil, add the onion and cook until well browned. Remove from the pan and set aside.

⊕ To prepare the curry sauce, in a dry pan roast the chilies, peppercorns, and coriander, cumin and mustard seeds and cinnamon stick until they are very aromatic and beginning to pop and jump about in the pan. Shake and stir frequently as they roast, so they color evenly. Pour into a spice grinder or mortar and grind to a fine powder—if you prefer a milder dish, break open the chilies and shake out and discard the seeds before using.

⊕ Reheat the pan, add some of the retained oil and the chopped onion and cook for 3 to 4 minutes, until well browned. Add the ground spices, plus the garlic and fry for 1 minute, stirring, then pour in the coconut cream and add the tamarind and 1 cup of water. Stir well and bring to a boil. Simmer for 6 to 8 minutes.

⊕ Return the chicken and sliced onion and bring to a boil again, then reduce the heat to medium-low and simmer for about 35 minutes.

⊕ Rinse and trim the amaranth or spinach. Add to the curry with the fried cashews. Cook for 2 to 3 minutes, then check seasonings, adding salt, pepper and sugar as needed.

Red Duck Curry with Lychees

or if roasted duck was prepared in advance

Makes 4 servings, or more if sharing several dishes

This is a quick and easy curry if you can purchase a ready-roasted duck from an Asian barbecue restaurant. You may alternatively, roast a fresh duck after rubbing the skin with some dark soy sauce and red curry paste, using a purchased curry paste or our recipe. This slightly sweet curry goes well with something hot and crisp, such as a Thai Fried Fish with Hot Sauce, on page 94, and steamed jasmine rice to accompany.

¹/₂ Chinese-style roasted duck, about 1¹/₂ pounds

¹/₂ recipe Thai Red Curry Paste (page 248)

2 cups coconut cream

4 fresh, medium red chilies, halved lengthways and seeded

2 kaffir lime leaves, torn in half, or ¹/₂ lime peel, cut into strips

¹/₂ cup water

12 fresh lychees (or cherry tomatoes or Chinese jujube fruit [red dates])

1¹/₂ tablespoons sugar

2 tablespoons fish sauce

Salt and freshly ground black pepper

¹/₃ loosely packed cup sweet basil leaves, picked from their stems

Using a Chinese cleaver or heavy knife, cut the cooked duck into bite-sized pieces and set aside.

Heat the coconut cream in a medium-size saucepan and add the curry paste. Bring to a boil, reduce heat and simmer for 5 to 6 minutes. Add the chilies, lime leaves and water (add red dates at this stage, if using instead of lychees) and simmer for 6 to 8 minutes.

Put in the duck pieces and lychees (or tomatoes) and heat through. Season to taste with the sugar and fish sauce, salt and pepper. Simmer for 2 to 3 minutes, then add the basil leaves and transfer to a deep bowl.

Fiery Diced Duck and Sausage in Lettuce Parcels

Makes 6 servings

18 small lettuce cups (cup-shaped leaves)

2 duck breasts (see sidebar)

1 tablespoon dark soy sauce

1 teaspoon sugar

1 tablespoon Chinese cooking (rice) wine or sake

3/4 cup vegetable oil

1/2 cup rice vermicelli, broken

3 Chinese dried pork sausages (lap cheong)

2 cloves garlic, minced

1 1/2 teaspoons grated fresh ginger

5 tablespoons minced scallion (green and white parts)

3 tablespoons very finely chopped bamboo shoots

3 tablespoons very finely chopped straw mushrooms or soaked Chinese black mushrooms

Salt and freshly ground black pepper

Sauce

2 tablespoons hoisin sauce

3 teaspoons light soy sauce

1/2 teaspoon sugar

1 to 1 1/2 teaspoons chili oil

2 teaspoons cornstarch

1 1/2 tablespoons cold water

Extra hoisin sauce

I usually purchase whole ducks, trim the breasts and save the remainder for dishes like Padang Braised Duck (page 136) and Red Duck Curry with Lychees (page 133). If the duck breasts are very fat, trim off excess fat and gently simmer it in a small nonstick saucepan to render the fat. This can be kept in the refrigerator to use instead of oil next time you stir-fry.

⊕ Cut the duck meat into very small dice and marinate in the soy sauce, sugar and wine for 20 minutes. Combine the sauce ingredients, except the cornstarch and water, in a bowl.

⊕ Heat the oil in a wok or pan and fry the rice vermicelli for just a few seconds until it expands and turns white and crisp, remove with a slotted spoon and set aside. Pour off all but 2 tablespoons of the oil.

⊕ Very thinly slice the sausages then fry over medium heat for 2 minutes, stirring continuously, remove and set aside.

⊕ Increase the heat and add the duck meat, garlic and ginger. Stir-fry for 3 minutes, until almost cooked, then add half the scallions, bamboo shoots and mushrooms and stir-fry for 1 minute.

⊕ Stir the sauce ingredients and pour into the pan, simmer for 1 to 2 minutes, then return the sausage and add $1/2$ cup water. Cook on high heat until the liquid has evaporated and the mixture is well cooked. Check seasoning, adding salt and pepper to taste. Mix the cornstarch into the $1^1/2$ tablespoons of cold water, pour into the sauce and stir until thickened and translucent.

⊕ Finally, stir in the crushed vermicelli and remaining scallions and heat briefly, then transfer to a serving dish.

⊕ To eat, place a portion of the filling in the center of a lettuce cup, roll up and dip into *hoisin* sauce before eating.

Padang Braised Duck

Makes 6 servings

Padang is a simple style of cooking from central Java in Indonesia. Padang dishes are usually quite pungent, which is well suited to the richness of duck. You could also make this recipe using pork underbelly, or you could use turkey and increase the volume of coconut cream to compensate for its drier texture. Serve with Nasi Goreng (page 277) or boiled shortgrain white rice. Spinach or kangkong (water spinach) stir-fried with garlic and dried shrimp, like the recipe on page 226, would complete the simple country-style menu.

1 duck, approximately 4¼ pounds (or substitute pork or turkey)

2 medium onions, coarsely chopped

5 cloves garlic, peeled

4 to 5 green chilies, seeded and chopped

2 stems lemon grass, one coarsely chopped, one slit in half lengthways

1½ inch-piece fresh ginger

1-inch piece fresh galangal, or ¾ teaspoon ground laos (optional)

2½ tablespoons vegetable or peanut oil

1½ cups coconut cream

1 to 2 teaspoons white peppercorns, crushed

1½ teaspoons salt

Tamarind water, or lemon juice to taste

Sweet basil or Vietnamese mint leaves

⊕ Use a Chinese cleaver or large, heavy knife to cut the duck into serving pieces. Place in a saucepan and cover with hot water. Bring to a boil, then drain and set the duck aside.

⊕ In the meantime, place the onion, garlic, chilies, chopped lemon grass, ginger and *galangal* in a blender or the small bowl of a food processor fitted with the metal blade and chop to a paste with some texture.

⊕ Heat the oil in a large saucepan and fry the seasoning paste for about 5 minutes, stirring constantly. Add the pieces of duck and cook, still stirring, to brown them lightly. Pour in the coconut cream and add the slit lemon grass and the pepper and salt. Cover tightly and cook for 10 minutes on medium heat. Turn the duck pieces, and cover again. Continue to cook in this way, turning the duck every ten minutes, until the duck is completely tender and the sauce reduced to a coating on the duck, about 35 minutes.

⊕ Sprinkle on a little water from time to time during cooking, if needed, to prevent the duck from sticking to the pan. In the last few minutes, skim off any fat that has accumulated in the pan, add tamarind water to taste, check seasonings, and stir in the basil or mint leaves.

⊕ Transfer to a serving plate.

Crisp and Spicy Duck

Makes 8 servings

This spicy duck is fried to a crispy crunchiness that is deliciously textured and aromatic. A great festive dish, it's easier to prepare than a first glimpse at the recipe might suggest. Just allow plenty of time.

1 large duck, approximately
  5 pounds

1½ whole star anise

6 thick slices fresh ginger

2 scallions (green and white parts),
  trimmed

8 to 10 cups vegetable oil for deep
  frying

Chinese pepper-salt dip
  (page 246)

Cilantro (fresh coriander) sprigs

Seasonings

¼ cup Chinese cooking (rice) wine
  or sake

¼ cup light soy sauce

1½ tablespoons dark soy sauce

1 tablespoon ground Sichuan
  peppercorns

2 tablespoons hoisin or sweet bean
  paste

¼ teaspoon ground cloves

1 teaspoon ground cinnamon

⅓ teaspoon ground star anise

1½ tablespoons minced scallion
  (white parts only)

1 tablespoon finely grated fresh
  ginger

Rinse the duck with cold water and drain well. Pour 5 to 6 cups of boiling water over the duck, while holding it over the sink or a large bowl to drain. Combine the seasoning ingredients and spread over the duck, rubbing them into the skin. Place the star anise, ginger and scallions in the cavity.

Prepare a large steamer. If necessary improvise as a Chinese cook might with a wok, a metal stand inside and its domed lid. Set the duck on a plate in the steamer and steam over gently simmering water for about 3½ hours, replenishing the water as necessary.

Remove the duck from the steamer and allow it to drain for about 30 minutes. Before you fry it, make sure there is no liquid left inside that can cause splattering in the oil.

⊕ Heat the oil in a very large wok or a large, deep pan to 385°F; the oil will be shimmering. Carefully lower the duck into the very hot oil, then use a large spoon to continually ladle the oil over the duck so the entire surface is constantly in contact with the hot oil. You will need to fry it for about 6 minutes in all, to ensure it is thoroughly crisped.

⊕ When the duck is a deep golden brown, carefully lift it from the oil and drain well. Use a Chinese cleaver, poultry shears or a heavy large knife to cut it into bite-sized pieces. The bones will be quite soft from the lengthy cooking. Arrange the pieces on a platter, emulating the original shape of the duck, and surround with the cilantro sprigs. Serve with the pepper-salt dip.

Duck Vindaloo

Makes 6 to 10 servings

Fiery vindaloos originated in the Portuguese enclave of Goa, on India's central west coast. Their distinct tart-hot flavor comes from a multitude of spices in a vinegary marinade. Goans' favorite is made with pork, but duck comes a close second. Plan to make this ahead of time to allow the vivid flavors to mellow. Flavor and color rice with saffron, a few cloves, a cinnamon stick and a little butter, to accompany the vindaloo and serve with plain yogurt flavored with chopped cilantro.

1 large duck, approximately 4½ pounds

2 medium onions, chopped

1 small bunch cilantro (fresh coriander)

3 tablespoons vegetable oil or ghee (clarified butter)

1½ teaspoons salt

Vindaloo Paste

1½ tablespoons black peppercorns

2¼ tablespoons coriander seeds

3 teaspoons cumin seeds

2½-inch piece cinnamon stick

½ teaspoon fenugreek seeds

¾ teaspoon fennel seeds

5 whole cloves

1 teaspoon brown mustard seeds

6 to 10 dried red chilies

¾ teaspoon aamchur (dried mango powder), optional

3 teaspoons jaggery, palm sugar or dark brown sugar

6 cloves garlic, chopped

One 2-inch piece fresh ginger, grated

1½ tablespoons mustard or vegetable oil

⅓ cup white vinegar

⊕ Cut the duck into bite-size pieces, rinse in hot water and set aside to drain.

⊕ To prepare the vindaloo paste, place the peppercorns, the coriander and cumin seeds and the cinnamon stick in a pan without oil and dry roast over medium heat until they are very aromatic, about 2½ minutes, stirring and shaking the pan frequently to ensure they cook evenly. Add the fenugreek and fennel seeds, the cloves, mustard seeds and dried chilies and toast 3 minutes more. Grind the dried spices to a fine powder in a mortar or spice grinder. Transfer the spices to a blender or the small bowl of a food processor fitted with the metal blade, or if preferred leave them in the mortar to complete the preparation of the paste.

❀ Add the aamchur, sugar, garlic and ginger and grind again to a thick paste, then slowly incorporate the oil and vinegar a few teaspoons at a time, pounding or grinding vigorously between each addition, until you have a thick emulsion.

❀ Spread the vindaloo paste evenly over the duck and cover with plastic wrap. Refrigerate for 3 to 4 hours to allow the seasonings to thoroughly penetrate the meat.

❀ Heat the oil in a large saucepan and brown the onions. Remove the onions. Brown the duck in the same pan, several pieces at a time. Return the onions and all of the duck and add any of the vindaloo paste that remains in the bowl. Add cold water to about 1 inch below the level of the duck. Add the salt and bring to a boil, then reduce heat to medium-low and cook until the duck is very tender, about 1¼ hours, stirring occasionally and scraping the bottom of the pan to prevent sticking.

❀ Use a large spoon to skim off the fat that has accumulated on the surface. It can be saved to use in another dish. Remove the curry from the heat and set aside for several hours, then gently reheat to serve.

❀ Pick the leaves from the cilantro and stir them into the curry. Check seasonings and transfer to a deep bowl.

Jungle Curry

Makes 6 to 8 servings

This northern Thai curry is packed with vibrant flavor. It is an excellent recipe for rich game meats, like wild boar, venison or game birds. In Australia, I tried kangaroo meat, to surprisingly good effect. I have made it here with tender roasting pigeons.

Curry Paste

1 to 3 green chilies, unseeded and
    chopped

5 cloves garlic, peeled

1-inch piece fresh galangal or
    2 teaspoons powdered laos,
    or young fresh ginger

10 pieces cilantro (fresh coriander)
    root, rinsed

1 1/2-inch piece young fresh ginger,
    peeled and chopped

10 red or golden shallots, peeled

1 stem lemon grass, trimmed and
    chopped

1 1/2 tablespoons shrimp paste*

1 tablespoon dried shrimp, rinsed
    and dried

1 1/4 teaspoons black peppercorns

1 1/3 teaspoon salt

1 1/2 tablespoons vegetable oil

Curry

2 to 3 dressed squab, 6 to 8 quails,
    or 2 small chickens, each about
    1 1/4 pounds

4 tablespoons vegetable oil

3 tablespoons fish sauce

2 hot green chilies, seeded and sliced

6 kaffir lime leaves, torn in half, or
    the peel of 1 lime

3 ounces pea eggplant**

3 ounces sliced bamboo shoots,
    drained

3 ounces snake or green beans, cut
    into 2-inch pieces

6 stems fresh peppercorns, or
    1 1/3 tablespoons green
    peppercorns

3 fresh galangal stems (optional)

3 ounces small straw mushrooms or
    champignons

6 small cherry tomatoes (optional)

1 small bunch fresh basil (preferably
    holy basil)

*Option for shrimp paste and dried shrimp is 2 to 3 tablespoons mashed anchovies.

**Underripe gooseberries or tomatillos are a good substitute for these tiny tart eggplants, or you can use slender Oriental eggplant, cut into 1-inch cubes.

◈ To make the curry paste, place all of the ingredients in a blender, in the small bowl of a food processor fitted with the metal blade, or into a spice grinder or stone mortar. Grind to a smooth paste, adding just enough water to moisten. Set aside.

◈ Cut the squab or chickens in half. Trim off the wing tips and necks. Place these trimmings in a saucepan with water to barely cover, bring to a boil, then reduce heat and simmer for 30 minutes to make a game stock. Cut the squab in half again, and the chickens into serving pieces. If you are using quail, cut them in half.

◈ Heat 2 tablespoons of the oil in a saucepan and brown the poultry pieces over high heat, cooking for 4 to 5 minutes. Then strain on the stock, add the fish sauce, chilies and lime leaves and simmer gently for 25 to 30 minutes, until barely tender. At this point, if you prefer, the meat can be removed from the stock and deboned.

◈ Heat the remaining oil in a wok or medium-size saucepan and fry the curry paste for 5 minutes over medium heat. Add the pea eggplant or cubed eggplant, bamboo shoots, beans, peppercorns and *galangal* and cook briefly, stirring. Add the poultry and its cooking stock and simmer for 5 to 6 minutes. Add the mushrooms and cherry tomatoes and cook for 2 to 3 minutes. Check seasoning, adding salt if needed. Pick the leaves from the basil and stir into the curry just before serving.

◈ Plain steamed jasmine or other long grain white rice, or 'sticky' (glutinous) white rice are the traditional companions for a 'jungle' curry in Thailand, with small dishes containing boiled and sliced salted duck eggs and pickled garlic or shallots on the side.

Chapter 7

Main Flavors: Beef, Lamb and Pork

Pork Dishes

Thai Sauté of Pork with Basil and Chilies

Spicy Pork with Sichuan Vegetables

Shanghai "Twice-Cooked" Sliced Pork
with Peppers

Thai Pork and Long Beans in Hot Chili Sauce

Fiery Shredded Pork with Mushrooms
and Bamboo Shoots

Pork Vindaloo

Malaccan "Devil" Pork

Indonesian Babi Kecap

Garlic Black Bean Braised Ribs

Beef Dishes

Chinese Country-Style Shredded Beef
and Peppers

Ma Po Tofu

Sichuan Chili Beef

Crisp Chili Beef with Orange Rind
and Sichuan Peppercorns

Sumatran Beef

Indonesian Beef Rendang

Braised Beef Hunan Style

Lamb Dishes

Sizzling Mongolian Lamb

Coconut Lamb Curry

Hunan Lamb Shanks

Lamb Koftas in Curry Sauce

Other Meats

Red Curry of Venison

A Fiery Sauté of Kidneys and Peppers

Sichuan Peppered Liver

Of Muttabaks and "Wok Hei"

I am standing transfixed watching the *muttabak* maker throwing his pastry across a circular work top of oiled aluminum. It stretches and floats downwards thin as silk, and as it touches he deftly flicks it upwards again, each action stretching the dough farther, until it's so transparent he could read his *Straits Times* through it. Satisfied, he looks up to his customer for approval, and a nod..."curry or egg?" The latter! Cracking an egg into the center, he pierces the yolk then with a series of neat tucks and folds, the pastry, which seconds earlier covered a square yard of work top, is now one neat parcel sizzling to gold on a griddle slicked with *ghee*. The man was an artist, a traveling food circus with a show not to be missed. An itinerant food stall operator who might be found at a streetside market anywhere in Malaysia. That morning I ordered lamb filling, usually preferring to bite into a searing curry when I eat a *muttabak*. There's an inspired contrast between the bland chewiness of the layered dough and a fabulously hot filling.

That particular visit to Malaysia, my fourth I think, was profoundly significant. First, there was my near-drowning in Penang. Replete from one of those multi-course lunches we food writers can unabashedly call "research," I had dozed off in the sun-filtering shade of a group of coconut palms on a quiet beach. The turning tide that edged up and lapped over me was of such perfect body temperature I didn't feel a thing until I was gagging on salt water and struggling upright. Coughing up water that sparkled with phosphorescence, I came to just in time to wade out for my bag holding passport, notebook and camera, which was slowly floating seawards. Next was the incident that confirmed my commitment to a life in the food industry. This trip I was on an assignment in Malaysia for an English publisher, gathering favorite recipes from restaurants all over the country. On arriving at a particular Malay restaurant, in the holiday retreat region of the Cameron Highlands, I was whisked straight into the kitchen by an excited chef, who promptly produced a much-stained and dog-eared edition of my first Asian cookbook. This, he informed me with as much pride as I was beginning to feel myself, was their kitchen manual! Nearly expired one day, on the top of the heap the next. Wow!

Malaysian food, and that of its neighbor Singapore, is uniquely cross cultural, a harmonious blend of local and acquired tastes, ingredients and cooking styles. The Indian food there has a Malay influence; the Chinese a decided obsession with chilies; and the Malay plenty to suggest close links with Indonesian cooking. It's good, honest hands-on food with pronounced flavors and often an excellent mouthfeel. *Cha kwai teow* is typical, and always one of the first meals I seek out—fleshy, ribbon-wide rice noodles

tossed in a wok over roaring flames. *"Wok hei"* is the objective here, the flames licking into the pan impart "the air of the wok" a wondrous smoky-charred flavor that is an essential element for the perfection of this simple noodle dish.

In Malaysia, an omelet is never plain, but spiked with chili and herbs (page 45) or packed with succulent oysters. Vegetables are used with imagination, like our recipe for stir-fried bean sprouts with Chinese sausage and chili shreds (page 225). Desserts are a fascinating melange of unusual flavors, and curries are hot with chili and pepper, but also richly fragrant with spices like the Indian curries that predate them.

From the Indians they also learned to eat curry in the traditional way, no cutlery, just the fingers. In Malaysia and Singapore you can sit down to eat curry and rice this way from the original, ecologically responsible disposable plate, a twelve-inch disk of banana leaf. It's a wonderfully drippy, messy experience that I try not to miss on any visit. There's a practiced knack to shaping a ball of rice with thumb and tips of your first two fingers and using this edible sponge to mop up the curry gravy, with each bite also incorporating some of the meat or vegetables. Over the years I've become quite adept at the art, but at a cost of many terminally turmeric-stained silk blouses.

Thai Sauté of Pork with Basil and Chilies

Makes 3 to 4 servings

Serve with steamed white rice or stir-fried rice noodles.

1 1/4 pounds lean pork

2 1/2 tablespoons vegetable oil

1 large fresh hot red chili, seeded and sliced

1/2 to 1 tablespoon Thai "bird's eye" (small, hot) chilies

1 1/2 tablespoons fish sauce

1 teaspoon dark soy sauce

1/2 teaspoon shrimp paste or 1/2 canned anchovy, mashed (optional)

2 to 3 teaspoons sugar

1 1/2 cups sweet basil leaves, loosely packed

Seasoning

3 teaspoons fish sauce

2 teaspoons mashed garlic

1 teaspoon freshly ground black pepper

◉ Cut the pork into very thin slices, then into pieces about 1 × 2 inches. Place in a dish. Combine the seasoning ingredients and mix with the pork. Leave for 20 minutes.

◉ Heat the oil in a wok or large skillet and sauté the pork over medium-high heat for about 2 1/2 minutes, until almost cooked. Add the chilies and sauté for 40 seconds, then add the fish sauce, soy sauce, shrimp paste and sugar, and sauté for 1 minute. Add the basil leaves, and stir just long enough for them to wilt.

◉ Transfer to a plate and serve immediately.

Spicy Pork with Sichuan Vegetables

In the north of China, they enjoy a spicy pork dish like this, stuffed into sesame-flavored pocket bread to eat like a sandwich. Try it filled into warmed whole wheat pita pocket bread, or serve over noodles (see sidebar).

Spicy Pork with Sichuan Vegetables can be the base of a great noodle dish. Soften bean thread vermicelli in boiling water and drain well. Add to the cooked pork dish then stir-fry over medium heat for a few minutes. Check seasonings. You may need to add a little extra soy or oyster sauce. This is a dish that loves chili, so toss in a generous addition of chopped fresh chilies or dried flaked chilies.

3 tablespoons vegetable oil

1 1/2 pounds lean pork, coarsely ground (minced)

2 ounces pork fat, very finely diced (optional)

1/4 cup chopped scallions, green and white parts

1 tablespoon light soy sauce

2 to 3 teaspoons minced garlic

3 teaspoons minced pickled ginger

4 ounces Sichuan hot pickled vegetables, mustard greens, pickled radish or Korean kim chi, very finely diced

1 tablespoon oyster sauce

2 teaspoons dark soy sauce

1 1/2 teaspoons sesame oil

2 fresh hot red chilies, seeded and minced

1 1/2 teaspoons cornstarch

2/3 cup water or chicken stock

Salt and freshly ground black pepper

2 tablespoons chopped cilantro (fresh coriander)

Heat the oil in a wok or large skillet and stir-fry the pork, plus the pork fat if you are using it, for about 3 minutes over high heat until it firms and lightens. Add the scallions, light soy sauce and garlic and continue to stir-fry until the pork is lightly browned, about 3 minutes more.

Add the ginger and pickled vegetables and stir-fry briefly, then stir in the oyster and soy sauces, the sesame oil and the chilies. Stir-fry 1 to 2 minutes more over high heat. Combine the cornstarch and water or stock in a small bowl and pour into the pan, stirring until the sauce thickens and clings to the meat. Check for seasonings, adding salt and pepper, as needed, then add the cilantro and mix well.

Shanghai "Twice-Cooked" Sliced Pork with Peppers

Makes 4 to 6 servings

I have stepped up the heat here. The Shanghainese might be horrified, but this is a great vehicle for chili flavors. Serve onto a plate with rice and Chinese greens, or the Stir-fried Bean Sprouts with Chinese Sausage and Chili Shreds on page 225.

1½ pounds fresh bacon (pork belly) with skin

6 slices fresh ginger

2 scallions (green and white parts), trimmed and halved

1 teaspoon black peppercorns

½ star anise, broken into points

1 small piece cassia bark or cinnamon stick

2 tablespoons dark soy sauce

2 tablespoons Chinese cooking (rice) wine or sake

To Finish the Dish

2 tablespoons vegetable oil

½ large green bell pepper

½ large red bell pepper

2 to 3 medium-hot fresh red chilies, seeded and sliced

4 scallions, cut into 1-inch (green parts); or 8 Chinese chives, cut into 2-inch pieces

4 cloves garlic, sliced

1 tablespoon Chinese cooking (rice) wine

1 tablespoon hot bean paste, or soy bean paste for a milder dish

1 tablespoon hoisin sauce

1½ tablespoons light soy sauce

2 teaspoons sugar

¼ cup chicken stock or water

1½ teaspoons cornstarch

Salt and white pepper

⊕ Score the skin of the pork at ½-inch intervals with a sharp knife. Put the pork into a saucepan in which it fits snugly and add the ginger, scallions, peppercorns, star anise, cassia, soy sauce and wine. Cover with water and bring to a boil, then reduce the heat to very low and simmer for about 1 hour, making sure the water does not bubble briskly, but just gently simmers.

Lift out the pork, drain it and allow it to rest for 10 minutes, before slicing it thinly with a very sharp knife.

 Cut the peppers into ³/₄-inch squares. Heat the oil in a wok or large skillet and stir-fry the sliced pork over very high heat for about 1¹/₂ minutes. Remove the meat from the pan. Reheat the pan and stir-fry the peppers, chilies, scallions and garlic for about 2 minutes, until they have begun to soften. Return the pork and sizzle the wine into the pan, stirring until it evaporates. Add the sauces and sugar and stir-fry for 1¹/₂ minutes.

 Combine the cornstarch and water, pour into the pan and stir over medium heat until the sauce thickens and becomes translucent. Check seasonings, adding salt and pepper, as needed.

Note: In Shanghai where they value the flavor and gloss of oil in a dish, they would dress the finished dish with a tablespoon of piping hot vegetable oil and a dash of sesame oil just seconds before it goes to the table.

Thai Pork and Long Beans in Hot Chili Sauce

Makes 6 to 8 servings, if sharing several dishes

This is one of the most pungent dishes you'll find in Thailand. So a little goes a long way. The shrimp-chili paste can be made in advance and refrigerated in a small, well-sealed glass container for up to three weeks. This quantity makes enough for two dishes. I like to include at least one potent dish in a menu in which the other dishes are less challenging in heat, making it a fiery highlight mid meal. You can use less chili and reduce the volume of shrimp-chili paste to make a milder dish to serve four with rice in a one-course meal. When asparagus is in good supply and inexpensive, it goes well in this dish instead of the beans.

Shrimp-Chili Paste

1 tablespoon dried shrimp

10 dried red chilies, soaked for 20 minutes in hot water

2 to 3 fresh hot red chilies, seeded and chopped

6 shallots or 1 small onion, chopped

3 cloves garlic

1/2-inch piece fresh galangal, or young fresh ginger, chopped

1 small stem lemon grass, trimmed and chopped

1 1/2 teaspoons soft shrimp paste

1 teaspoon sweet paprika or mild chili powder

1/2 teaspoon salt

1/2 teaspoon freshly ground white pepper

To Finish the Dish

14 ounces boneless pork, with some fat

1 teaspoon mashed garlic

1 1/2 teaspoons grated fresh ginger

3 tablespoons vegetable oil

2 to 3 long beans, cut into 2-inch pieces

1 1/2 tablespoons fish sauce

1 tablespoon sugar

4 kaffir lime leaves, finely shredded or 1 tablespoon finely shredded lime rind.

6 to 18 Thai "bird's eye" (small, hot) chilies, chopped

Wedges of salted duck egg or hard-boiled egg

Purchased sweet pickled shallots or pickled vegetables (page 97)

⊕ Prepare the shrimp chili paste by first grinding the dried shrimp to a floss in a blender or mortar, or the small bowl of a food processor fitted with the metal blade. Add the dried chilies and grind until they are powdered, then add the remaining ingredients and grind to a paste. Add a little vegetable oil in preference to water, to moisten the paste.

⊕ Cut the pork into very thin slices, then into strips of about $3/4 \times 1^1/2$ inches. Heat the oil in a wok or large skillet and stir-fry the pork for about $2^1/2$ minutes; add the garlic and ginger and stir-fry another 40 seconds.

⊕ Add the shrimp-chili paste and the beans and cook over medium heat for about 4 minutes, stirring frequently with a wooden spoon or wok spatula to ensure the spices do not catch on the pan.

⊕ Add 3 to 4 tablespoons of water, the fish sauce, sugar, lime leaves and chilies and continue to cook, stirring frequently, until the sauce is thick and paste-like and the pork cooked through. Serve onto a plate, garnishing with the sliced salted duck egg and the pickled vegetables.

Fiery Shredded Pork with Mushrooms and Bamboo Shoots

Makes 4 servings

Serve, garnished with the shreds of scallion and chili. Chinese steamed buns, white rice or grilled scallion cakes all go well with this dish.

12 ounces lean boneless pork

2 tablespoons cornstarch

1 egg white, beaten

1 to 1½ tablespoons water

2½ ounces bamboo shoots

3 large pieces dried black "wood ear" fungus, soaked in hot water for 15 minutes

3 scallions (green and white parts), finely sliced

1¼ tablespoons finely shredded fresh ginger

3 cloves garlic, minced

1 large hot green chili, seeded and finely sliced

2½ cups vegetable oil for deep frying

Sauce

3 teaspoons soy bean paste, or Japanese red miso

1½ teaspoons Chinese cooking (rice) wine, sake or dry sherry

3 teaspoons light soy sauce

2 to 3 teaspoons minced chili or chili paste

½ teaspoon sugar

Salt and freshly ground black or Sichuan peppercorns

2 tablespoons chicken stock or water

1 teaspoon cornstarch

Garnish

Finely shredded red chili and scallion greens chilled in ice water to curl

The Chinese technique for cutting meat shreds is to hold the meat firmly on the cutting board with the flat of one hand and slide a very sharp cleaver horizontally beneath the hand to make very thin slices. These are then stacked in groups of four to six slices and the stacks cut through to make shreds finer than a matchstick.

Cut the pork into wafer-thin slices, then into very fine shreds (see sidebar). Combine the cornstarch, egg white and water in a bowl, add the pork and mix thoroughly with the fingers or a wooden spoon so each piece of pork is coated. Set aside.

⊕ Finely slice the bamboo shoots and black fungus, discarding any hard and woody parts. Prepare the scallions, ginger, garlic and chili and set aside in a small dish ready for use. Mix the sauce ingredients, except chicken stock and cornstarch, in a bowl. Combine the chicken stock and cornstarch in another small bowl. Set aside.

⊕ In a wok or large skillet, heat the oil to very hot, 375°F. Slide the pork into the oil, then very quickly stir it with chopsticks or a narrow spatula so the threads of pork separate. Cook for about 1 minute, then remove with a wire strainer and set aside in the strainer over a bowl to drain.

⊕ Pour off all but 2^1/$_2$ tablespoons of the oil. Reheat it briefly, then over high heat stir-fry the scallions, ginger, garlic and chili for about 40 seconds. Add the sauce mixture and stir-fry for 30 seconds, return the pork and stir fry for about 1^1/$_2$ minutes. Add the bamboo shoots, fungus, and the stock and cornstarch mixture. Stir-fry, still over high heat, until the ingredients are well mixed and thoroughly heated and the sauce and seasonings glaze every strand of the pork and vegetables.

Pork Vindaloo

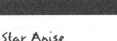

Makes 6 servings

Serve with white rice and a salad of diced cucumber, tomatoes and onion in a herb and yogurt dressing, or the pineapple salad on page 221.

1³/4 *pounds boneless pork shoulder*
3 *medium onions, finely chopped*
¹/3 *cup vegetable oil*
3 *points star anise (see sidebar)*

1 *teaspoon dark brown sugar*
15 *curry leaves or 2 bay leaves*
Salt and freshly ground black pepper

Vindaloo Paste

2 *teaspoons sweet paprika*
1 *teaspoon chili powder or flakes*
1 *teaspoon cumin seeds*
2 *teaspoons white poppy seeds or ground almonds*
6 *whole cloves*
8 *black peppercorns*
3-*inch cinnamon stick*
10 *to 16 dried red chilies, soaked in hot water for 15 minutes*

6 *to 8 cloves garlic, chopped*
2¹/2 *tablespoons finely chopped or grated fresh ginger*
1¹/2 *teaspoons tamarind concentrate, or 1 tablespoon lemon juice*
1 *tablespoon white vinegar*
2 *points star anise*

⊕ Cut the pork into 1-inch cubes and place in a glass or stainless steel bowl. Set aside.

⊕ To make the vindaloo paste, dry roast the cumin seeds, until they pop and splutter in the pan. Drain the chilies and set aside. In a blender or mortar, a food processor fitted with the metal blades, or a spice grinder, grind the paprika, chili powder, dry-roasted cumin, poppy seeds, 2 cloves, the peppercorns, and half the cinnamon stick to a fine powder. Add the drained chilies, garlic and ginger and grind to a paste, adding the tamarind and vinegar. Grind until smoothly emulsified. Stir at least half of the vindaloo paste into the pork and set aside to marinate for 30 minutes.

Star Anise

This Chinese spice, with a distinct licorice flavor and aroma, is only rarely featured in Indian curries, and then in moderation. Its irregular, star-shaped pod is composed of five or six split "points" or "petals" each holding a small seed. But it's the woody pod itself, rather than the seeds, that has the characteristic flavor. Use whole star anise, or break off a few points to add to your dish, and don't even think about buying the powdered spice as it loses much of its glory in the spice grinder. If a recipe calls for powdered, grind it yourself so it's absolutely fresh and full flavored.

⊕ Fry the onions in the oil over medium-high heat, stirring occasionally, until well browned. Add the remaining vindaloo paste with the remaining cloves and cinnamon stick and the star anise and fry for a few minutes, stirring constantly, and adding just enough water to prevent catching.

⊕ Add the marinated pork and cook, stirring, over medium heat for about 5 minutes, then add water to cover and salt to taste and cook slowly until the meat is tender, about 50 minutes. Half way through, add the sugar and curry or bay leaves and check seasonings, adding salt and pepper to taste.

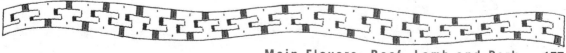

Malaccan "Devil" Pork

When the Portuguese colonized Malacca in the sixteenth century, they brought with them many cultural traditions, particularly those related to the church and the kitchen. This is a much-evolved version of an old diable or devilled dish, pepped up with curry spices. Serve with white or saffron rice, and a dish of sweet fruit chutney.

2¼ pounds boneless lean pork, from leg or shoulder

12 red shallots, peeled and thinly sliced

1¾ tablespoons finely shredded fresh ginger

½-inch piece fresh galangal, cut into fine shreds (optional)

1½ cups light beef stock or water

Seasoning

2 tablespoons white vinegar

1 tablespoon thick soy sauce or 2 tablespoons dark soy sauce

1 tablespoon crumbled palm sugar or soft brown sugar

1 tablespoon minced garlic

Curry Paste

8 dried red chilies, soaked in hot water for 20 minutes

2 stems lemon grass, trimmed of outer leaves

1 teaspoon fenugreek seeds (optional)

1 teaspoon brown mustard seeds

1 teaspoon cumin seeds

1 tablespoon coriander seeds

3 tablespoons vegetable oil

1 teaspoon shrimp paste or ½ anchovy, mashed

1 teaspoon ground turmeric or 1 tablespoon grated fresh turmeric

1½ teaspoons salt

½ teaspoon freshly ground black pepper

8 candlenuts or 12 macadamia nuts, ground to a paste

To Serve

Sweet fruit chutney

Hard-boiled eggs, cut into wedges

Sliced cucumber

⊕ Cut the pork into 2-inch cubes. Combine the marinade ingredients in a shallow bowl large enough to accommodate the pork. Use a wooden spoon to spread the seasoning evenly over the pork, cover and set aside for at least 30 minutes.

⊕ To make the curry paste, drain the chilies, and slit open and scrape out the seeds. Roughly chop the chilies and lemon grass, then place in a mortar, blender, the small bowl of a food processor fitted with the metal blade, or a spice grinder and grind to a paste.

⊕ In a dry pan, dry roast the whole spices for about 2¹/₂ minutes over medium heat, until they are very aromatic and beginning to pop. Grind finely. Heat the oil in a large saucepan with a heavy base. Fry the shrimp paste for a few seconds, then add the chili/lemon grass paste and the turmeric and fry 30 seconds more. Add the ground spices with salt, pepper and ground nuts and fry for 1 minute.

⊕ Add the pork and shallots to the pan, stirring to coat them evenly with the curry paste. Cook over medium-high heat to seal the surface, then add the ginger and *galangal* with the water or stock.

⊕ Cover tightly, reduce heat to medium low and simmer for about 1³/₄ hours, until the pork is very tender. Do not open the lid for at least the first 30 minutes of cooking—shake the pan occasionally to turn the meat. Then stir up, scraping the bottom of the pan. Uncover the pan for the last 30 minutes of cooking. When done, the liquid should be well absorbed into the meat. If it is drying out too quickly, it may be necessary to add a few tablespoons of extra liquid during cooking, to prevent the meat from sticking to the pan.

⊕ Check seasonings, adding extra salt or pepper, and if needed a squeeze of lime juice. Transfer the pork to a shallow serving dish and surround it with wedges of hard-boiled egg and sliced cucumber, with the fruit chutney in small dishes on the side.

Indonesian Babi Kecap

Makes 6 servings

I have the fondest memories of learning how to prepare this dish in an open-sided, palm-thatched outdoor kitchen. My teacher was a housewife in a small village in the hills of Bali, near Ubud.

Pork belly, with its layers of fat, is the traditional choice for this dish; however, if you prefer a leaner cut, expect the meat to be a little drier than is preferable. I always make a big pot of Babi Kecap; the next day it reheats beautifully in the microwave to serve over white rice, for a quick lunch. Serve with white or coconut-flavored rice (see sidebar) the Chili Sambal on page 263, or the Shrimp Paste and Coconut Sambal on page 262.

2¹/₂ pounds fresh bacon (pork belly)

1¹/₂ teaspoons freshly ground black pepper

5 tablespoons vegetable oil

12 shallots, halved

1¹/₂-inch piece fresh ginger, very thinly sliced

1 to 2 fresh hot red chilies, seeded and sliced

²/₃ cup sweet soy sauce (kecap manis), or ¹/₂ cup dark soy sauce and ¹/₃ cup dark corn syrup

2 teaspoons palm or soft brown sugar

2 teaspoons ground coriander

1¹/₄ cups coconut milk

Salt

Garnish

Finely shredded red chili

Thinly sliced scallion greens

In Indonesia, they enjoy coconut-flavored rice with many of their curries. To make, measure 1¹/₂ to 2 cups of long-grain white rice into a saucepan with a heavy base. Add 2 to 2³/₄ cups of coconut milk or diluted coconut cream and 1¹/₂ teaspoons of salt. Cover tightly, bring to a boil and reduce heat to the lowest point. Cook for about 17 minutes, or until all of the liquid has been absorbed and the rice is tender and fluffy. Stir up lightly before serving.

◉ Cut the pork into 1¹/₂-inch cubes and season with pepper. Heat the oil in a heavy skillet or frying pan over high heat and brown the pork pieces, for about 5 minutes, and transfer to an ovenproof dish. Preheat the oven to 350°F.

◉ In the same pan, lightly brown the shallots for about 1¹/₂ minutes, add the remaning ingredients and bring almost to a boil, scraping the bottom of the pan.

◉ Pour over the pork, cover and cook in the oven for about 1¹/₄ hours, or until the pork is very tender. Skim excess fat from the surface of the dish, and check for salt, adding a little extra if needed.

◉ Serve in the oven dish or transfer to a serving bowl.

Garlic Black Bean Braised Ribs

Makes 8 or more servings

This is a great easy and economical party dish, so I have given a generous recipe. It can be marinated and cooked beforehand for reheating in the oven or microwave on the day. This same recipe can be applied to chicken wings (cook for about 35 minutes) or chicken legs (cook for about 45 minutes). This is also the most popular Chinese method for cooking tripe, which they serve as a breakfast or lunch dish at dim sum restaurants.

3 pounds Chinese-style meaty ribs of pork (fresh bacon on the bone)

5 scallions, using the white ends and half of the green tops, cut into 1-inch pieces

8 cloves garlic, minced

2 tablespoons finely minced or grated fresh ginger

1 to 3 fresh mild red chilies, seeded and sliced

2½ tablespoons fermented black beans, rinsed, dried and finely chopped

1 tablespoon fine white sugar

½ cup light soy sauce

2 tablespoons hoisin sauce

⅓ cup Chinese cooking (rice) wine or sake, or 2 to 3 tablespoons ginger wine (see sidebar, page 104)

½ cup water

To Finish the Dish

Chopped scallion greens

Chopped cilantro (fresh coriander)

⊕ Use a cleaver or large, heavy knife to cut the meat into 2-inch pieces, or ask your butcher to do it for you. Place in an ovenproof dish or casserole. Scatter on the scallions, garlic, ginger, chilies and black beans. Mix the sugar, soy and hoisin sauces, wine and water in a bowl. Pour evenly over the pork and cover with foil or the lid of the dish. Refrigerate for at least 2 hours to marinate.

⊕ Preheat the oven to 400°F. Put in the pork to cook for about 20 minutes, then reduce heat to 360°F and cook for 35 minutes. Turn the meat and return to the oven for a further 20 to 25 minutes.

⊕ Finally, increase the heat again, uncover the dish and cook for about 15 minutes or until tender, basting occasionally with the pan juices. Use a large spoon to skim off the surface oil.

⊕ Stir in extra chopped scallions and cilantro and serve in the dish or casserole with a hot chili sauce or sambal and plenty of rice. If you prefer, thicken the sauce with a solution of cornstarch and water, stirring over medium heat until the sauce becomes translucent.

Chinese Country-Style Shredded Beef and Peppers

Makes 4 servings, or 6 if sharing several dishes

It is a joy to watch a skilled Chinese chef as he shreds the ingredients for a dish like this. His meat will be sliced so thin you could read a newspaper through it, then he stacks it to cut into the finest of shreds. Serve with fried rice, or stir-fried egg noodles.

14 ounces lean boneless beef

1/2 medium carrot

1/2 large green bell pepper

1/2 large red bell pepper

1/4 cup sliced bamboo shoots (optional)

1 rib celery

1 small Chinese squash or cucumber

4 scallions (green and white parts), shredded

2 tablespoons vegetable oil

Salt and freshly ground black pepper

Seasoning for Beef

1 tablespoon light soy sauce

1 tablespoon Chinese cooking (rice) wine, sake or dry sherry

1/2 teaspoon baking soda

1/2 teaspoon sugar

Sauce

1 tablespoon light soy sauce

1 1/2 tablespoons dark soy sauce

3 teaspoons Chinese black vinegar, or 2 teaspoons balsamic vinegar

1 teaspoon sugar

1 to 2 teaspoons hot chili sauce

2 tablespoons chicken stock or water

1 teaspoon cornstarch

◉ Slice the beef very thinly, then slack the slices together and cut across them to make very fine shreds. Place in a bowl, add the seasoning ingredients and mix well. Refrigerate for 30 minutes for the meat to marinate and tenderize.

◉ Cut the vegetables into fine shreds and place in reach of the wok or pan.

◉ Combine the sauce ingredients in a small bowl and set aside.

◉ Heat the oil in a wok or large skillet and stir-fry the beef shreds over very high heat for about 40 seconds, remove to a plate and set aside. Add the vegetables, lower the heat slightly and stir-fry for about 1 1/2 minutes, or until crisp tender.

✦ Increase the heat and return the meat. Stir up the sauce ingredients and pour into the pan. Cook, stirring and turning with the spatula in the Chinese way, until the dish is well blended and each strand of meat and vegetables is glazed with the sauce. Check seasoning, adding salt and pepper as required.

Ma Po Tofu

This is the most famous dish of China's Sichuan province. It contrasts tender, bland tofu (bean curd) with hot and spicy ground (minced) beef or pork. Flavor highlights are provided by slivers of pickled mustard greens or pungent chili pickled radish. Serve it with a big bowl of white rice and something crunchy to accompany, perhaps Chinese greens or asparagus sautéed with oyster mushrooms. For a meatless treat, try the Vegetarian Ma Po Tofu on page 238. Serve in a shallow bowl, garnished with the reserved scallion greens.

12 ounces soft fresh tofu (bean curd)

3 tablespoons vegetable oil

1¼ pounds ground (minced) beef (or pork)

3 scallions, (green and white parts), chopped (reserve some of the green tops for garnish)

3 to 4 cloves garlic, minced

1 tablespoon minced or grated fresh ginger

1 tablespoon Chinese cooking (rice) wine, sake or dry sherry

1½ teaspoons fine white sugar

1 tablespoon light soy sauce

1 teaspoon dark soy sauce

1½ tablespoons Sichuan chili sauce or hot bean paste, or 1 tablespoon red miso paste and 2 teaspoons chili sauce

¾ cup chicken or beef stock

3 teaspoons cornstarch

1 tablespoon chopped cilantro (fresh coriander)

⊕ Cut the tofu into ⅓-inch cubes and set aside.

⊕ Heat the oil in a wok or large skillet over high heat and stir-fry the beef or pork for 2 to 3 minutes, until lightly browned. Add the scallions, garlic and ginger and stir-fry a further 1 minute. Add the wine, sugar and sauces and cook for about 1 minute, stirring.

⊕ Combine the stock and cornstarch and pour into the pan. Cook, stirring, until the sauce thickens and becomes translucent.

⊕ Finally, add the bean curd and cilantro and gently heat it through.

Sichuan Chili Beef

Serve with steamed white rice or rice noodles stir-fried with bean sprouts and small spinach leaves or chives. Or to complete a delicious Sichuan menu, serve with the Sichuan Braised Spicy Eggplant on page 235.

If you partially freeze the beef for about 30 minutes, it's much easier to achieve fine slices. Use a very sharp knife with a thin blade to slice finely; then if you need shreds, stack the slices and cut through the stack to make fine shreds.

1 pound lean beef steak

1 medium onion

2 tablespoons vegetable oil

1½ teaspoons sesame oil

1 fresh mild red chili, seeded and minced

3 cloves garlic, minced

2 teaspoons grated fresh ginger

1½ tablespoons Sichuan chili paste or sambal ulek

1½ teaspoons fine white sugar

1 teaspoon cornstarch

⅓ cup chicken stock or water

1 teaspoon Chinese black vinegar or balsamic vinegar

1 tablespoon very finely minced scallions, white parts only

Salt and freshly ground black pepper

Marinade

1 tablespoon Chinese cooking (rice) wine, or dry sherry

1 tablespoon vegetable oil

3 teaspoons light soy sauce

1 teaspoon baking soda

Slice the beef (see sidebar), place in a dish and add the marinade ingredients. Refrigerate for about 1 hour.

Peel the onion, slice off the top and bottom and then cut the onion into narrow wedges.

Heat the vegetable and sesame oils in a wok or large skillet and stir-fry the beef over very high heat for about 1½ minutes. Remove and set aside, keeping warm. Reduce the heat slightly, add the onion and stir-fry until it softens, about 2½ minutes. Return the meat, add the chili, garlic and ginger and stir-fry briefly.

Add the chili sauce and sugar. Combine the cornstarch and stock or water and pour into the pan. Cook, stirring continually, until the sauce thickens, becomes translucent, and coats the meat. Add the vinegar and check seasonings adding salt and pepper to taste, stir in the scallions.

Crisp Chili Beef with Orange Rind and Sichuan Peppercorns

Serve this tangy, peppery beef dish with rice and a side dish of pickled cucumber (page 130).

12 ounces beef tenderloin (fillet)

1¹/₂ cups peanut or vegetable oil

3 large dried red chilies

1¹/₂ teaspoons Sichuan peppercorns

4 pieces dried tangerine peel, soaked in hot water for 20 minutes, or the rind of half a fresh, sweet orange

4 scallions (green and white parts), trimmed and sliced, reserving some of the green tops for garnish

1 tablespoon dark soy sauce

2 teaspoons hoisin sauce

1 teaspoon sesame seeds, toasted

Marinade

1 tablespoon finely grated fresh ginger

1 tablespoon Chinese cooking (rice) wine or sake

1 teaspoon dark soy sauce

2 teaspoons light soy sauce

1 teaspoon sugar

1 tablespoon cornstarch

⊕ Very thinly slice the beef (see sidebar, page 165), then cut into pieces of 2 × 1-inch and place in a dish. Wrap the grated ginger in a piece of clean cloth and squeeze the juice over the beef. Add the remaining marinade ingredients and a tablespoon or two of cold water. Mix lightly, cover, then refrigerate for 30 minutes.

⊕ A few minutes before cooking, transfer the meat to a strainer over a bowl to drain off excess marinade liquid.

⊕ Cut each chili into 4 to 5 pieces and discard the seeds, if preferred. Heat the oil in a large wok or large deep, skillet over high heat. When ready, the oil should be shimmering. Fry the beef for about 1¹/4 minutes, stirring with wooden chopsticks to ensure the slices of beef do not stick together. Remove with a slotted spoon and set aside, keeping warm.

❋ Pour off all but 2 tablespoons of the oil, add the chilies, peppercorns and drained tangerine peel and stir-fry until the chilies turn a deep purple and the tangerine peel is crisp, about 1½ minutes.

❋ Return the beef and the reserved marinade, and add the scallions and soy and hoisin sauces. Cook until the beef is crisp and glazed a rich amber. Add the sesame seeds and transfer to a serving dish. Garnish with finely sliced scallion greens.

Sumatran Beef

Makes 6 servings

Serve with rice flavored with turmeric and coconut milk and finished with a teaspoon each of brown mustard seeds and cumin seeds fried in butter.

2 pounds lean, boneless braising beef, such as shin or round

2 to 3 tablespoons vegetable oil

1¹/₂ teaspoons minced fresh ginger

1¹/₂ teaspoons minced garlic

2 large onions, minced

1¹/₃ teaspoons shrimp paste, or 1 anchovy, mashed, or 1¹/₃ tablespoons fish sauce

1 to 3 teaspoons chili flakes

1 teaspoon ground turmeric

2 tablespoons ground candlenuts or macadamias

1¹/₂ teaspoons palm or soft brown sugar

1 bay leaf or 5 curry leaves

1 stem lemon grass, slit in half lengthways

1 cup coconut cream

Salt and freshly ground black pepper

1 small bunch basil or Vietnamese mint leaves

1¹/₂ cups sliced green beans

Tamarind water or lemon juice

⊕ Trim the beef and cut into 1-inch cubes. Heat the oil in a medium/large, heavy saucepan and brown the meat over high heat, in several batches. Remove and set aside. Cook the ginger, garlic and onions, stirring, for 3 minutes over medium heat, then add the shrimp paste and cook lightly before adding the chili flakes, turmeric, nuts and palm sugar. Stir well.

⊕ Add the meat and stir to coat with the spices, then add the bay leaf or curry leaves, the lemon grass and salt. Add the coconut cream and water to barely cover. Bring to a boil, reduce the heat and simmer until the meat is very tender, about 2 hours.

⊕ Add the basil or Vietnamese mint leaves a few minutes before serving, or alternatively, add sliced green beans about 6 minutes before the meat is cooked.

⊕ Check the seasonings, adding a little tamarind water or a squeeze of lemon juice, and additional salt and pepper, as needed.

Indonesian Beef Rendang

Aromatic spiciness rather than chili heat is preferred for this popular Indonesian dish. But you can add just as much chili as you like.

2¹/₃ pounds lean boneless braising beef (round, shin, skirt)

2¹/₂ cups coconut milk

6 to 8 curry leaves or 1 bay leaf

3 medium onions

2¹/₂ tablespoons vegetable oil

3 to 4 cloves garlic

³/₄-inch piece fresh ginger

1 stem lemon grass, trimmed and chopped

¹/₂-inch piece galangal, or 1 teaspoon powdered laos (optional)

1 to 2 teaspoons sambal ulek

1¹/₃ tablespoons coriander seeds

1¹/₄ teaspoons cumin seeds

1 small piece cassia bark or cinnamon stick

12 black peppercorns

2 tablespoons finely shredded coconut

2 teaspoons tamarind concentrate, or 1¹/₂ tablespoons lemon juice

1¹/₂ teaspoons palm sugar or soft brown sugar

Salt

⊕ Cut the beef into 2-inch cubes and place in a saucepan with hot water to barely cover. Bring to a boil, then strain the water into a bowl and set aside. Add the coconut milk and curry leaves to the beef. Bring to a boil, then reduce the heat to medium-low and leave to cook gently while the other ingredients are prepared.

⊕ Finely slice half the onion. Heat the oil in a small sauté pan and fry them over medium-high heat until very well browned, about 6 minutes, then set aside.

⊕ Chop the remaining onions coarsely and place in a food processor fitted with the metal blade. Add the garlic, ginger, lemon grass, *galangal* and *sambal ulek* and grind to a paste. Stir into the coconut milk in the saucepan and continue cooking over medium-low heat.

⊕ Dry roast the spices and the coconut in a wok or saucepan without oil, over medium heat, stirring frequently. Cook for about 5 minutes until the coconut is golden brown. Pour into a mortar or spice grinder and grind to a fine powder. Pour over coconut milk and beef, stir in and continue cooking.

⊕ Increase heat until the liquid boils, then reduce heat to a simmer to cook until the beef is tender and the sauce well reduced (it should need at least 1¹/₂ hours cooking time). Combine the tamarind and sugar with a little of the sauce. Stir this also into the coconut milk and beef and add salt to taste. Simmer until the sauce has reduced to a thick glaze on the meat.

Braised Beef Hunan Style

Makes 6 servings, or more if sharing several dishes

Serve with a big bowl of steamed white rice.

3 pounds boneless braising beef
(shin, skirt)

5 cups water

3 whole star anise

2 to 3 pieces dried tangerine peel or
peel of ¹/₂ fresh sweet orange

2 pieces cassia bark, or 1 cinnamon
stick

1¹/₂-inch piece fresh ginger, thickly
sliced

3 scallions, (white and green parts),
trimmed and cut in half

Seasonings

4 dried red chilies, soaked for
15 minutes in hot water, or
2 teaspoons Sichuan chili paste

2¹/₂ tablespoons vegetable oil

1 tablespoon chopped garlic

2 teaspoons Sichuan peppercorns

2 teaspoons white peppercorns

¹/₂ cup dark or mushroom soy sauce

¹/₄ cup Chinese cooking (rice) wine,
or sake

¹/₃ cup Chinese bean paste, or hoisin
sauce

3 scallions (white and green parts),
chopped

¹/₄ cup sugar, or to taste

Salt and freshly ground black pepper

⊕ Trim the meat of any excess fat and cut it into 2 inch cubes. Place in a saucepan with the stock ingredients. Cover and bring to a boil, boil for 1 minute, then skim the froth from the surface, reduce heat and simmer very gently, barely allowing the water to boil, for 2 to 2¹/₂ hours. If you have used a fat cut of meat, cool for a half hour, then skim off the fat that has come to the surface.

⊕ In the meantime, drain the chilies, seed if preferred, and grind to a paste in a mortar. Heat the oil in another saucepan and fry the chili paste and garlic over medium-high heat for about 30 seconds, stirring. Add the peppercorns, soy sauce and wine and cook briefly.

⊕ Strain on the broth from the meat, then add the meat. Bring to a boil, add the bean paste, reduce heat and simmer until the meat is so tender it can be easily shredded with two forks. Add the scallions or cilantro, cook briefly, then check seasonings adding sugar, salt and pepper as needed.

Sizzling Mongolian Lamb

Makes 4 servings

To make it easier to achieve the thin slices needed for this dish, freeze the lamb for about 30 minutes before slicing (see sidebar, page 165).

1 pound lean boneless lamb

1¹/₂ teaspoons sesame seeds

2 tablespoons vegetable oil

2 small white onions

¹/₂ red bell pepper

3 tablespoons water or chicken stock

1 teaspoon cornstarch

¹/₂ teaspoon Sichuan pepper or white pepper

Marinade for Lamb

2 teaspoons vegetable oil

1 tablespoon sesame oil

2 tablespoons dark soy sauce

2 teaspoons sugar

¹/₂ teaspoon five-spice powder

3 teaspoons Chinese cooking (rice) wine, sake or dry sherry

◉ For this dish to be most effective, you will need a steak sizzling pan with a wooden base that can be served onto the table. Preheat the oven to 380°F, and put the sizzle pan or a heavy skillet with an ovenproof handle in to heat.

◉ Cut the lamb into 1¹/₂-inch squares. Combine the marinade ingredients in a bowl, add the lamb and mix well, cover and set aside for at least 1 hour.

◉ In a dry wok or skillet, dry roast the sesame seeds until golden, stirring and shaking the pan as they cook so they color evenly. Pour into a bowl and set aside.

◉ Peel the onion, cut off the top and bottom, cut into narrow wedges and separate the layers. Cut the pepper into small diamond-shaped pieces. Heat the oil in a wok or large skillet over medium-high heat and fry the onions and peppers until they have softened and are very lightly browned about 4 minutes. Remove.

◉ Reheat the pan if necessary, add the lamb and stir-fry quickly over high heat, stirring and tossing in the Chinese way, until it is very lightly cooked about 1¹/₂ minutes. Combine the cornstarch with the stock and pour into the pan, stir until the sauce thickens, and becomes translucent, then sprinkle on the sichuan pepper and add the sesame seeds.

◉ Remove the sizzling pan from the oven and place on its stand. Cover with the onions and peppers and spoon the lamb evenly over. Take immediately to the table to serve from the hot pan, with white rice.

Coconut Lamb Curry

Makes 4 to 6 servings

As an accompaniment, cook long-grain rice with a pinch of turmeric, and stir in chopped scallion greens and toasted flaked almonds when done.

2 pounds lean boneless lamb

3 tablespoons ghee (clarified butter), or vegetable oil

1 large onion, finely chopped

2 cloves garlic, minced

2 tablespoons Madras Curry Paste (page 249), or other hot curry paste, to taste

2 teaspoons ground coriander

1¹/₂ cups coconut milk

³/₄ cup beef stock or water

2 bay leaves

2 whole cloves

2-inch piece cinnamon stick

Salt and freshly ground black pepper

1 teaspoon tamarind concentrate

¹/₄ cup chopped cilantro (fresh coriander) leaves

⊕ Cut the lamb into 1-inch cubes. Heat the *ghee* or oil in a medium/large heavy saucepan over medium-high heat for 5 to 7 minutes. Set aside.

⊕ Brown the onion over medium heat in the same pan for about 4 minutes. Add the garlic, curry paste and coriander and stir for about 40 seconds. Pour in the coconut milk and stock and bring to a boil, reduce heat and return the lamb, adding the bay leaves, cloves and cinnamon stick.

⊕ Partially cover and cook for about 40 minutes, then uncover, add the salt and pepper to taste and tamarind and cook very slowly until the lamb is tender and the sauce well reduced. In the last few minutes of cooking, stir in the cilantro.

Hunan Lamb Shanks

Makes 6 to 8 servings

Take these tender flavorsome shanks to the table in an informal earthenware serving dish with plenty of white rice and stir-fried vegetables.

4 pounds meaty lamb shanks (6 to 8 pieces)

2 medium onions, chopped

5 cloves garlic, peeled

1-inch piece fresh ginger, thickly sliced

2 tablespoons vegetable oil

2 teaspoons sesame oil

4 pieces cassia bark or 1 large cinnamon stick

3 whole star anise

2 cloves

2 teaspoons Sichuan peppercorns

1 teaspoon cracked black pepper

2 kaffir lime leaves, or 1 teaspoon grated lime rind

4 dried red chilies

1/4 cup crushed Chinese rock sugar, or light brown sugar

2 tablespoons dark soy sauce

1/2 cup light soy sauce

1/4 cup Chinese cooking (rice) wine, or dry sherry

Stock

Peel of 1 orange or tangerine/mandarin

1 medium onion, quartered

2-inch piece fresh ginger

1 teaspoon black peppercorns

1 teaspoon salt

7 cups water

⊕ Blanch the lamb shanks for a few minutes in boiling water, then drain. Return to the saucepan. Add the stock ingredients and bring to a boil. Reduce heat and simmer for 1 hour.

⊕ When almost done, in another large saucepan, cook the onions, garlic and ginger in the oils for about 4 minutes over medium-high heat. Strain on the broth from the shanks, and add the remaining ingredients.

⊕ Lift out the shanks with tongs and place in the broth.

⊕ Bring the broth back to a boil, then reduce heat and simmer until the meat is so tender it will fall from the bone, about 1 1/4 hours. Carefully transfer the shanks to a serving platter. Bring the broth to a rapid boil and cook until well reduced and syrupy. Adjust seasoning as needed, then strain over the shanks.

Lamb Koftas in Curry Sauce

Makes 6 servings

You can transform this into a vegetarian dish by substituting mashed potato for the lamb in the koftas and coating them in a besan (chickpea flour) or cornmeal batter before frying. Alternatively, add cubes of fried tofu (bean curd) to the curry sauce and supplement with peas or sliced green beans and florets of cauliflower or broccoli. A salad of cucumber, crisp fruit such as apples, Japanese pears and celery, dressed with chaat masala (page 247) is an interesting accompaniment.

Curry Sauce

2 large onions

2 large cloves garlic

3/4-inch piece fresh ginger

3 tablespoons ghee (clarified butter) or vegetable oil

1 1/3 tablespoons coriander seeds

1 1/2 teaspoons cumin seeds

1 to 2 dried red chilies

3 cloves

2 green cardamom pods

2-inch piece cinnamon stick

1 1/4 cups chopped tomatoes

1 3/4 cups chicken stock or water

12 strands saffron

2 tablespoons boiling water

1 teaspoon sweet paprika

1 tablespoon garam masala, or mild curry powder

3/4 cup yogurt

1/3 cup heavy cream

2 to 3 tablespoons chopped cilantro (fresh coriander)

Salt and freshly ground black pepper

Lamb Kofta

2 pounds finely ground (minced) lean lamb

1 pound minced onions

2 large cloves garlic, minced

1 teaspoon salt

2 teaspoons garam masala, or mild curry powder

2 teaspoons ground coriander

1/4 teaspoon ground cloves

1/2 teaspoon ground mace

1/2 teaspoon ground cinnamon

2 tablespoons chopped cilantro (fresh coriander) leaves

1 1/2 cups vegetable oil

⊕ Make the curry sauce first. Coarsely chop the onions and place in a food processor fitted with its metal blades. Add the garlic and ginger, chop finely, but do not puree. Heat the *ghee* or oil in a medium-large saucepan and cook the onion mixture for about 5 minutes, stirring frequently, over medium heat.

⊕ In another small pan, without oil, dry roast the coriander, cumin and dried chilies until they are aromatic, and beginning to pop and splutter in the pan, then grind to a powder in a spice grinder or mortar. Add the ground spices and the whole spices to the onion mixture and cook for about 1¹/₂ minutes over medium heat, stirring frequently.

⊕ Add the tomatoes and stock or water and bring to a boil. Reduce heat and simmer for at least 12 minutes. Transfer the contents of the pan to a food processor or blender after retrieving the whole spices, and blend to a puree, then strain back into the saucepan. Set aside while the *koftas* are made.

⊕ Place the *kofta* ingredients in a large food processor (or in a smaller food processor, in two batches). Grind until reasonably smooth, but retaining some texture. Using oiled hands, shape the mixture into balls about the size of walnuts. Heat the oil and fry the meatballs in three or four batches, until well browned.

⊕ Reheat the sauce. Pour boiling water over the saffron and set aside. Stir the paprika, *garam masala* and yogurt into the sauce and reheat gently. Add the cream and cilantro, then salt and pepper to taste. Put in the *koftas* and heat them very gently in the sauce for a few minutes, sprinkle on the saffron water and transfer to a serving bowl.

Red Curry of Venison

This speedy red curry can be made with a good grilling steak instead of the venison. (To make slicing easier, you can partially freeze the beef, for about 30 minutes, see sidebar, page 165.)

4 cups coconut milk

3 tablespoons Thai Red Curry Paste
(page 248), or purchased red
curry paste, to taste

2¼ pounds venison steak or round

3 kaffir lime leaves, torn into strips,
or 4 to 5 strips of lime peel

8 to 12 pea eggplants or 3 to
4 tomatillos (see sidebar)

3 fresh mild red chilies, seeded and
sliced

½ cup coconut cream

Salt and fish sauce to taste

½ cup firmly packed sweet basil
leaves

Pea eggplants grow in small clusters and look like miniature unripe cherry tomatoes which can be substituted in a recipe, as can tomatillos. They have a firm and granular texture and a sharp, tart taste. They are a characteristic ingredient in some Thai curries, but are not vital to the success of the dish.

⊕ Pour the coconut milk into a medium-large saucepan and bring to a boil, slowly stirring with a wide paddle or ladle. Reduce heat so that it continues to very gently bubble. Cook for about 12 minutes, until it is reduced and there is a layer of oil floating on the surface. Add the curry paste and cook another 3 to 4 minutes.

⊕ Cut the beef into thin slices, then into strips about 4 × 2 inches. Put into the curry sauce, with the kaffir lime, pea eggplants and chilies and increase heat until almost boiling. Reduce the heat again and simmer for about 10 minutes until the meat is tender. Add coconut cream, salt and fish sauce to taste, and stir in the basil leaves before serving. Serve with steamed jasmine rice, and a crunchy seafood dish, such as the Crisp-Fried Shrimp with Four Peppers on page 106.

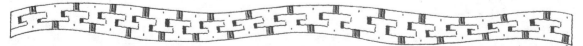

A Fiery Sauté of Kidneys and Peppers

Makes 4 servings, or more if sharing several dishes

In my view, there are only two ways to cook kidneys—as the Chinese do with plenty of pepper or chilies, or in the French classic style with a rich cognac-and-cream sauce. In this recipe, the sliced kidneys are first flash-fried over intense heat then stir-fried with the peppery sauce.

Serve with steamed white rice and a simple assortment of stir-fried vegetables or the stir-fried bean sprout recipe on page 225.

1 pound lamb kidneys

1 tablespoon light soy sauce

3 teaspoons Chinese cooking (rice) wine, or sake

1 teaspoon Chinese black vinegar, or balsamic vinegar

1/2 cup stock, preferably made from lamb bones

2 tablespoons cornstarch

1 1/2 cups vegetable oil

2 tablespoons minced scallion, white part only

1 teaspoon minced fresh ginger

1 to 3 teaspoons minced red chili

1/2 teaspoon freshly ground black pepper

Salt

Skin the kidneys and cut in half. Use kitchen shears to trim away the fatty core, then cut the kidneys into thin slices. Combine the soy sauce, wine, vinegar, stock and 1 teaspoon of cornstarch in a small bowl.

Sprinkle the kidneys with the remaining cornstarch. Heat the oil in a wok or large skillet over high heat, until a haze of smoke appears over the oil. Add the kidneys to fry for about 1 minute, then remove with a wire ladle or slotted spoon. Pour off all but 1 tablespoon of the oil.

Add the scallion, ginger, chili and pepper and cook briefly, then pour in the sauce and stir until it clears. Return the meat and stir to coat with the sauce. Check seasonings, adding salt if necessary.

Sichuan Peppered Liver

Makes 4 servings

Serve with fresh rice noodles, and perhaps the sautéed spinach on page 226.

12 ounces calf's liver or pork liver

¹/₃ cup vegetable oil

1¹/₂ teaspoons Sichuan peppercorns

2 points star anise

2 whole garlic cloves, peeled

3 scallions (green and white parts), chopped

2 teaspoons minced fresh ginger

¹/₂ cup beef stock or water

1¹/₂ teaspoons cornstarch

¹/₂ teaspoon ground Sichuan peppercorns

1 teaspoon chili oil

Seasoning

2 tablespoons cornstarch

1 tablespoon light soy sauce

2 teaspoons Chinese cooking (rice) wine, or ginger wine

¹/₃ teaspoon white pepper

⊕ Cut the liver into thin slices. Place in a dish with the seasoning ingredients and mix thoroughly. Set aside for 10 minutes.

⊕ Heat the oil in a wok or large skillet over medium heat then fry the peppercorns, star anise and garlic for about 1¹/₂ minutes, until the oil is very fragrant, then discard the star anise and garlic, retaining the peppercorns, if preferred.

⊕ Increase the heat to very high, put in the sliced liver and fry just long enough to seal the surface, about 1 minute. Remove it and pour off all but 1 tablespoon of the oil. Add the scallions and ginger and fry briefly, return the liver and add the stock mixed with cornstarch.

⊕ Stir until the sauce thickens enough to coat the meat. Sprinkle on ground Sichuan peppercorns and chili oil.

Chapter 8

Great Grills

Seafood

Asian Blackened Tuna with Soy and Wasabi Vinaigrette

Swordfish Kebabs on Spicy Peanut Sauce

Grilled Seafood Parcels

Kettle-Baked Whole Fish

Char-Grilled Stuffed Masala Shrimp

Poultry

Tandoori Chicken Tikka

Grilled Chicken Breast with Peppered Avocado Sauce

Chicken Yakitori with a Kick

Thai Barbecued Chicken

Grilled Chicken Wings

Tandoori-Roasted Chicken Legs

Crisp-Skin Cornish Game Hens or Baby Chickens

Kettle-Roasted Chicken with Wild Rice Stuffing and Asian Spices

Grilled Quail with Chili and Sichuan Pepper

Char-Grilled Breast of Duck with Lime Sauce

Tandoori Turkey Steaks

Pork

Butterfly Pork Steaks with Fiery Peach Chutney

Pork Tenderloin with Green Peppercorn Sauce

Grilled Pork Chops with Chili Plum Glaze

Beef

Pepper Steaks with Shiitake Mushroom Sauce

Beef Skirt with Asian Marinade

Korean Barbecued Beef Ribs

Lamb

Lamb Cutlets in Coconut and Cilantro Sauce

Honey Curry Lamb Kebabs

Kettle-Roasted Leg of Lamb Stuffed with Onion Chutney

Vegetables

Grilled Corn on the Cob with Chili Tomato Sauce

The Passion for Pepper

Long before chilies burned their way into the hearts of southeast Asians, they had pepper to add fire to their food. For centuries the Malabar Coast of east India, and the Indonesian islands flourished on a red-hot pepper trade with Europe, that's still firing worldwide today. Pepper adds bursts of bright heat, and a deep, concentrated flavor that can't be replaced by chili. If you want it really hot and spicy, use them both.

Pepper comes in three forms: green, black and white. Fresh-picked green pepper berries go to market on the stem in small, tight clusters. They are preserved in brine for retail and export sale. Green peppercorns are allowed to ripen in two stages to obtain black and white pepper. Berries of medium maturity are picked and sun or kiln dried, and in a few days shrivel and turn black. White peppercorns stay on the tree longer, until turning red, then they are soaked to remove this outer red skin, leaving the smoother white peppercorn which is a milder, smoother seasoning than black pepper.

Cooks around Asia are particular about which one they choose to use. Northern Thais give their jungle curry (page 142) its characteristic punch by adding whole stems of green pepper berries. In China, Cantonese cooks choose to season stir-fries with white pepper for its more subtle flavor, while in Shanghai, they may cook with black, but dust white pepper liberally over favorite dishes like eel or fish braised in rich brown sauces. In Sichuan province, they use an indigenous pepper product, below. Curry cooks in Malaysia, Indonesia and central-southern India prefer the bold taste of black pepper, and have made it an essential ingredient in their curry pastes and powders (see pages 22 and 248–49). In the south of India, where the pepper tree originated, they lavish pepper into many a dish as its prime seasoning. So fond are they of its fiery heat that they even begin the day with a fiercely hot black pepper soup, *rasam* (page 20) or *sambar* a searing, watery curry which is eaten with *dosa*, a unique thin crepe made from fermented rice and lentil batter. Vietnamese rarely cook with chilies or pepper, opting to add seasonings at the table. But I have had some exceptionally peppery sweet-and-sour dishes in Saigon, and a majestic peppered crab (page 111) long ago became a favorite in our household.

Sichuan peppercorn is the small, red-brown berry of the prickly ash tree. Sichuan cooks are so fond of this little kitchen treasure that they have adopted it as their own, even though it grows right through the central and northern regions of China. It also grows in Japan, where they prefer to use its exquisitely furled young leaves as a decoration, rather than cook with the spice. It doesn't taste like common pepper, being not at all related, but

the dried berries have a delightful peppery taste, a subtle and pleasing aroma, and a delicate astringency.

In Chinese cooking, Sichuan peppercorns, botanically named *Xanthoxylum*, and also called *fagara*, are tossed in whole, often with star anise and cassia, the native equivalent of cinnamon, to produce a fragrant sauce base or stock for braised and poached dishes. They are fried in oil, sometimes with garlic, to infuse the cooking oil with their powerful aromatics (see Sichuan Peppered Liver, page 178, and Crisp Chili Beef with Orange Rind and Sichuan Peppercorns, page 166). But Sichuan pepper is equally important as a condiment, and a potent one at that. Sichuan cooks sprinkle it willy nilly over finished dishes, which can turn them into an explosive powder keg for the unwary, (see Sichuan Piquant Chicken, page 120). Once you're past that initial, delicious taste, an excess of Sichuan pepper can cause an unpleasant numbing of the lips and throat.

Sichuan pepper teams with roasted salt to make Pepper-Salt (page 246), a dipping condiment that's the perfect partner for char-grilled quail, plump shrimp grilled in their vibrant red shells, or meaty little pork cutlets on the bone cooked over a charcoal barbecue.

You might not find Sichuan peppercorn in every Asian supermarket, but it's worth hunting down. Buy the whole berries, rather than ground spice, and look for those that are a light brown with a distinct blush of pink. To maintain freshness, store them in a well sealed spice jar away from heat and damp and grind as needed.

Asian Blackened Tuna with Soy and Wasabi Vinaigrette

Serve with soba noodles and stir-fried snow peas.

3 tablespoons cracked black pepper

3 tablespoons cracked white peppercorns

1 teaspoon (ground) Sichuan peppercorns (optional)

½ teaspoon crushed coriander seeds

½ teaspoon crushed fennel seeds

½ teaspoon chili flakes

Four ¼-pound tuna steaks (or swordfish, sea bass, etc.)

1 large carrot, peeled

½ daikon (giant white/Japanese radish), peeled

½ fennel root, finely sliced

Soy and Wasabi Vinaigrette

¼ cup light olive oil

6 tablespoons fresh lemon juice

2 tablespoons light soy sauce

1 to 2 Thai "bird's eye" (small, hot) chilies, seeded

1 teaspoon minced fresh ginger

1 teaspoon minced cilantro (fresh coriander)

1 teaspoon wasabi, or to taste, or use pure horseradish

Garnish

Sprigs of dill or fennel

Sprigs of cilantro (fresh coriander)

⊕ Prepare and light the coals in a charcoal barbecue and allow time for the coals to burn to a dull glow.

⊕ Combine the peppers, coriander and fennel seeds and chilies and spread on a plate. Press the fish steaks into the dressing to coat them thickly and evenly. Set aside while the vinaigrette and vegetables are prepared.

⊕ Cut the carrot and daikon into fine julienne. Blanch all of the vegetables together in boiling water for 40 seconds. Drain and refresh in cold water, then drain again thoroughly.

⊕ Whisk the vinaigrette ingredients in a bowl until emulsified. Toss the vegetables in the vinaigrette.

⊕ If using a gas or electric barbecue, heat ten minutes before it is needed. Set a flat cast iron plate on a griddle on the barbecue and wipe it with a cloth dipped in vegetable oil.

⊕ Cook the tuna steaks just long enough to sear the surface, leaving them pink inside. Cut them into 1/3-inch thick slices.

⊕ Serve some of the vegetables onto each plate and arrange the fish over them. Spoon over any remaining dressing and garnish with sprigs of herbs.

Swordfish Kebabs on Spicy Peanut Sauce

6 swordfish (tuna or mackerel)
    steaks

Marinade

2 tablespoons fresh lime juice

2 teaspoons ground coriander

1/2 teaspoon ground turmeric

2 tablespoons vegetable oil

Salt and freshly ground black pepper

12 metal skewers, brushed with oil,
    or 12 bamboo skewers soaked in
    cold water for 2 to 3 hours

Sauce

1 cup raw peanuts, shelled
    (or 2/3 cup peanut butter)

1 cup peanut or vegetable oil

1 tablespoon minced shallots

2 teaspoons minced garlic

1 tablespoon minced red chili

2 teaspoons concentrated tamarind
    or 1 1/2 tablespoons lemon juice

3 teaspoons palm sugar or soft brown
    sugar

1 teaspoon ground coriander

1/4 teaspoon ground turmeric

1/2 stem lemon grass, bruised

1 kaffir lime leaf, scored with the
    point of a knife (optional)

3/4 cups water

3/4 cup coconut cream

3/4 teaspoon salt

1/3 teaspoon freshly ground black
    pepper

To Serve

Fried rice or Pickled Vegetables
    (page 272)

Sweet Chili Sauce (page 253)

◉ Cut the fish steaks into 1-inch cubes and place in a bowl. Combine the marinade ingredients, pour over the fish and stir with a wooden spoon to coat each cube of fish. Cover with plastic wrap and set aside for at least 25 minutes. Prepare and light the coals of a charcoal barbecue and allow to burn down until they are glowing red beneath a layer of grayish.

◉ To make the sauce, heat the oil in a wok or medium saucepan over high heat and fry the peanuts for about 5 minutes, until golden brown. Remove with a wire skimmer and spread on a double layer of paper towel to drain. When drained, transfer to a clean kitchen cloth and rub them to remove their skin.

◉ Rinse and drain the peanuts, then grind to a smooth paste; or if you prefer a textured sauce, grind coarsely, then remove half and grind the remainder to a smooth paste.

◉ Wipe out the pan and return 1 tablespoon of the oil to the pan. Sauté the shallots, garlic and chili, stirring over high heat, for 2 minutes, then add the remaining sauce ingredients and cook until it comes to a boil. Reduce heat to low and simmer, stirring, for 5 minutes. To make the sauce very smooth, first discard the lime leaf and lemon grass and then puree the sauce in a blender or food processor.

◉ Place a cast iron griddle or rack on the barbecue and brush with vegetable oil. Light heat and gas in electric barbecue. Thread the cubes of fish onto the skewers and place on the heat. Grill the kebabs for about 6 minutes, turning frequently. Brush with extra vegetable oil, if necessary, to ensure the kebabs remain moist.

◉ Make a bed of pickled vegetables or fried rice on each warmed plate. Place two kebabs over each and spoon on the sauce. Serve with soy sauce in small dishes on the side.

Grilled Seafood Parcels

Makes 6 Servings

Use any combination of seafood that pleases. The fresher, the better! Serve the parcels, unopened, with lemon wedges for squeezing.

Garlic and Chili Butter

1 stick (1/2 cup) unsalted butter

3 large cloves garlic, mashed with
   1/2 teaspoon salt

1 tablespoon chopped cilantro (fresh
   coriander) or fresh dill

1 1/2 teaspoons finely minced red chili

The Seafood

Prepare the following or a selection of your choice, including both fish and shellfish.

12 large shrimp (prawns), shelled

12 small squid, cleaned and skinned
   (no tentacles)

6 large fresh sea scallops

6 large fresh clams

12 ounces tuna

12 ounces sea bass, bream or other
   white fish fillets

6 ounces crabmeat chunks

3 scallions (spring onions), trimmed
   (green and white parts)

6- × 12-inch squares aluminum foil

2 to 3 teaspoons vegetable oil

1 lemon

6 sprigs fresh dill

Salt and freshly ground black pepper

Mash the butter ingredients together, form into a sausage shape and roll in foil. Chill until firm.

Devein the shrimp (see sidebar, page 64). Cut the squid in half lay out flat on a board the inner side facing up. Use a sharp knife to score the flesh closely in the inside in the Chinese way, cutting at a 45° angle at close intervals first in one direction, then cross hatch making sure you do not cut right through. This will tenderize the squid, and cause it to curl up attractively as it cooks.

Remove scallops and clams from their shells, if necessary. Cut the fish into 2- × 1-inch pieces. Cut the scallions into 1 1/2-inch pieces.

Lay the squares of foil on a flat work surface and brush the shiny side of the foil with vegetable oil. Arrange equal amounts of the seafood and scallions on each piece of foil. Cut the butter into six portions and slice the lemon. Place a portion of butter, a slice of lemon and a sprig of dill in each parcel, then season the seafood generously with salt and pepper. Close the parcels, folding the edges of the foil together to seal in the juices. Refrigerate while the barbecue or broiler heats.

 Grill the seafood parcels for about 12 minutes turning once or twice. Prepare and light the coals for charcoal barbecue and allow them to burn down to a glow, or light a gas or electric barbecue and allow about 10 minutes for it to heat.

Do Ahead Note: The parcels can be prepared in advance and frozen or kept overnight in the refrigerator before cooking.

Kettle-Baked Whole Fish

Makes 6 to 8 servings

A large fish cooked whole and presented on a big platter surrounded by herbs and chili "flowers" makes a spectacular feature dish for a dinner party. If you don't want to barbecue, you can cook the fish indoors in the oven at 350°F, for about 30 minutes. Serve with coconut rice and the pineapple salad on page 221.

One 2-pound whole snapper or sea bass, cleaned and scaled

2 lemons

1 small bunch sweet basil

2 chopped scallions, (green and white parts)

2 medium-hot green chilies, seeded and sliced

Aluminum foil or an aluminum roasting tray to fit the fish (a turkey roasting tray would be perfect)

2 tablespoons unsalted or clarified butter, melted

Marinade

2-inch piece fresh young ginger

³/₄ teaspoon ground turmeric

1¹/₂ teaspoons salt

1¹/₂ teaspoons finely ground black pepper

2 teaspoons ground coriander

1 teaspoon crushed fennel seeds

1 tablespoon corn or canola oil

Garnish

Chili "flowers" (see sidebar, page 31)

Sliced cucumber

Sliced lemons

Fresh herbs such as dill, basil, chervil

Prepare the coals for a kettle barbecue, light and allow to heat until you have a deep mass of hot coals covered with a fine white ash. There should be enough coals to maintain heat for at least 30 minutes.

⊕ Rinse and drain the fish and pat dry with paper towels. Make deep slashes diagonally across each side, 1 inch apart. To make the marinade, finely grate the ginger onto a piece of clean, fine cloth and squeeze the juice into a small dish. Reserve the ginger pulp. Add the turmeric, salt, pepper, fennel, coriander and the oil to the ginger juice. Rub evenly over the fish on both sides and in the cavity.

⊕ Cut one lemon into quarters. Place the quartered lemon, reserved ginger pulp, basil, scallions and chilies in the cavity of the fish and secure the opening with fine metal or wooden skewers.

⊕ Make a tray from a double thickness of aluminum foil, turning up and pinching the edges, or use the foil baking tray, and brush it generously with melted butter. Place the fish in the tray and surround with sliced lemon. Set it on the grid of the barbecue. Brush with melted butter. Cover the barbecue and allow the fish to cook gently for 15 minutes, brushing occasionally with butter to keep the fish moist. Turn and cook for 15 minutes on the other side.

⊕ Finally, remove the skewers, and discard the herbs into cavity of the fish, stand the fish upright in the tray by splaying the sides of the cavity. Finish the cooking in this way so the fish cooks evenly on both sides. Test if the fish is cooked by inserting a skewer into the thickest part near the head. When done, the meat pierces easily.

⊕ Use two large spatulas to carefully transfer the fish onto a large platter. Surround it with overlapped slices of lemon and cucumber and decorate with chili "flowers" and fresh herbs.

Char-Grilled Stuffed Masala Shrimp

Makes 4 to 6 servings

These spicy shrimp (prawns) have much more flavor if you leave their heads and shells on when you broil (grill) them, although it's not easy to find them in American markets this way. Serve them straight from the hot plate with finger bowls of warm water floating slices of lime or lemon.

18 large fresh shrimp, in their shells

2 scallions, white part only, chopped

2 cloves garlic, peeled

2 thin slices fresh ginger, chopped

1 tablespoon chopped fresh dill

1/2 to 1 teaspoon chili paste, harissa, or sambal ulek

2 teaspoons ground coriander

1 teaspoon garam masala, or mild curry powder

1/3 teaspoon whole black peppercorns

1/2 teaspoon fennel seeds

1/2 teaspoon salt

2 tablespoons ground almonds or raw cashew nuts

Before You Grill

2 tablespoons vegetable oil

1/2 teaspoon ground turmeric

1/4 teaspoon hot paprika

1/2 teaspoon ground coriander

✦ Prepare and light the coals in a charcoal barbecue and allow to burn to a dull red glow.

✦ Use kitchen shears to trim off the legs of each shrimp, then with a large, sharp knife cut along the underside, cutting deeply into the meat. Place the remaining ingredients into a blender, mortar, a food processor fitted with the metal blades, or a spice grinder, and grind to a thick paste. Press the stuffing into the slit made in each shrimp, smoothing the surface.

✦ If using a gas or electric barbecue, heat about 10 minutes before it's needed.

✦ Before you grill, combine the oil, turmeric, paprika and coriander in a bowl and brush over each shrimp. Char-grill the shrimp until their shells turn orange-red and the meat is firm to the touch, 3 to 4 minutes. Remove with tongs, shell if you prefer, and arrange on steamed white rice flavored with cardamom.

✦ If you are cooking shelled shrimp, they will require about 2 1/2 to 3 minutes cooking time. Garnish with lemon or lime wedges.

Tandoori Chicken Tikka

Makes 6 servings

See the Butter Chicken recipe on page 123, for another way to use this smoky, spicy chicken recipe.

Serve chicken tikka as a first course with lemon wedges for squeezing, and marinated salad onion (see sidebar). As a main course, serve these delicious golden nuggets of chicken with rice or freshly baked flatbread and marinated onion, see side bar, or a crisp cucumber, tomato and onion salad. Offer the Tamarind Sauce or Mint Yogurt Sauce from pages 268 and 256 on the side.

1¹/₂ pounds boneless chicken breasts

Tandoori Marinade

6 cloves garlic, peeled and mashed

1 tablespoon fresh lemon juice

2 teaspoons ginger juice (see sidebar, page 96)

¹/₂ teaspoon salt

¹/₂ teaspoon hot chili sauce or chili paste

1 teaspoon sweet paprika

1 teaspoon garam masala or 1 extra teaspoon mild curry powder plus ¹/₄ teaspoon ground cinnamon and a pinch of ground cloves

¹/₄ teaspoon ground turmeric

3 teaspoons mild curry powder

2 teaspoons finely minced cilantro (fresh coriander) leaves

3 tablespoons plain yogurt

1 tablespoon vegetable oil

Pinch of orange-red tandoori or other food coloring

Skin the chicken breasts and cut into 2-inch pieces. Combine the marinade ingredients in a glass or stainless steel bowl. Add the chicken, and mix with a wooden spoon until the chicken pieces are evenly coated with the marinade. Cover with plastic wrap and refrigerate for at least 2 hours.

Heat a charcoal, gas or electric barbecue to medium and brush the grill with oil to prevent the chicken sticking. Cook the chicken until done, about 20 minutes, using tongs to carefully turn it several times. Remove from the heat and let it rest for a few minutes before serving.

Marinated salad onion is the perfect accompaniment to grilled and tandoori-roasted meat, especially chicken. Peel and thinly slice medium-size salad onions and place them in a glass dish. Sprinkle generously with salt and fine white sugar, then add just enough vinegar to moisten. Add plenty of chopped mint or coriander and let sit for at least 20 minutes before using.

Grilled Chicken Breast with Peppered Avocado Sauce

Makes 4 servings

4 pieces boneless, skinless chicken breast

1 tablespoon light olive or vegetable oil

Marinade

1 teaspoon garlic salt

1½ teaspoons ground black pepper

1½ tablespoons fresh lemon juice

1½ tablespoons light olive oil

Peppered Avocado Sauce

2 teaspoons freshly ground black pepper

⅓ teaspoon brown mustard seeds

1 tablespoon light olive oil

2 cups mashed avocado (start with 2 ripe whole avocados)

2 tablespoons fresh lemon juice

2 tablespoons plain yogurt

3 teaspoons chopped scallions (green and white parts)

1½ teaspoons chopped cilantro (fresh coriander) leaves

½ to 1 teaspoon Tabasco sauce or chili oil

¾ teaspoon fine white sugar

Salt to taste

⊕ Trim the chicken breasts of any fat and sinew. Place in a flat dish and sprinkle with the marinade ingredients. Set aside for 15 minutes.

⊕ Heat a heavy skillet or ribbed pan/griddle and brush with oil. Cook the chicken breasts over medium-high heat, top side first, until golden brown. Turn and reduce the heat slightly to allow the meat to gently cook through, about 8 minutes, depending on the thickness of the chicken breasts.

⊕ Make the sauce while the breasts are cooking. Sauté the pepper and mustard seeds in the oil, stirring over high heat for about 45 seconds or until the mustard seeds begin to pop, then remove from the heat and pour into a small dish to cool.

⊕ Add lemon juice to the mashed avocado to prevent discoloration. Stir the pepper and mustard seeds with their oil into the avocado, adding the yogurt, scallions and cilantro. Add Tabasco sauce or chili oil, sugar and salt to taste and beat with a fork until creamy. Serve over the sliced chicken breasts.

Chicken Yakitori with a Kick

Makes 4 servings

4 boneless and skinless half chicken
   breasts
1½-inch piece fresh ginger
¼ cup mirin (Japanese sweet wine)*
3 teaspoons Chinese rock sugar,
   crushed

¼ cup light soy sauce
1 tablespoon hoisin sauce
½ teaspoon chili oil
2 tablespoons corn or canola oil
12 thin bamboo skewers, soaked for
   2 to 3 hours in cold water

Accompaniments

Red pepper flakes or Japanese pepper
   seasoning

Peppery salad of arugula or other
   greens, in an oil and vinegar
   dressing with garlic and a splash
   of sesame oil

⊕ Cut the chicken into ¾ inch strips and place in a bowl. Grate the ginger onto a piece of fine cloth and squeeze the juice over the chicken; leave for 20 minutes.

⊕ In the meantime, heat the *mirin* and sugar in a small saucepan until the sugar dissolves. Remove from heat and stir in the soy and *hoisin* sauces and the chili oil and corn or canola oil. Pour over the chicken and marinate for 1 hour.

⊕ Prepare and light the coals for a charcoal barbecue and allow time for the coals to heat to a dull red glow or light a gas or electric barbecue about ten minutes before needed. Heat a hotplate or heavy flat iron griddle on the barbecue, and brush with oil (or use a heavy hotplate or pan over the stove). Brush the griddle with oil.

⊕ Thread the chicken onto the skewers and place them on the grill. Cook them, turning frequently, for 6 to 10 minutes, depending on the thickness of the meat, brushing with the remaining marinade until it has all been used up.

⊕ Sprinkle on pepper flakes or seasoning and serve with the salad.

 Note: *Sake* **or Chinese cooking (rice) wine can be used instead of** *mirin*, **adding an extra 1 teaspoon of sugar to the recipe.**

Thai Barbecued Chicken

Makes 2 servings, or 4 if sharing other dishes

Kai Yang is a popular marketplace or streetside snack in Thailand, where it is often accompanied by Green Papaya Salad (page 220). Serve with a salad and the Chili-Garlic Vinegar Sauce from page 253.

2 small chickens, each approximately 1½ pounds	3 cilantro (fresh coriander) roots
2½ teaspoons black peppercorns	1 teaspoon salt
2 teaspoons coriander seeds	1 tablespoon vegetable oil
6 cloves garlic, peeled	Chili-Garlic Vinegar Sauce (page 253)

✸ Rinse, and drain the chickens and pat them dry. Cut the chickens in half. Trim off wing tips, plus any excess fat. Prick the skin all over with a sharp skewer.

✸ In a small pan without oil, dry roast the peppercorns and coriander seeds, for about 4 minutes on medium heat, until very aromatic. Grind to a fine powder in a mortar, blender or spice grinder, or in the small bowl of a food processor fitted with the metal blades, then add the garlic, coriander roots and salt and grind to a paste. Mix in a little oil to make an emulsion. Spread this thickly over the chickens on both sides, rub in with the fingers and set aside for 30 minutes.

✸ Prepare and light the coals in a charcoal barbecue and allow the coals to subside to a dull glow, or heat a broiler (grill) to medium 10 minutes before cooking starts. Brush the griddle with oil to prevent the chicken from sticking. Grill the chickens, turning several times, until well cooked with crisp golden skin, about 20 minutes.

Grilled Chicken Wings

Makes 4 to 6 servings

A fiery chili dip gives this popular treat grown-up appeal. Serve by themselves, or with steamed white rice, the chili sauce and a simple vegetable dish.

24 chicken wings   Vegetable oil

Marinade/Glaze

3 tablespoons corn or canola oil $1\frac{1}{4}$ teaspoons salt
3 tablespoons hoisin sauce $\frac{1}{3}$ teaspoon white pepper
3 to 4 teaspoons minced garlic

Chili Sauce

$\frac{1}{2}$ cup hoisin sauce   2 teaspoons brown sugar
3 tablespoons tomato ketchup   1 tablespoon minced scallion
1 to 2 tablespoons hot chili sauce   (white and green parts)

⊕ Place the wings in a flat dish. Combine the marinade ingredients and brush evenly over the wings. Cover with plastic wrap and set aside for at least 3 hours, or overnight, in the refrigerator. Combine the sauce ingredients and serve into several dipping dishes.

⊕ Prepare and light the coals in a charcoal barbecue and allow the coals to subside to a dull red glow or light a gas/electric barbecue about ten minutes before it is needed. Brush the griddle with oil or clarified butter to prevent the wings from sticking. Grill the wings for 12 to 15 minutes turning frequently, until evenly cooked and golden brown on the surface.

Tandoori-Roasted Chicken Legs

Makes 4 to 6 servings

Serve with steamed white rice or warm flatbread, and Tamarind Sauce for dipping.

12 chicken legs

1 tablespoon vegetable oil

Tandoori Marinade

2 tablespoons vegetable oil

2 tablespoons fresh lemon juice

2 teaspoon minced fresh ginger
   or ginger juice (see sidebar,
   page 96)

3 teaspoons minced garlic

1³/₄ teaspoons hot chili sauce or
   chili paste

2 teaspoons sweet paprika

1 tablespoon minced cilantro
   (fresh coriander) leaves

1¹/₂ tablespoons mild (korma) curry
   paste or 1¹/₂ tablespoons mild
   curry powder, moistened with
   vegetable oil or white vinegar

¹/₃ cup plain yogurt

To Serve

Lemon wedges

Tamarind Sauce (page 268)

⊕ In a bowl large enough to place the chicken legs side by side, combine the marinade ingredients, thinning with water to the consistency of cream. Put in the chicken and stir around until each piece has been coated with the marinade. Cover with plastic wrap and refrigerate for 4 to 5 hours or overnight. Turn several times while marinating.

⊕ Prepare and light the coals in a charcoal barbecue and allow the coals to subside to a dull red glow, or light a gas or electric barbecue about ten minutes before it is needed. Brush the griddle with oil. Remove the chicken from the marinade with tongs and place on the barbecue. Cook, turning frequently and brushing with the remaining marinade for 15 to 20 minutes, until cooked through and red-gold on the surface.

⊕ Arrange the chicken on a plate and surround with lemon wedges. Serve with Tamarind Sauce.

Crisp-Skin Cornish Game Hens or Baby Chickens

Makes 4 to 6 servings

Crisp-skin baby chickens, seasoned with Sichuan pepper and aromatic spices, give balance to a menu of curried dishes and add flavor highlights to a simple noodle meal.

risply barbecued game hen or chicken can be served in the manner of Peking Duck, finely sliced and wrapped in thin crepes with the usual accompaniments of hoisin sauce and sliced scallions (spring onions) or cucumber sticks.

2 to 3 Cornish game hens, or small chickens, each about 1³/₄ pounds

1¹/₂ tablespoons Chinese cooking (rice) wine or sake

1 tablespoon light soy sauce

2¹/₂ teaspoons spiced salt

1 teaspoon ground Sichuan peppercorns or finely ground white pepper

1¹/₂ tablespoons melted butter or light olive oil

To Serve

Spiced Salt (page 246), or Soy Green Chili Sauce (page 255)

⊕ Use a Chinese cleaver, poultry shears or a heavy knife to cut the hens in half. Rinse with cold water, drain and pat dry with paper towels. Place them skin side up on a tray or large plate. Combine the cooking wine and soy sauce and brush the mixture evenly over them, then sprinkle on the spiced salt and Sichuan pepper or white pepper. Place uncovered in the refrigerator for at least 1 hour and preferably longer, to allow time for the seasonings to be absorbed and the skin to dry.

⊕ Prepare and light the coals in a charcoal barbecue and allow the coals to subside to a dull red glow or light a gas/electric barbecue about ten minutes before it is needed. Heat a barbecue to medium. Brush the chickens with melted butter or oil, place on the barbecue skin side down and grill until the skin is golden, turn and continue to grill until evenly cooked through, then cook the skin a final few minutes, to crisp.

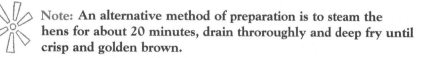

Note: An alternative method of preparation is to steam the hens for about 20 minutes, drain throroughly and deep fry until crisp and golden brown.

Kettle-Roasted Chicken with Wild Rice Stuffing and Asian Spices

Makes 4 to 6 servings

You can cook this chicken in the oven, if you do not have a kettle or other type of covered barbecue, but it will not have the same wonderful smoky flavor. When planning this recipe, allow time to precook the wild rice.

All you need to accompany this generous meal is a Chinese-style vegetable. Try one of these—steamed baby bok choy with a drizzle of oyster sauce, the Sautéed Spinach with Garlic and Dried Shrimp on page 226, or snow peas stir-fried with a hint of ginger!

1 large chicken, approximately 3¹/₂ pounds

1 teaspoon salt

¹/₂ teaspoon Chinese five-spice powder

1-inch piece fresh ginger

1 tablespoon dark soy sauce

1 tablespoon vegetable oil, plus 2 to 3 teaspoons extra

Wild Rice Stuffing

¹/₂ cup wild rice

¹/₃ cup minced onion

¹/₂ teaspoon minced garlic

¹/₄ cup minced celery or water chestnuts

1¹/₂ tablespoons vegetable oil

¹/₃ cup long-grain white rice

1 lap cheong (Chinese sausage) or ¹/₄ cup pancetta or fat bacon, very finely chopped

¹/₄ cup chopped straw mushrooms, or Chinese black mushrooms, previously soaked for 25 minutes

2 tablespoons chopped roasted peanuts

2 to 3 teaspoons minced cilantro (fresh coriander) leaves

1¹/₂ teaspoons Spiced Salt (page 246) or 1¹/₄ teaspoons salt and ¹/₂ teaspoon Chinese five-spice powder

Rinse and thoroughly drain the chicken. Pat dry with paper towels. Season with the salt and five-spice powder on the skin and inside the cavity, and refrigerate for 1 hour, uncovered.

Put the wild rice on to cook, according to the directions on the package. Cook until almost tender, then drain well. Cook the fat bacon, if used, the onion, garlic and celery, stirring in the oil in a large pan over medium-high heat for about 2 minutes, then add the uncooked white rice and stir until it is coated with the oil.

Add ¹/₂ cup water and cook, stirring occasionally until the water is absorbed, about 6 minutes. Remove from the heat and add the sliced pancetta or sausage, the wild rice and the other ingredients for the stuffing.

◉ Fill the chicken with the prepared stuffing and secure the opening with poultry pins or fine skewers. Grate the ginger onto a piece of fine cloth and squeeze the juice into a bowl. Add the soy sauce and oil and mix well, then brush evenly over the chicken.

◉ Return the chicken, uncovered, to the refrigerator while the barbecue is being prepared. This will dry out the skin, making it crisper when roasted.

◉ Prepare and light the coals for a kettle-style barbecue, ensuring there are sufficient coals to maintain heat while the chicken cooks. When ready, push them aside and insert a drip container into the center of the barbecue. Position the grid over and brush with oil. Place the chicken, breast upwards, on the grid, close the barbecue and cook for 20 minutes, then turn the chicken first to one side, then to the other, to ensure it cooks evenly. Cook for 20 minutes on each side, then a final 20 to 30 minutes, breast up again. Test by inserting a skewer into the thickest part of the thigh. If no pinkish liquid runs off, the chicken is done.

◉ If cooking in the oven, preheat oven to 390°F. Place chicken on a rack in a roasting pan breast upwards and roast for 25 minutes. Reduce heat to 370°F. Turn the chicken and roast 30 minutes, then turn and roast a further 30 minutes or until cooked.

◉ To serve, pull out the skewers cut the chicken in half and remove the wild rice stuffing. Divide the chicken into serving portions and serve with the stuffing.

Grilled Quail with Chili and Sichuan Pepper

Makes 6 servings

This is one of the simplest and most delicious ways to serve quail, but also great with other small game birds or baby chickens. Serve with extra pepper-salt, for dipping.

6 dressed quail

1¹/₂ teaspoons Pepper-Salt, (page 246)

Vegetable oil

Basting Ingredients

¹/₂ teaspoon chili oil

1¹/₂ teaspoons sesame oil

1¹/₂ tablespoons corn or canola oil

1 medium-sized hot red chili, finely minced

1 scallion (green and white parts), minced

1 teaspoon minced ginger

Cut the quails in half and rinse in cold water, drain and pat dry with paper towels. Sprinkle evenly with the pepper-salt and place, uncovered, in the refrigerator for 2 hours.

Prepare and light the coals for a charcoal barbecue and allow them to subside to a dull red glow or heat a gas/electric barbecue to medium-hot and brush the grid with oil. Use a small brush to dab the mixed basting ingredients evenly over the quails. Place on the barbecue to cook. Turn and baste the quail frequently while they grill for at least 7 minutes, until well browned.

Arrange the quails on warmed plates over lettuce or mixed salad greens, and pour over any remaining basting ingredients.

Char-Grilled Breast of Duck with Lime Sauce

Makes 4 servings

Serve with molds of mixed white and wild rice, fine slices of yellow sweet potato crisp-fried, and steamed sugar snap or snow peas.

4 duckling breasts, each about 5 ounces

1 teaspoon salt

¹/₂ teaspoon white pepper

1¹/₃ teaspoons ground coriander

2 teaspoons freshly squeezed lime juice

1 tablespoon vegetable oil

Lime Sauce

Juice and zest of 2 large limes, about ¹/₃ cup juice

2 to 3 tablespoons fine white sugar

¹/₃ cup water

1¹/₂ tablespoons fish sauce

1 small clove garlic, finely minced

1 teaspoon Chili Chutney (page 266)

1 teaspoon cornstarch

Salt and freshly ground black pepper

1 to 2 fresh kaffir lime leaves, very finely shredded

⊕ Prepare the duck breasts by trimming off any fat. Rub them with the salt and pepper, the ground coriander and lime juice and set aside for 20 minutes.

⊕ Prepare and light the coals for a charcoal barbecue and allow them to subside to a dull glow, or light a gas/electric barbecue about 10 minutes before cooking starts. Brush the barbecue grill with oil. Brush the duck breasts lightly with oil and place, skin downwards, on the grill. Cook for about 2 minutes, then turn and cook the underside for 2 to 3 minutes. Lastly, turn again and cook until the meat is done and the skin is crisp and amber in color. Remove from the barbecue and let sit, keeping warm, for a few minutes.

⊕ To make the sauce, combine the ingredients, except cornstarch and lime leaves, in a small saucepan and simmer over low heat until partially reduced. Mix cornstarch with 2 to 3 teaspoons of cold water, stir in and cook until the sauce thickens and becomes translucent. Taste for seasoning, adding salt and pepper if needed, and the shredded lime leaves.

⊕ Use a sharp knife to very finely slice the duck breasts. Fan onto plates and spoon on the sauce.

Tandoori Turkey Steaks

Makes 6 servings

Serve with Marinated Onion Rings, wedges of lemon, and warmed naans or flatbread, or try the Hot and Aromatic Okra on page 228, with rice, as accompaniments.

1¼ teaspoons salt

1 teaspoon chili powder

6 turkey breast steaks, each 5 to 6 ounces

2 to 3 tablespoons ghee (clarified butter), melted, or butter or margarine

2 to 3 teaspoons vegetable oil

Tandoori Marinade

½ cup plain yogurt

¼ cup thin cream or half and half

2 tablespoons fresh lemon juice

2 teaspoons minced garlic

3 teaspoons minced ginger

1 tablespoon ground coriander

1 teaspoon ground cumin

1 teaspoon garam masala or curry powder (mild or hot)

⅓ teaspoon crushed carom (ajwain) seeds, or aniseed (optional)

Orange-red tandoori or other food coloring

Garnish

Marinated Onion Rings (page 272)

Lemon wedges

Combine the salt and chili powder and rub into the turkey steaks, then set aside for 15 minutes.

Mix the tandoori marinade. Place the turkey steaks on a flat plate or tray and coat thickly with the marinade, cover with plastic wrap and refrigerate for 4 to 5 hours. Turn the turkey several times while it is marinating, spreading the marinade evenly over it each time.

Prepare and light the coals for a charcoal barbecue and allow them to subside to a dull glow, or light a gas/electric barbecue about 10 minutes before cooking starts. Heat a barbecue to medium-hot, and brush the grid with oil. Grill the turkey steaks, turning several times until cooked through, with the surface amber-red and flecked with dark brown. Brush the turkey steaks with the melted butter or margarine as often as needed to keep them moist and succulent. (Tandoori turkey steaks can also be oven baked at 400°F, brushing frequently with melted butter.)

Butterfly Pork Steaks with Fiery Peach Chutney

Makes 4 to 6 servings

Serve this elegant pork barbecue onto warmed plates with the chutney, accompanied by herbed rice.

4 to 6 butterfly-cut pork steaks
  (see note)

2 teaspoons ginger juice (see sidebar, page 96)

1/2 teaspoon finely ground black pepper

1 tablespoon ghee (clarified butter), butter or oil, plus 2 to 3 teaspoons extra

Salt

Fiery Peach Chutney

4 large ripe peaches

1/2 teaspoon minced garlic

1/2 teaspoon minced fresh ginger

1 teaspoon minced red chili

2 tablespoons rice or cider vinegar

3 teaspoons sugar

1 hot red chili, seeded and chopped (optional)

Salt and freshly ground black pepper

⊕ Season the pork with ginger juice and pepper and set aside for 15 to 20 minutes.

⊕ Prepare and light the coals for a charcoal barbecue and allow them to subside to a dull glow, or light a gas/electric barbecue about 10 minutes before cooking starts.

⊕ Peel the peaches, cut in half and remove the pits, then slice thinly. In a small saucepan of nonreactive metal, simmer the chutney ingredients over medium heat until the peaches are tender, about 15 minutes, stirring occasionally. Season to taste with salt and pepper. Remove from the heat and transfer to a bowl to cool.

⊕ Brush the barbecue grid with oil or clarified butter. Grill the steaks for about 3 minutes on each side, or until done to preference, seasoning them lightly with salt half way through grilling.

Note: **To make butterfly-cut pork steaks, debone plump pork chops and slice them laterally, then fold out into thin escalopes. Or alternatively, slice escalopes from the leg.**

Pork Tenderloin with Green Peppercorn Sauce

Makes 6 servings

This Green Peppercorn-Hoisin Sauce is an excellent dipping sauce for Chinese roast pork or duck purchased from a Chinese barbecue shop.

1¹/₂ pounds pork tenderloin (select 2 or 3 even sized pieces)

2 tablespoons hoisin *sauce*

1 teaspoon salt

2 teaspoons mashed garlic

2¹/₂ tablespoons vegetable or peanut oil

1¹/₂ pounds baby bok choy *(small Chinese white cabbage)*

Green Peppercorn-Hoisin Sauce

6 teaspoons green peppercorns in brine, drained

4 tablespoons hoisin *sauce*

1¹/₂ teaspoons dark soy sauce

⊕ Make the peppercorn sauce a little ahead of time to meld the flavors. In a mortar, grind 4 teaspoons of the peppercorns to a paste. Scrape into a bowl and combine with the *hoisin* sauce and dark soy sauce. Mix well, then stir in the whole peppercorns and set aside.

⊕ To prepare the pork, trim it of any surface silver skin, and cut into six evenly sized pieces. Butterfly each piece by cutting deeply along one side and opening out. Bat the steak firmly once or twice with the flat side of a cleaver blade. Combine the *hoisin* sauce, salt and 1¹/₂ teaspoons of the garlic, brush thickly over the pork steaks and set aside for 15 to 20 minutes.

⊕ Prepare a barbecue or heat a grill or ribbed heavy pan. Moisten with oil to prevent sticking. Cook the pork over reasonably high heat for about 3 minutes on each side. While the pork is cooking, poach the baby *bok choy* for 3 to 4 minutes in lightly salted water; drain well. Heat a pan with 1 tablespoon vegetable or peanut oil and add the remaining ¹/₂ teaspoon of garlic. Fry very, very briefly, then add the *bok choy* and cook on high heat, stirring and turning, for 1 mintue. Season with salt and a sprinkle of sugar and toss again for a few seconds.

⊕ Arrange the vegetables on plates with a pork steak. Spoon on the sauce and serve.

Grilled Pork Chops with Chili Plum Glaze

Makes 6 servings

I use this glaze on spare ribs as well, but also when I do a pork roast, brushing it on a leg of pork, or a boned and rolled loin as it roasts.

6 pork chops (about 2 pounds)
2 teaspoons mashed garlic

2 teaspoons grated fresh ginger
1¹/₂ teaspoons salt

Chili Plum Glaze

¹/₂ cup Chinese plum sauce
1 tablespoon sambal ulek or other chili paste

1 tablespoon light corn syrup
1 tablespoon water

✦ Season the pork chops with the garlic, ginger and salt and set aside for 15 to 20 minutes. Combine the remaining ingredients in a bowl.

✦ Heat a barbecue or grill. Brush the chili plum glaze over the chops and grill on medium-high heat for about 4¹/₂ minutes on each side.

✦ Turn the chops frequently, basting each time.

✦ Serve on warmed plates, with any remaining glaze heated in a small pan and poured over.

Pepper Steaks with Shiitake Mushroom Sauce

Makes 4 servings

Serve these pepper-crusted steaks straight from the barbecue, or make up the rich and creamy mushroom sauce to accompany them.

4 sirloin or porterhouse steaks

1¹/₂ tablespoons canola oil or melted butter

Pepper Crust

2 tablespoons black peppercorns

1 tablespoon white peppercorns

¹/₂ teaspoon yellow mustard seeds

¹/₂ teaspoon caraway seeds

¹/₂ teaspoon cumin seeds

¹/₂ teaspoon sea salt flakes

1 small hot red chili, seeded and minced

2 cloves garlic, mashed

Shiitake Mushroom Sauce

12 dried shiitake mushrooms or Chinese black mushrooms, soaked in cold water for 25 minutes

1¹/₄ cups dry white wine

1 shallot, minced

1 clove garlic, minced

1¹/₂ cups cream

¹/₂ cup liquid from soaking mushrooms

Salt

⊕ Combine the pepper crust ingredients. Brush the steaks with oil or melted butter, sprinkle on the pepper ingredients evenly and press them in lightly. Set aside for 20 minutes.

⊕ Prepare and light the coals for a charcoal barbecue and allow them to subside to a dull glow, or light a gas/electric barbecue about 10 minutes before cooking starts.

⊕ Prepare the sauce by first draining the mushrooms and reserving ¹/₂ cup of the liquid. Trim off the stems, then slice the mushrooms finely and set aside. In a small saucepan simmer the white wine with the shallot and garlic over medium heat

until the wine has reduced to about 2 tablespoons, about 10 minutes. Add the cream and the mushrooms, plus 1/2 cup of the reserved soaking liquid and simmer over medium heat until this sauce has reduced to about 1 cup, about 8 minutes. Add salt to taste and keep warm.

⊕ Grill the steaks over high heat, until the surface is well seared and the pepper crust slightly blackened and very aromatic.

Beef Skirt with Asian Marinade

Makes 6 servings

Stack the grilled beef on a platter, garnish with sprigs of fresh herbs, tomato wedges and slices of lime and serve with herbed rice and the hot barbecue sauce.

1½ pounds beef skirt steak

2 to 3 tablespoons ghee (clarified butter) or vegetable oil

Asian Marinade

2 tablespoons ground cumin

1 teaspoon cracked black pepper

1 teaspoon ground white pepper

½ teaspoon ground allspice

3 teaspoons crushed garlic

¼ cup chopped cilantro (fresh coriander)

2 teaspoons harissa or other hot chili sauce

½ cup vegetable oil

Hot Barbecue Sauce

⅓ cup bottled barbecue sauce

2 tablespoons hoisin sauce

2 teaspoons harissa or other hot chili sauce

1 small onion, very finely chopped

1 clove garlic, very finely chopped

2 teaspoons chopped cilantro (fresh coriander)

Garnish

Sprigs of fresh cilantro (fresh coriander) or basil

Sliced lime and tomato wedges

⊕ Cut the beef into 1-inch × 6-inch strips and place in a wide dish. Combine the marinade ingredients and use a wooden spoon to thoroughly mix the meat with the marinade. Cover and refrigerate overnight, or at least 6 hours, turning the meat several times.

⊕ Heat a charcoal barbecue and brush the grid with oil or clarified butter.

⊕ Cook the beef until the surface is well crisped, turning several times and occasionally basting with oil or clarified butter, 4 to 5 minutes on each side.

⊕ Combine the sauce ingredients, mixing thoroughly. Spoon into a sauce bowl.

Korean Barbecued Beef Ribs

Makes 6 to 8 servings

Serve with white rice and the Kim Chi from page 269, or a salad.

4 pounds beef short ribs

²/₃ cup vegetable oil

Marinade

¹/₄ cup dark soy sauce

¹/₂ cup light soy sauce

¹/₄ cup sesame oil

1 tablespoon Roasted Chili Paste (see sidebar)

1 tablespoon minced garlic

1 tablespoon minced ginger

¹/₄ cup minced scallions (green and white parts)

2 tablespoons sugar

1¹/₂ tablespoons sesame paste

¹/₄ cup vegetable oil

1 teaspoon freshly ground black pepper

Have your butcher cut the ribs into 2-inch pieces. Combine the marinade ingredients in a large bowl, stirring until the sesame paste and sugar are completely mixed. Add the ribs, then knead and stir with the hands until each piece of rib is coated with the sauce. Cover and refrigerate for at least 5 hours, stirring occasionally.

Prepare and light the coals for a charcoal barbecue and allow them to subside to a dull glow, or light a gas/electric barbecue about 10 minutes before cooking starts.

Prepare and heat a barbecue hotplate, or a suitable tabletop hot plate such as an electric skillet or a ribbed hotplate. Brush with vegetable oil. Place the ribs on the hotplate to cook until done, about 12 minutes, turning frequently and brushing with any marinade that remains in the bowl.

Roasted Chili Paste

Korean cooks use chili with generosity. This roasted chili paste adds brilliant color and intense flavor. Heat a small, heavy skillet or sauce pan over medium heat. Put in 2 tablespoons sweet paprika and 1 tablespoon chili flakes or coarsely ground dried chilies, and stir constantly as they cook. I usually wear glasses while preparing this, to keep fumes from my eyes. When the chili is well heated, about 1 minute, add 2 tablespoons of Japanese miso or Chinese bean paste and 1 tablespoon oil. Stir over medium heat, until it is all well mixed, adding a sprinkle of water to help the paste amalgamate. It can be stored in a small jar in the refrigerator for several months.

Lamb Cutlets in Coconut and Cilantro Sauce

Makes 6 servings

Coconut groves adorn the southwestern coast of India, so naturally they are an important element in the cuisine, as well as providing materials for cooking utensils, housing and table decoration. This is a favorite recipe. Arrange the cutlets on a serving platter, spoon on the sauce and pour over the fried ingredients, then serve at once.

1½ pounds trimmed lamb cutlets

2½ tablespoons ghee (clarified butter) or butter, melted, or vegetable or peanut oil

½ teaspoon ground turmeric

Coconut and Cilantro Sauce

4 cloves garlic, peeled

1 small onion, peeled and quartered

¾-inch piece fresh ginger, coarsely chopped

2 green chilies, seeded and coarsely chopped

½ cup chopped cilantro (fresh coriander)

1 tablespoon white poppy seeds, or 1 tablespoon ground almonds

¼ teaspoon ground cinnamon

½ teaspoon grated nutmeg or ground mace

⅛ teaspoon ground cloves

Salt and freshly ground black pepper

½ to ¾ cup water

Fried Ingredients

½ teaspoon brown mustard seeds

½ teaspoon coarsely cracked black pepper

1½ tablespoons ghee (clarified butter) or 1 tablespoon vegetable or peanut oil

Scrape the cutlet bones free of any meat, then set the cutlets aside. To make the sauce, place the garlic, onion, ginger and green chilies in the small bowl of a food processor fitted with the metal blade, or in a blender and grind to a paste. Add the cilantro and grind again to a reasonably smooth paste. Toast the poppy seeds

in a dry pan until golden, grind finely with the cinnamon, nutmeg and cloves and mix with the other sauce ingredients. Set aside.

⊕ Prepare and light the coals for a charcoal barbecue and allow them to subside to a dull glow, or light a gas/electric barbecue about 10 minutes before cooking starts.

⊕ Heat a barbecue grill, or a heavy skillet, and brush the surface with a little of the *ghee* or oil. Mix the turmeric with half the remaining *ghee* or oil and brush over the cutlets, then cook to preference, ideally rare. Remove to a plate and keep warm.

⊕ If you have cooked the cutlets on a hotplate, you will now need a large skillet or sauté pan to finish the dish. Heat the remaining *ghee* and fry the prepared sauce ingredients for about 2 minutes, sprinkling on a little water to prevent burning. Add $1/2$ to $3/4$ cup water to make a sauce the consistency of cream. Season to taste with salt and pepper and stir well.

⊕ Cook until the sauce is well blended, then return the cutlets to briefly warm in the sauce.

⊕ To finish the dish, fry the mustard seeds and cracked pepper in the *ghee* or oil until the mustard seeds begin to pop. Serve the cutlets onto a platter, cover with the sauce and pour on the hot spiced oil.

Honey Curry Lamb Kebabs

Makes 6 servings

Serve the skewers on a bed of rice, with your choice of Indian style vegetables. Choose from the Indian Spiced Cauliflower on page 227, Pumpkin Fugarth on page 232, or Masala Potatoes on page 231.

1½ pounds lean boneless lamb

6 small onions

1 red bell pepper

Melted butter or vegetable oil

12 metal skewers, oiled, or 12 thin
    bamboo skewers soaked in cold
    water

Marinade

¼ cup honey

1 tablespoon vegetable oil

1 to 2 teaspoons vindaloo paste
    (or Thai red curry paste)

1 teaspoon ground cumin

⅓ teaspoon ground cinnamon

1 tablespoon whole grain mustard

½ teaspoon cracked black pepper

1 teaspoon salt

🌐 Cut the lamb into 1-inch cubes. In a stainless steel or glass dish combine the marinade ingredients, mixing thoroughly. Add the lamb and stir with a wooden spoon until each piece of lamb is coated with the marinade. Cover with plastic wrap and refrigerate for at least 3 hours.

🌐 Peel the onions and cut in half. Cut the pepper into 1-inch squares.

🌐 Thread the meat, onion halves and pepper squares onto the skewers.

🌐 Prepare and light the coals for a charcoal barbecue and allow them to subside to a dull glow, or light a gas/electric barbecue about 10 minutes before cooking starts. Heat a barbecue with a flat or ridged hotplate. Place the skewers on the hotplate and brush with oil or butter. Grill until done, frequently turning and brushing with the oil or butter and any remaining marinade.

Kettle-Roasted Leg of Lamb Stuffed with Onion Chutney

Makes 6 servings

My Onion Chutney from page 265 has proved useful to have on hand. Here, I use it to stuff a boned leg of lamb, which I roast in a kettle barbecue. You can cook the lamb in the oven, or wrap it in a parcel of foil and cook slowly over an open barbecue. It goes equally well with barbecue-grilled vegetables or a salad.

4-pound butterflied leg of lamb

1 recipe Onion Chutney (page 265)

2 teaspoons coarse salt

2 teaspoons cracked black pepper (coarsely ground)

1 tablespoon mashed garlic

Vegetable oil, ghee (clarified butter) or butter

⊕ Heat a kettle or other covered style of barbecue.

⊕ Cut two deep pockets within the cavity along the length of the lamb leg where the bone was removed. Fill this cavity with chutney. Re-shape the lamb leg and tie with string at 1¹/₂-inch intervals.

⊕ Place the lamb leg in the kettle barbecue, cover and cook, turning every ten minutes. Rub the surface with the salt, pepper and mashed garlic. Brush occasionally with melted butter or vegetable oil while it cooks. If you plan to cook the lamb in foil, use a double layer of foil and brush it with butter or oil. Place the leg in the center of foil, and wrap, folding the edges together to seal. Turn the lamb every 8 to 10 minutes so it cooks evenly. After about 45 minutes, open the parcel, draining the juices into a bowl. Place the lamb directly on the barbecue grid and continue to cook until the surface has crisped and browned, basting occasionally with the reserved juices and extra oil or butter.

⊕ Allow the roast to rest for 6 to 7 minutes before carving into thick slices.

Grilled Corn on the Cob with Chili Tomato Sauce

Makes 8 servings

8 fresh ears of corn

2 tablespoons butter, melted

Chili Tomato Sauce

Makes 1 3/4 cups

1 large onion, very finely chopped

2 teaspoons minced garlic

1 large mild red chili, seeded and minced

2 tablespoons vegetable oil

1 teaspoon chili flakes

1 teaspoon sweet paprika

3/4 teaspoon salt

2 teaspoons red wine vinegar

1 tablespoon white sugar

One 14-ounce can Italian-style tomatoes

1 tablespoon chopped fresh basil or cilantro (fresh coriander)

Husk the corn, then brush with butter and place on a moderately hot grill. Turn frequently as they cook, and brush occasionally with extra butter.

To make the sauce, place the onion, garlic and chili in a medium saucepan with the oil. Cook, stirring, over medium-high heat for about 4 minutes, stirring frequently. Add the chili flakes, paprika, salt, vinegar and sugar and stir for 1 minute over medium heat, then add the tomatoes and cook for about 10 minutes.

Transfer the contents of the saucepan to a blender or food processor fitted with the metal blades, and puree until reasonably smooth. Pass through a sieve and return to the heat. Simmer until the sauce has thickened, about 10 minutes more. Check seasonings, add the herbs and serve hot or at room temperature, with the grilled corn.

Greens and Grains

Dal, Dhal and Daljit—Reminiscences of India

You have to take to the streets to find real food in India. Not that you can't eat spectacular food in restaurants there, you can. But there is a blurring of the edges of regionality that frustrates the serious foodie. Not that that makes India different from most other countries. Restaurants, and particularly those on major tourist routes, tend to play it safe, offering a spread of dishes to suit everyone. So to find out what's really happening on any local food scene, you have to get out there among the people, and eat where they eat.

I had been spoiled with good Indian food long before I first set foot there. First in my teens, sharing student accommodation with a friend from southern India, whose idea of weekend relaxation was to cook up dishes that reminded of home. After that Daljit came into my life, my first Indian cooking teacher, who schooled me in the characteristics of Punjabi cooking and taught me to make a perfect *chupati*. I'd shared feast days with my local Sikh community, and *dhansak* with Parsis, I cooked a mean *kofta* curry (page 174), and knew a *sambar* (page 16) from a *rasam* (page 20). I'd talked and listened, and prepared a wish list of dishes I was determined to eat in India.

So in every hotel where I stayed, I asked the chefs where they ate, and many offered to take me to their favorite eating places. That is, if I didn't mind eating late, or starting early to do a market round with them. Most were small food stalls with just one or two specialties—this one made *vadais* like no one else, that one small *puris* stuffed with spiced chickpeas (page 236), the envy of the marketplace. I didn't drink the water, I didn't touch salads or unpeeled fruit, but I did eat whatever cooked food took my eye, or tantalized my nose. I seared my palate with the fiery, chili-laden vegetarian food of the south, savored the elegantly spiced Moglai foods of the central north, reveled in the coconut-seafood combinations of the west coast, and the pungent mustard oil-cooked foods of the east. I dined in many of India's first-class restaurants, but also where everyday people ate, and that way came to know India, and its food, a little more intimately.

You don't go to Kashmir to eat hot food, though at ripening time scarlet banners of chilies hang from beneath the eaves and the protruding wooden balconies of almost every home there. Kashimiri chilies are enormous, but lack the heat of the varieties that proliferate in the south. You go for food that's subtly spiced, for cherries in season, and tiny apples and breathtaking views of snowclad mountains. For several years, Kashmir was a delightful annual retreat for our family, a haven from the rigors of life in more frenetic parts of Asia. We'd take a houseboat on the vast and tranquil Dal lake, preferring the hospitality of the entrepreneurial

S. Gulam Wangnoo, whose visitors' book attested to the worldwide popularity of his comfortably appointed craft. Madam Wangnoo, his wife, was chief cook for the houseboat guests, her kitchen a makeshift arrangement on the bank of the lake. Their houseboat had two spacious bedrooms, and an expansive living room, with a large sunning deck above. Every panel, pole and ceiling of the wooden craft was elaborately carved in traditional Indian style, the rear verandah a superb work of art. We'd spend several hours there each day bartering with visiting salesmen and trade persons who'd row up in slender *shikaras* completely outfitted with the tools of their trade. The flower seller's boat would be stacked high with lotus blossoms plucked from the lake, the spice merchant would have his wares in rainbow mounds from which he scooped into a cone of newspaper when he made a sale. There were tailors who'd come on board to measure, then return 24 hours later with shirts, skirts or sari underclothes beautifully stitched by hand. I was intrigued by the products offered by the vegetable merchants. Unlike most other parts of India, where the vegetables are often diminutive and of poor quality, those we bought on the lake were magnificent. Their secret, an ingenious semi-hydroponic arrangement of vegetable gardens that floated on the lake. Built up of soil and mulch layered on an accumulation of lotus and other water plants, the gardens had been skillfully constructed to form huge floating rafts, to which their attendants would row each morning. I particularly recall the kohlrabi, with a sweetness I'd never tasted elsewhere. But my most vivid memory of food in Kashmir was of lamb. We ate it at just about every meal, usually companioned by crispy *pakoras* of diced vegetables (page 86) coated in a chickpea flour batter. Mrs. Wangnoo was of short and stocky build, her girth accentuated by the many layers of skirts, underskirts, shirts, waistcoats and jackets that are a typical mode of dress for the region. Over all of these she would wrap a voluminous apron much impregnated with the stifling, lanolin odor of lamb. As she was happy to pass on her cooking techniques, I took to hanging around her work area before mealtime. Pleased with my companionship, perhaps she had no daughters of her own, or because of my obvious appreciation of her food, she'd spontaneously gather me in her arms for a bear hug, pinning my face deep into the folds of that rank apron. I'd endure, breath held, and would happily do so again to learn a few more of her cooking secrets.

Indonesian Fruit and Vegetable Salad

Makes 4 to 6 servings

1 jicama or yam bean (bangkwang)

1 Japanese nashi pear, or 1 to 2
    firm, ripe pears

1 large, unripe mango

2 thick slices pineapple or jackfruit

2 star fruit (carambola), optional

1½ cups bean sprouts

1 small bunch long beans or young
    green beans

1 cucumber

2 tablespoons vegetable oil

2 pieces firm, fresh tofu (bean curd),
    each 2 x 2 inches

1 tablespoon Crunchy Garlic Crisps
    (page 279)

2 hard-boiled eggs, sliced

Lime wedges

Dressing

1 teaspoon dried shrimp paste

3 cloves garlic, finely chopped

4 shallots, finely chopped

1½ teaspoons minced fresh ginger

1¼ teaspoons ground coriander

1 to 2 teaspoons sambal ulek or chili
    sauce

⅓ cup sweet soy sauce (kecap
    manis)

1¼ tablespoons crunchy peanut
    butter

1 tablespoon palm sugar or soft
    brown sugar

3 teaspoons tamarind concentrate or
    about 1½ tablespoons lemon
    juice

2 to 3 tablespoons water

Juice of ½ to 1 lime

⊕ Peel the jicama, pear and mango and discard the central seed core and stem of
the pear and the stone of the mango. Slice the fruit thinly and place in a bowl, or
arrange in separate groups on a platter. Peel the pineapple or jackfruit and cut into
bite-sized chunks. Slice the star fruit thinly, if using. Mix them with the other fruit
in the bowl, or arrange on the platter.

⊕ Blanch the bean sprouts briefly in boiling water, drain and refresh under cold
water. Drain again. Cut the beans into 2-inch pieces. Parboil in lightly salted water
for 2 minutes, then drain and refresh under cold water; drain again. Cut the
cucumber in half lengthways and scoop out the seeds with a teaspoon. Slice the
cucumber thinly.

⊕ Add the vegetables to the salad bowl, or arrange on the platter.

⊕ Heat the oil in a small skillet and fry the tofu over medium heat, until golden brown, turning twice, about 2 minutes. Remove and drain, then cut into sticks. Add to the salad bowl, or to the plates.

⊕ To make the dressing, first wrap the shrimp paste in a piece of aluminum foil and place in a dry skillet or wok. Cook over medium-high heat for 1 to 1½ minutes, turning frequently. Grind the garlic and shallots in a mortar or blender, the small bowl of a food processor fitted with the metal blades, or a spice grinder, then add the shrimp paste and grind briefly and transfer to a small mixing bowl, add the remaining dressing ingredients and stir until thoroughly amalgamated. Check seasoning and consistency, adding extra sugar, tamarind or a little salt to balance the flavors. Add a squeeze of fresh lime juice, and taste the dressing. It should have a pleasant tang.

⊕ Spoon the dressing over the salad, or serve separately in a bowl. Sprinkle on fried garlic and add a slice or two of the hard-boiled egg and a wedge of lime.

Green Papaya Salad

Makes 6 servings

In Thailand, this tangy, peppery salad, Som Tam, is often included in the menu to add vibrant flavor and texture points to a curry meal. It can be made with either green (unripe) mango or papaya (pawpaw). I have often served it as a stimulating start to a summer menu, in tall, stemmed glasses, with one perfect large shrimp (prawn) hanging over the rim.

4 cups coarsely grated unripe mango or papaya (from 2 large mangoes or 1 medium papaya)

1 large tomato, sliced into thin wedges

1 small white onion or 1 to 2 red salad onions, finely chopped

2 tablespoons finely chopped cilantro (fresh coriander) or mint leaves

3 tablespoons freshly squeezed lime juice

1/3 cup fish sauce

3 tablespoons fine white sugar

1/2 teaspoon chili flakes

To Serve as an Appetizer

6 crisp lettuce leaf cups

6 large cooked and peeled shrimp

6 small lime wedges

6 sprigs of fresh herbs (mint, fennel, dill, cilantro)

Some people can experience a painful allergic reaction to the juice of unripe mangoes and papaya. As a precaution, use disposable latex gloves while peeling and handling them. However, the dressing neutralizes sharp fruit acids, so you should encounter no problems in serving or eating this delicious salad.

⊕ You can simply combine the ingredients in a salad bowl, or do as they do in Thailand and place the mango or papaya in a stone mortar and pound it lightly and briefly with the pestle (or chop very briefly in a food processor using the pulse control). Add the tomato, onion and herbs and pound or chop again, very briefly. Done this way the salad may not be as attractive on the plate, but the pounding or chopping helps to meld the flavors. Mix the lime juice, fish sauce, sugar and salt, add to the salad and mix well, or if using the mortar, pound again briefly. Cover with plastic wrap and chill for at least 20 minutes.

⊕ To serve as a salad, simply pile into a shallow dish and garnish with fresh herbs or shredded chilies.

⊕ As an appetizer, line each cocktail glass with a lettuce leaf, mound the salad high in the glass, and garnish each with a shrimp, a lime wedge and a sprig of herbs.

Pineapple Salad

Serve the salad in the pineapple shells, and scatter on the toasted coconut, to garnish.

large fresh pineapple

1 medium cucumber

1 large scallion (green and white parts)

1 large fresh mild red chili

2 to 3 tablespoons shredded coconut, toasted

Dressing

3/4 teaspoon shrimp paste*

1 tablespoon vegetable oil

1 teaspoon finely minced garlic

1 teaspoon finely minced fresh ginger

3 tablespoons sweet soy sauce (kecap manis)

1 1/2 tablespoons white vinegar

1 1/2 teaspoons palm sugar or dark brown sugar

Cut the pineapple in half. Use a small sharp knife, ideally with a curved blade, to remove the flesh from the pineapple. Retain the pineapple shells. Trim away the core, then cut the pineapple into bite-sized chunks and place in a mixing bowl.

Use a vegetable carving tool to score grooves along the length of the cucumber, then cut in half, scoop out the seeds and slice thinly. Finely chop the scallion. Finely slice the chili, discarding the seeds if preferred. Mix with the pineapple.

Fry the shrimp paste in the vegetable oil in a very small pan, for about 40 seconds over medium heat. Pour into a bowl, mash smooth and add the remaining dressing ingredients, whisking until thoroughly amalgamated.

Pour the dressing over the salad and mix well before piling into pineapple shells.

You may prefer to substitute 3 teaspoons of fish sauce for the shrimp paste, deleting the vegetable oil from the recipe as well.

Chickpea and Cilantro Salad

Makes 4 sevings or more as a side dish

Serve as a side dish with curries or grilled meat. Whipped yogurt, flavored with cumin or aniseed, or with chopped fresh dill, goes beautifully with this salad.

2 medium potatoes, peeled

1½ cups cooked chickpeas, approximately 1½ cans, or ¾ cup dried

1 medium ripe tomato

1 large scallion (green and white
parts), chopped

¼ cup chopped cilantro (fresh
coriander) leaves

2 medium hot green chilies, seeded
and chopped

1⅓ teaspoons sugar

3 teaspoons fresh lemon juice

2½ teaspoons chaat masala
(page 247)

⊕ Cut the potatoes into small cubes and boil in lightly salted water until barely tender. Drain and set aside to cool.

⊕ Place the chickpeas in a salad bowl. Cut the tomato in half, gently squeeze out the seeds, then chop the tomato into small dice. Mix the tomato, potato, scallions, cilantro and chili with the chickpeas, adding the sugar, lemon juice and *chaat masala*. Use wooden spoons to carefully mix the salad, then cover with plastic wrap and chill for at least half an hour before serving.

Chili Coconut Cabbage

Makes 4 to 6 servings

As part of an interesting vegetarian menu, serve Chili Coconut Cabbage with the Sri Lankan Eggplant recipe on page 234, plain yogurt and white rice.

1 pound white cabbage

2 tablespoons vegetable or coconut oil

1 teaspoon brown mustard seeds

2 green chilies, seeded and shredded

1/4 cup finely shredded coconut

3/4 cup coconut milk

Salt, freshly ground black pepper and chili powder

⊕ Finely shred the cabbage, cutting away and discarding the thick white ribs.

⊕ Heat the oil in a medium saucepan over medium-high heat. Fry the mustard seeds until they begin to pop, then add the cabbage and fry, stirring, for about 1¹/₂ minutes. Add the remaining ingredients, reduce heat to medium-low, cover and simmer until the cabbage is tender, about 8 minutes, stirring and shaking the pan occasionally. Serve in a shallow bowl.

Stir-fried Vegetables with Spicy Peanut Sauce

Makes 4 to 6 servings

This makes a delicious and substantial vegetarian meal served over batons of fried tofu (bean curd) with steamed white rice.

4 ounces sliced green or long beans

2 cups fresh bean sprouts

1/4 cup vegetable oil

1 1/2 cups chopped spinach or bok choy *leaves*

1 1/2 cups coarsely chopped Chinese cabbage (wombok)

3 scallions, green and white parts, cut into 1-inch pieces

1 medium carrot, thinly sliced

1/2 red bell pepper, sliced

1 green chili, seeded and sliced

Spicy Peanut Sauce

1/3 cup crunchy peanut butter

1 to 2 teaspoons sambal ulek or other chili paste

1 teaspoon dark soy sauce

2 1/2 teaspoons ground coriander

1/2 teaspoon ground laos (galangal) (optional) or 1 1/2 teaspoons finely shredded galangal

1/2 teaspoon tamarind concentrate or 2 teaspoons lemon juice

1 tablespoon palm sugar or soft brown sugar

1/2 teaspoon salt

1/3 teaspoon freshly ground black pepper

1/2 to 3/4 cup coconut milk

To Serve

Sweet Chili Sauce (page 253)

⊕ Cook the beans in lightly salted water until *al dente*, drain, refresh in cold water and drain again. Blanch and drain the beansprouts.

⊕ Heat the oil in a wok or very large skillet over high heat and stir-fry the vegetables for about 3 minutes, then if they require additional cooking, add 2 to 3 tablespoons of water, cover the pan and leave over medium heat for 2 to 3 minutes, stirring occasionally.

- Use a slotted spoon to remove the vegetables to a serving plate.
- Combine the sauce ingredients in a small nonstick saucepan and bring barely to a boil over medium-high heat. Reduce the heat to medium and cook, stirring, for about 1¹/₂ minutes.
- Spoon evenly over the vegetables, drizzle on a little sweet chili sauce, or serve it separately.

Stir-fried Bean Sprouts with Chinese Sausage and Chili Shreds

Makes 4 to 6 servings

12 ounces fresh bean sprouts

2 Chinese lap cheong sausages or
  ¹/₂ cup chopped pancetta

2 tablespoons vegetable oil

¹/₂ teaspoon sesame oil

3 scallions, white parts only, finely
  sliced

1 fresh hot red chili, seeded and
  finely shredded

3 thin slices fresh ginger, finely
  shredded

¹/₂ teaspoon dark soy sauce

Salt and white pepper

¹/₄ cup chicken stock

1 teaspoon cornstarch

- Rinse and drain the bean sprouts. Place the sausages in a steamer to steam over gently simmering water for 6 to 7 minutes. Remove from the steamer, and when partially cooled, slice very thinly.
- Heat the oils in a wok or large skillet over high heat and stir-fry the sausage, or *pancetta*, scallions, chili and ginger for 2 minutes. Add the beansprouts and stir-fry for 1 minute, then add the soy sauce, salt and pepper.
- Combine the stock and cornstarch, pour into the pan and stir-fry until the sauce has formed a glaze on the ingredients, about 1¹/₂ minutes. Serve.

Sautéed Spinach with Garlic and Dried Shrimp

Makes 4 servings

1 pound fresh spinach or kangkong (water vegetable)

1 tablespoon dried shrimp or 1 1/2 teaspoons fresh soft shrimp paste

2 tablespoons vegetable oil

2 cloves garlic, minced

1 dried red chili, minced

1 tablespoon oyster sauce

1/3 teaspoon sugar

1/4 teaspoon freshly ground black pepper

Salt, if needed

1 teaspoon fish sauce (optional)

⊕ Rinse the spinach or water vegetable thoroughly. Pick off and discard the stems (trim the ends of water vegetable stems, and cut into 2-inch pieces). Wrap in a kitchen towel and squeeze gently to remove excess water.

⊕ Grind the shrimp in a food processor fitted with the metal blades, a mortar or blender until it is reduced to a floss. Heat the vegetable oil in a wok or large saucepan, over medium-low heat. Add the ground dried shrimp, garlic and chili and cook, stirring, for 2 minutes until very aromatic.

⊕ Add the spinach or water vegetable with 1 tablespoon water. Cover and cook for about 2 minutes until the vegetables wilt, then remove the lid, increase the heat to high and stir-fry until cooked.

⊕ Stir in the oyster sauce, sugar, pepper, salt and fish sauce, if used, and stir-fry again briefly. Serve.

Indian Spiced Cauliflower

Makes 6 servings as a side dish

Indian Spiced Cauliflower is a versatile dish to serve as an accompaniment to curries and grilled meats, or as part of a vegetarian menu. Serve with lemon or lime wedges for squeezing over the vegetables at the table.

1¼ pounds cauliflower

5 ounces small fresh mushrooms

2 tablespoons ghee (clarified butter) or 1½ tablespoons vegetable oil

1 teaspoon brown mustard seeds

1 teaspoon cumin seeds

Pinch of asafoetida (optional)

1 teaspoon salt

¼ to ½ teaspoon cracked black pepper

2 teaspoons garam masala (page 247), or mild curry powder

To Serve

Lemon or lime wedges

⊕ Cut the cauliflower into small flowerets. Bring a pan of lightly salted water to a boil and add the cauliflower. Cook for 5 minutes, then pour into a colander to drain.

⊕ In the meantime, wipe the mushrooms with a clean cloth. Cut larger ones in halves or quarters and set aside. Heat the *ghee* or oil in a wok or large, heavy skillet, over high heat. Add the spices beginning at the top of the list and allowing about 30 seconds between each addition. They will pop and splutter, so stir carefully with a long-handled wooden spoon while they cook.

⊕ Add the cauliflower and mushrooms and stir frequently. Reduce the heat to medium-high until the vegetables are cooked, about 2½ minutes.

Hot and Aromatic Okra

Makes 3 to 4 servings as a vegetarian main course, or 6 as a side dish

In India, they refer to okra as "ladies fingers." Serve as an accompaniment to meat dishes or as part of a vegetarian meal, accompanied by plain yogurt flavored with chopped cilantro.

12 ounces small fresh okra

2¹/2 to 3 tablespoons ghee (clarified butter) or 2 tablespoons vegetable oil

1/3 teaspoon fenugreek seeds (optional)

1 teaspoon cumin seeds

1¹/4 teaspoons brown mustard seeds

4 curry leaves or 1 bay leaf

2 large green chilies, seeded and chopped

1-inch piece fresh ginger, very finely shredded

2¹/2 teaspoons mild curry paste or powder

1 to 2 teaspoons mild to medium-hot chili powder

Salt and freshly ground black pepper

Tamarind water or lemon juice

❋ Trim the okra stems and use a small, sharp knife to cut each okra in half from the tip towards the stem end, without severing it. If using larger okra, cut them into 1/2-inch slices. Set aside.

❋ Heat the *ghee* in a pan and fry the whole spices and curry or bay leaves for 1 minute. Add the chilies and ginger and sauté for 30 seconds, then add the okra and the curry and chili powders. Stir thoroughly, then add 1/2 cup water and seasonings to taste.

❋ Cover the pan, and simmer gently until the okra is tender, 15 to 20 minutes. Add tamarind water or lemon juice to slightly acidulate the dish, which helps to accentuate the unique fresh flavor of the okra.

Spicy Beans with Garlic

The Koreans enjoy the health-giving benefits of garlic, which they use unsparingly in many dishes, such as this full-flavored bean dish to partner other vegetarian dishes or to complement a grill.

1 pound green beans	¹/₂ to 2 teaspoons chili paste (see note)
3 teaspoons sesame seeds	
1¹/₂ tablespoons sesame oil	1 tablespoon light soy sauce
3 teaspoons minced garlic	¹/₂ teaspoon sugar
1¹/₂ tablespoons minced scallions (green and white parts)	Salt

Cut the beans into 1¹/₂-inch pieces, slicing them at a sharp diagonal.

Heat a wok or skillet without oil over high heat and toast the sesame seeds until golden and aromatic, shaking the pan frequently to ensure they cook evenly. Remove to a mortar or spice grinder and grind to a semi-fine powder. Set aside.

Wipe out the pan and reheat. Add the beans, with water to barely cover. Bring quickly to a boil and simmer for about 3 minutes to crisp-tender. Drain the pan and wipe dry. Return to medium heat.

Add the sesame oil and when heated add the garlic and cook, stirring, for about 20 seconds . Return the beans and cook for about 1 minute on slightly higher heat, tossing and stirring in the Chinese way.

Add the scallions, chili paste, soy sauce and the sugar and salt to taste. Increase the heat to high, and cook for another ¹/₂ to 1 minute stirring and turning the beans before transferring to a serving plate.

 Note: Any chili paste based on mashed chilies and salt will do; *sambal ulek* is ideal.

Southern Indian Cabbage

The red lentils give this peppery dish an appealing crunch. Serve it with curries or grilled meats, or as part of a vegetarian menu.

1 teaspoon cumin seeds

1/2 teaspoon caraway or fennel seeds

2 tablespoons ghee (clarified butter) or vegetable oil

1 to 3 dried red chilies, broken and seeds shaken out

8 curry leaves or 1 bay leaf, broken

1/4 cup red lentils

1 1/4 pounds shredded cabbage

2 teaspoons minced green chili (optional)

Salt and freshly ground black pepper

2 tablespoons chopped cilantro (fresh coriander) leaves

Heat a medium saucepan over medium-high heat and add the seed spices and *ghee* or vegetable oil. Heat for 1 minute, stirring and shaking the pan, then add the chilies and curry leaves or bay leaf and the lentils. Stir in the hot oil for 1 1/2 minutes, then add the shredded cabbage and the minced chili.

Cover the pan and cook for 2 minutes, frequently stirring and shaking the pan to turn the cabbage and evenly coat each strand with the oil. Add 1/4 cup water and continue to cook covered, stirring occasionally, until the cabbage and lentils are both tender, about 12 minutes. Season to taste with salt and pepper and stir in the cilantro.

Masala Potatoes

This is an invaluable standby. Serve with curries or grilled meats, or to give substance to a vegetarian meal.

8 large potatoes, approximately 3 pounds, peeled

5 tablespoons ghee (clarified butter) or vegetable oil or light olive oil

1 medium onion, finely chopped

4 to 5 cloves garlic, very finely minced

2 teaspoons grated fresh ginger

1 to 2 teaspoons minced red chili

1 tablespoon garam masala (page 247), or mild curry powder

2 teaspoons ground coriander

1½ teaspoons salt

1 cup plain yogurt

½ cup water

To Finish the Dish

½ teaspoon brown mustard seeds

1 tablespoon minced cilantro (fresh coriander) leaves

⊕ Leaving the potatoes whole, fry them in the *ghee* over medium-high heat until they are golden on the surface, then remove to a covered oven dish and set aside. Remove 1 tablespoon of the *ghee* or oil and keep it aside.

⊕ Preheat the oven to 360°F.

⊕ Put the onion, garlic, ginger and chili in the pan and cook over medium heat, stirring constantly, for 3 minutes. Then add the *garam masala*, coriander and salt and cook briefly. Add the yogurt mixed with water, heat to boiling and pour over the potatoes. Cover the dish and place it in the oven.

⊕ Bake for about 40 minutes, until the potatoes are completely tender and have absorbed the pan liquids. Baste and turn them from time to time, during cooking.

⊕ Fry the mustard seeds in the reserved *ghee* or oil until they begin to pop and splutter. Sprinkle the fried mustard seeds and cilantro evenly over the potatoes just before serving.

Pumpkin Fugarth

Makes 4 to 6 servings

This spiced pumpkin is a triumph as the filling for handmade ravioli. Use the recipe for the cilantro-flavored dumpling dough on page 68 (Scallop and Cilantro Dumplings). You will only need about half of this recipe for the filling. Serve the ravioli doused with butter in which you have fried cracked pepitas (pumpkin seeds), and added plenty of cracked black pepper.

2 pounds pumpkin (1½ pounds
    peeled and deseeded weight)

2 tablespoons ghee (clarified butter)
    or vegetable oil

1 large onion, sliced

3 teaspoons grated fresh ginger

1 teaspoon minced garlic

1 teaspoon ground cumin

½ teaspoon ground turmeric

½ teaspoon hot chili powder

1 teaspoon salt

Lemon juice or heavy cream, to taste

To Finish the Dish

1 tablespoon finely chopped cilantro
    (fresh coriander) or mint leaves
    or ¾ teaspoon brown mustard
    seeds

6 curry leaves (optional)

1 to 2 tablespoons ghee (clarified
    butter) or vegetable oil

⊕ Peel, deseed and cube the pumpkin. Heat the *ghee* or oil in a medium saucepan over medium-high heat and cook the onion, stirring, until golden. Add the ginger, garlic, cumin, turmeric, chili powder and salt and cook, stirring constantly, for 1 minute.

⊕ Add the pumpkin pieces and stir until they are evenly coated with the *ghee* or oil. Add 2 to 3 tablespoons of water and cover the pan tightly. Cook over medium-low heat, shaking the pan frequently to turn the pumpkin, until it is completely tender.

⊕ Add the lemon juice or cream, then stir in the chopped herbs, or serve dressed with the fried mustard seeds and curry leaves (below).

⊕ In a small pan heat the *ghee* or oil and fry the mustard seeds and curry leaves until the mustard seeds begin to pop and splutter. Pour over the pumpkin together with the *ghee* or oil and serve at once.

Grilled Eggplant with Hot Asian Sauce

Makes 6 servings

1 large purple eggplant, about
   1³/₄ pounds

1¹/₂ to 2 teaspoons salt

2 tablespoons light olive oil

2 teaspoons sesame oil

Hot Asian Sauce

1 medium onion, very finely chopped

2 tablespoons vegetable oil or light
   olive oil

3 cloves garlic, crushed

1¹/₂ teaspoons grated fresh ginger

2 tablespoons hoisin sauce

2 tablespoons sesame paste (tahini)

2 teaspoons Chinese garlic-chili paste

1 tablespoon dark soy sauce

1 to 2 teaspoons fine white sugar, to
   taste

³/₄ cup water

⊕ Cut the unpeeled eggplant into ¹/₂-inch slices and spread on a cloth. Sprinkle on half the salt and leave for about 15 minutes. Turn and sprinkle the remaining salt over the other side, then leave another 15 minutes. Rinse off the salt and the beads of liquid the salt has drawn to the surface. Set aside to dry thoroughly on a cloth or paper towels.

⊕ To make the sauce, cook the onion in a small saucepan in 2 tablespoons oil, stirring, over medium-high heat until softened and lightly browned, about 3 minutes. Add the garlic and ginger and cook, stirring, for another 1 minute. Stir in the hoisin sauce, sesame paste, garlic-chili paste, dark soy sauce, sugar and water. Cook for about 3 minutes, stirring constantly until thickened. Check seasonings adding salt and pepper, or additional sugar, as needed. Set aside.

⊕ Heat a wide pan or cast iron skillet and add the olive and sesame oils. Fry the eggplant slices over high heat until well browned on both sides. Ensure the heat is sufficiently high so that the surface sears to prevent the eggplant from absorbing too much oil. Alternatively, the eggplant can be brushed with oil and grilled until softened and lightly browned, then finished with the sauce, as below.

⊕ Preheat a broiler or grill to hot. Arrange the eggplant on an oven or grill tray. Spread the sauce evely over the eggplant and place under the hot grill for about 1 minute, until very aromatic. Serve.

Sri Lankan Eggplant

Makes 6 or more servings as a side dish

I find this a tad too rich to serve on its own, but it's superb with other spicy vegetarian dishes or with creamy curries, and plenty of rice. It also makes a great side dish with plain grilled meat or tofu cutlets.

1¹/₂ pounds purple eggplant

1¹/₂ to 2 teaspoons salt

3 tablespoons ghee (clarified butter) or vegetable oil

2 large onions, sliced

2 teaspoons minced garlic

1¹/₂ teaspoons minced fresh ginger

3 teaspoons ground coriander

¹/₂ teaspoon ground cumin

¹/₂ teaspoon ground turmeric

2 teaspoons garam masala (page 247), or mild, roasted curry powder

¹/₂ teaspoon ground mace

8 curry leaves or 1 bay leaf, broken

3 well-ripened tomatoes

2 hot green chilies, seeded and sliced

2 fresh mild red chilies, seeded and sliced

¹/₂ cup water

1 teaspoon sugar

1 teaspoon tamarind concentrate or 3 teaspoons lemon juice

Salt and freshly ground black pepper

⊕ Cut the unpeeled eggplant into ¹/₂-inch-thick slices and spread on a cloth. Sprinkle with half the salt and leave for 15 minutes, then turn and sprinkle the remaining salt on the other side. Leave another 15 minutes, then rinse thoroughly and dry on a clean cloth or paper towels.

⊕ Heat a large nonstick pan over high heat and add 1 tablespoon of the *ghee* or oil. Heat well, then brown the eggplant, several pieces at a time. Do not use extra *ghee* or oil, as it will make the finished dish very rich.

⊕ When all of the eggplant is browned, set aside on a plate. Add the remaining *ghee* or oil, reduce the heat to medium and cook the onions, stirring, until they are well browned. Add the garlic and ginger and cook briefly, stirring. Add the spices and curry leaves and cook, stirring, for about 30 seconds.

⊕ Cut the tomatoes into wedges, add to the pan with the chilies, and cook on medium-high heat for a few minutes. Return the eggplant and add ¹/₂ cup water, the sugar and tamarind. Cover and cook for about 15 minutes, until the eggplant is tender and has absorbed the sauce. Add salt and pepper to taste.

Sichuan Braised Spicy Eggplant

Makes 4 to 6 servings

This robust dish from central China goes beautifully with plump wheatstarch noodles, and with brown or white rice. It's also particularly good in a vegetarian menu partnered with Vegetarian Ma Po Tofu (page 238).

1¹/₄ pounds purple eggplant

¹/₂ cup vegetable oil

1 tablespoon sesame oil

¹/₂ cup chopped scallions (green and white parts)

3 teaspoons minced garlic

3 teaspoons minced fresh ginger

3 teaspoons minced red chili

2 tablespoons hoisin or sweet bean sauce

2 tablespoons dark soy sauce

1 teaspoon sugar

¹/₂ teaspoon ground Sichuan peppercorns or white pepper

2 teaspoons cornstarch

¹/₄ cup chicken stock or water

¹/₂ teaspoon chili oil

Salt

1 to 2 teaspoons sesame seeds, toasted (see sidebar, page 16)

⊕ Cut the eggplant into 1-inch cubes. Heat a large skillet or sauté pan and cook the eggplant, stirring, in the oils over medium high heat for about 5 minutes. Remove with a slotted spoon and set aside on paper towels to drain.

⊕ Pour off half the oil. Put the scallions, garlic, ginger and chili into the pan and cook, stirring, for 2 minutes, then add the *hoisin* or sweet bean sauce, the soy sauce, sugar and pepper and cook briefly.

⊕ Return the eggplant, cover the pan and cook for 3 to 4 minutes, stirring occasionally. Combine the cornstarch mixed with chicken stock and pour into the pan. Cook, stirring, until the eggplant is tender and the sauce has reduced to a glaze on the eggplant. Sprinkle on the chili oil and add salt to taste, stir in lightly, then sprinkle on the toasted sesame seeds and serve.

Spiced Chickpeas with Tart and Hot Flavors

Makes 4 to 6 servings

The natural partners for spicy chickpeas are puris, balloon-shaped, crisply fried bread made from finely milled wholewheat flour, together with lightly spiced yogurt. For convenience, serve this dish with purchased flatbread, brushed with butter, sprinkled with salt and pepper and heated in the oven, or toasted crisp under a grill.

3¹/₂ cups canned or cooked chickpeas
    (about 1¹/₂ cups dried)

2 tablespoons vegetable oil

1 large onion, chopped

1¹/₂ tablespoons grated fresh ginger

1 unripe tomato, chopped

2 ripe red tomatoes, seeded and
    chopped

3 teaspoons ground coriander

¹/₂ teaspoon ground cumin

2 teaspoons chili powder

¹/₂ teaspoon aamchur (dried green
    mango powder) (optional)

Salt and freshly ground black pepper

2 tablespoons chopped cilantro (fresh
    coriander) leaves

Lemon juice to taste

❁ Drain the chickpeas and retain their liquid. Set aside.

❁ In a medium-large saucepan heat the oil over medium heat and cook the onion, stirring, until it is golden and translucent, about 3¹/₂ minutes. Add the ginger and tomatoes and cook for about 6 minutes, stirring frequently and scraping the bottom of the pan to prevent catching.

❁ Add the chickpeas and the spices, with ¹/₂ cup of the reserved chickpea liquid. Cook, stirring occasionally, for about 6 minutes, until the peas have absorbed the flavorings. Season with salt and pepper to taste, stir in the cilantro and lemon juice to taste—it should be quite tangy—and transfer to a serving dish.

Lentil Dal

This is a versatile recipe. Serve it as a dip with points of toasted flatbread or naans, as a side dish with vegetarian meals or meat dishes, or dilute it with water, stock or coconut milk to make a satisfying soup.

3/4 cup red lentils

1 medium potato, peeled and diced

1 medium onion, finely chopped

2 1/2 tablespoons ghee (clarified butter) or 2 tablespoons light olive oil

2 cloves garlic, minced

2 teapoons grated fresh ginger

2 1/2 teaspoons garam masala (page 247), or mild curry powder

1 1/2 teaspoons chili powder

2 1/2 teaspoons ground coriander

1/2 to 1 teaspoon sambal ulek or chili sauce

1 1/2 teaspoons salt

1/2 teaspoon freshly ground black pepper

1/4 cup chopped cilantro (fresh coriander) leaves

2 to 3 teaspoons lemon juice or 2 to 3 tablespoons heavy cream

Sweet paprika or finely ground garam masala

⊕ Pour the lentils into a bowl and cover with cold water. Stir around, then add the potatoes, and stir again to rinse off their excess starch. Drain and set aside.

⊕ In a medium saucepan over medium heat, cook the onion in the *ghee* or oil, stirring, until lightly browned, about 3 1/2 minutes. Add the drained lentils and potatoes, the garlic and ginger, and about 2 1/2 cups of cold water. Bring to a boil, then reduce heat and cook, uncovered, for about 20 minutes. Add the *garam masala*, chili powder and coriander and cook until the lentils and potatoes are tender enough to be easily mashed. The liquid should be well reduced.

⊕ Add the *sambal ulek* or chili sauce, salt and pepper, cilantro, and lemon juice or cream. The lentils are delicious when their texture is retained, but if you prefer, mash them smoothly with a potato masher, or puree in a food processor. Check seasonings, adding additional salt and pepper, or lemon juice as needed.

⊕ Pour into a shallow serving bowl, and decorate with a cross hatch design of sprinkled paprika or *garam masala*.

Vegetarian Ma Po Tofu

Makes 4 servings, or more if sharing several dishes

Vegetarian Ma Po Tofu is just as delicious as the traditional recipe on page 164. Serve it with plain white rice or over cooked bean thread noodles.

1¼ pounds firm fresh tofu (bean curd)

½ cup chopped scallions (green and white parts)

2 teaspoons minced garlic

3 teaspoons grated fresh ginger

2 tablespoons vegetable oil

¼ cup finely diced pickled turnip or cabbage (Sichuan pickles, or the Kim Chi on page 269)

¼ cup finely diced bamboo shoots

1 ounce black fungus (wood ears), soaked in hot water 15 minutes

1 tablespoon light soy sauce

1 to 1½ tablespoons hot bean paste or Sichuan chili sauce

1 teaspoon fine white sugar

2 teaspoons sesame oil

¾ cup water or chicken stock

3 teaspoons cornstarch

Salt and freshly ground black pepper

Sichuan peppercorns, finely ground

Cilantro (fresh coriander) leaves, whole or chopped

❀ Cut the tofu into small cubes and set aside. Cook the scallions, garlic and ginger in the oil, stirring, for about 40 seconds over high heat. Add the turnip or cabbage, bamboo shoots and finely chopped fungus and stir-fry for 1 minute.

❀ Add the soy sauce, bean paste or chili sauce, sugar and sesame oil and stir-fry briefly. Combine the stock and cornstarch, pour into the pan and bring to a boil then cook, stirring, until the sauce thickens and becomes translucent.

❀ Add the tofu and heat through, carefully stirring to mix it in without crushing the tofu. Finally, add salt and pepper to taste and serve in a shallow dish. Sprinkle on Sichuan pepper and cilantro leaves.

Tofu Cutlets with Spicy Peanut and Chili Sauces

Makes 4 servings

1 1/2 pounds firm, fresh tofu (bean curd)

1 medium onion

2 1/2 cups oil for deep frying

2 egg whites

1 tablespoon cornstarch

Spicy Peanut Sauce (page 224)

Sweet Chili Sauce (page 253)

⊕ Cut the tofu into 2 1/2-inch cutlets, 3/4-inch thick. Cut the onion into thick slices and separate into rings, discarding the smaller, inner rings. Bring a small pan of water to a boil, put in the onion to blanch for 40 seconds, then drain and dry on paper towels.

⊕ Heat oil over medium-high heat in a wok or large, deep pan suitable for deep frying to 365°F. Slide the tofu into the oil to fry for about 3 minutes, until the surface is crisp and golden. Remove from the oil and drain briefly. Alternatively grill the tofu on a hot plate or shallow-fry in a heavy skillet on both sides until the surface is deeply golden.

⊕ Beat the egg whites to soft peaks and fold in the cornstarch. Dip the onion rings into the batter and fry in the hot oil until puffy, crisp and golden. Remove and drain well.

⊕ Place several pieces of tofu on each plate and surround with Spicy Peanut Sauce. Arrange onion rings over, and drizzle on Sweet Chili Sauce.

Thai Vegetable and Tofu Curry

Makes 4 servings, or more if sharing several dishes

1 slender Oriental eggplant

1 teaspoon salt

2 medium carrots

2 small onions

4 ounces chopped Chinese cabbage

4 ounces sliced green or long beans

14 ounces firm tofu (bean curd)

2 1/2 tablespoons vegetable oil

1/2 teaspoon minced garlic

2 teaspoons minced fresh ginger

2 teaspoons minced lemon grass

2 tablespoons green curry paste

2 cups coconut milk

1/2 cup sliced bamboo shoots

1/2 cup sliced straw mushrooms or champignons

Fish sauce

Salt and white pepper

⊕ Cut the eggplant into 3/4-inch-thick slices and sprinkle on the salt. Set aside for 10 minutes, then rinse and drain thoroughly. Peel and thickly slice the carrots, quarter the onions, and roughly chop the cabbage into squares. Cut the beans into 2-inch pieces and the tofu into 3/4-inch cubes.

⊕ Heat the vegetable oil in a large saucepan over high heat and stir-fry the garlic, ginger and lemon grass for 1 minute, add the curry paste and fry for 2 minutes, then pour in the coconut milk and stir until it reaches a boil.

⊕ Add all of the vegetables with salt and pepper to taste. Bring back to a boil, then reduce heat and simmer for about 15 minutes or until the carrot and onions are tender. Add the bamboo shoots, mushrooms and tofu cubes and heat through gently. Check the seasonings adding fish sauce first, then additional salt and pepper as needed.

Red Curry of Tofu and Mushrooms

Makes 4 to 6 servings

If I have some fresh spinach or Chinese greens on hand, I sometimes prefer to cook it up in a vegetable curry instead of serving it plain. If you use Chinese greens, trim off stems and slice very finely to use in the dish, or cut them into 2-inch pieces and cook separately to serve as a vegetable.

2 medium onions, chopped

3 cloves garlic, minced

1-inch piece fresh ginger, minced

2 tablespoons vegetable or peanut oil

1 large tomato, skinned and seeded

3 teaspoons (or to taste) Thai Red Curry Paste (page 248)

1 cup coconut cream

1½ cups water

1¼ pounds firm tofu (bean curd)

4 ounces small straw mushrooms or use small canned or fresh champignons

4 ounces shredded or sliced bamboo shoots

3 scallions, white parts only, cut into 1-inch pieces

1 bunch spinach, Asian water spinach or Chinese greens, rinsed, drained and stems trimmed

Fish sauce or light soy sauce to taste

Salt and freshly ground black pepper

Garnish

Chopped cilantro (fresh coriander) or scallion greens

⊕ In a medium saucepan cook the onions, garlic and ginger in the oil, stirring over medium heat until lightly browned, about 3 minutes. Chop the tomato and add to the onion, together with the curry paste. Cook, stirring, for 1 minute, then pour in the coconut cream and stir well.

⊕ Cook for about 10 minutes on gentle heat. Add the water and bring to a boil, then reduce the heat and simmer for about 2 minutes. Finally, add the tofu, mushrooms, bamboo shoots and scallions, and also add spinach or other greens. Cook for about 6 minutes.

⊕ Check for seasoning, adding fish sauce or soy sauce, salt and pepper to taste. Transfer to a serving dish and scatter chopped cilantro or scallion greens over.

Tofu Indonesian Style

Makes 4 servings

Red and green chilies and sambal ulek *make this a potent dish. Serve as a highlight in a vegetarian meal, or as part of a curry meal of several courses.*

1 pound firm tofu (bean curd)

2¹/2 tablespoons vegetable oil

2 tablespoons sliced shallots

2 to 3 green chilies, seeded and sliced

2 fresh hot red chilies, seeded and sliced

1 tablespoon dried shrimp, soaked for 15 minutes, drained and chopped (optional)

3 teaspoons minced garlic

¹/2 stem lemon grass, very finely sliced

1 teaspoon sambal ulek or other chili paste

1 teaspoon tamarind concentrate or 3 teaspoons lemon juice

1 tablespoon light soy sauce

2 teaspoons palm sugar or soft brown sugar

¹/2 cup water

Salt and sugar

1 tablespoon chopped fresh cilantro (fresh corinader)

Garnish

1 to 2 hard-boiled eggs, cut into wedges

1 lime, cut into wedges

1 small tomato, cut into wedges

⊕ Cut the tofu into ¹/4-inch cubes. Heat the oil in a wok or large skillet over medium heat and fry the tofu, until golden on all sides, turning it carefully. Remove and set aside, keeping warm. Add the sliced shallots to the pan and cook, stirring, until they are deep brown and crisp, taking care they do not burn in the final minutes of cooking. Remove with a slotted spoon and set aside to drain on paper towels.

⊕ In the saucepan, stir-fry the chilies, shrimp, garlic and lemon grass for about 2 minutes, then add the *sambal ulek*, tamarind, soy sauce, sugar and water and stir to boiling. Check seasoning, adding salt and a pinch of sugar, as needed. Reduce the heat, return tofu and heat gently in the sauce for a few minutes.

⊕ Serve onto a plate, sprinkle on chopped cilantro and fried shallots surround with the garnish.

Chapter 10

On The Side

Spiced Salts, Masalas, Curry Pastes and Marinades

Spiced Salt, Five-Spice Salt, Pepper-Salt

Chaat Masala, Garam Masala

Thai Red Curry Paste

Madras Curry Paste

Tandoori Marinade

Citrus Marinade

Sauces, Dips and Dunks

Peanut Sauce

Sweet Chili Sauce

Chili-Garlic Vinegar Sauce

Vietnamese Dunking Sauce

Chinese Essentials: Sichuan Sauce, Soy Green Chili Sauce, Hot Hoisin Sauce

Mint Yogurt Sauce

Creamy Dips with Pizzaz: Sweet Chili Mayo, Spiced Mayo, Spiced Yogurt, Sour Cream and Chili Chutney

Dressings and Vinaigrettes

Wasabi Sabayon

Cilantro Pesto

Chili Vinaigrette

Wasabi Vinaigrette

Sambals, Relishes, Pickles and Chutneys

Indonesian Chili Coconut Sambal

Fresh Tomato and Onion Sambal

Shrimp Paste and Coconut Sambal

Chili Sambal

Hotter than Hellfire Sambal

Fresh Herb Chutney

continued

Quick Date and Ginger Chutney

Onion Chutney

Chili Chutney

Pumpkin Chutney

June's Chili Relish

Peach Relish

Tamarind Sauce

Chili Pickle

Kim Chi (Hot and Sour Cabbage Pickle)

Accompaniments

Raita

Kachumber

Pickled Vegetables and Marinated Onion Rings

Chili Fruit Compote

Garlic Chili Bread Sticks

Peppered Flatbread

Sichuan Hot Sauce Noodles

Nasi Goreng

Thai Fried Rice with Pepper and Crabmeat

Garnishes

Crisp Fried Onions

Crunchy Garlic Crisps

Eating in Asia is a multi-faceted experience. At any main meal, they rarely choose to serve a single main course, but a selection of dishes that form a harmonious collaboration. The texture component is important. If one dish or ingredient is firm and chewy, its counterpart must offer a melt-in-the-mouth, silken softness. If one is dry and crisp, the preceding or following dish should be moist and succulent. A smooth dish or ingredient calls for something textural, crunchy.

Colors and garnish are an integral part of the design—what appeals to the eye is equally attractive to the palate. But overriding these factors is the element of taste. The base flavors should flow in smooth rhythm with each other, each making its contribution without overpowering the other. Then there should be rich, sonorous tones for depth and interest, and bright, high notes, to stimulate and excite.

These extra flavor points are sometimes built into a dish, but more often are added at the table in the form of sweet and hot condiments. India comes first to mind when I think of pickles, relishes and chutneys. They embellish their meals with an artists' palate of brightly colored, powerfully flavored chutneys or preserves, tangy salads and creamy side dishes. It's never an idle selection. A sweet, fruity chutney or relish, or a smooth *raita* (page 270) serve to tame the ferocity of a chili-laden curry. A peppy lime

pickle brightens up a bland bean or vegetable dish, aiding digestion into the bargain. A tart and spicy *chaat* (page 247) adds interest to a mild and creamy northern-style curry, just as marinated onion rings make a *tandoori* roast more appealing. In the southern states, they counter the afterburn of chili and hot mustard seed with fresh-made chutneys of grated coconut or herbs, such as mint or cilantro (fresh coriander) (page 264).

Indonesian cooks choose, mostly, to keep their dishes in the mild-to-medium heat range. They may munch fresh green chilies on the side, and rely on *sambals* to widen the flavor spectrum. Some of their *sambals* are fearsome compilations of chili and pungent shrimp paste which should be approached with extreme caution. Others are more user-friendly blends of tomatoes, onion and grated fresh coconut (pages 261).

In most other parts of southeast Asia, no meal is complete without a sauce or condiment of some kind. The Vietnamese, who prefer their food relatively bland, always offer a mashed, salted chili paste at the table, and many of their foods come with a tasty, fish sauce-based dunking sauce (page 254). In Singapore, bottled chili sauces are generally preferred, though they have a penchant for green chilies sliced into soy sauce (page 255). In Thailand you may have the choice of a viscous, sweet chili sauce (page 253), a "*nam prik*" of mashed chili perhaps with garlic that's so powerful it could blister a lip on contact, or a sprinkle of roasted chili powder (page 253).

Everywhere you eat, there will be sauces for dipping and dunking, bottles of sauce for splashing on generously, or sprinkling on in cautiously measured drops. There are spicy dressings and dips for vegetables, pastries and grills, based on peanuts, tamarind, sweet thick soy, or Chinese bean pastes. There are fragrant, salty-peppery condiments, and rich, creamy dips to add flavor highlights or palate-soothing smoothness. There are tart and tangy salads, and fruity side dishes, all designed to elevate the eating experience.

No hot and spicy meal is complete without at least one of these on the side.

Spiced Salts, Masalas, Curry Pastes and Marinades

I keep spiced salts on hand in my spice rack to pep up plain grills, fries and potato skins. I serve them in small Chinese sauce dishes, as an aromatic, salty dip for fried quail, little skewers of boneless chicken and whole shrimp cooked in their shells.

Store them in small jars, and make sure they remain dry and cool to maintain their freshness.

Spiced Salt

1 tablespoon fine table or kosher salt

1/2 teaspoon hot chili powder

1 teaspoon sweet paprika

1 teaspoon ground coriander

1/3 teaspoon ground cumin

⊕ Combine the ingredients and store in a spice jar. Tightly sealed and kept dry, spiced salt will keep for up to a year.

Five-Spice Salt

2 tablespoons fine table or kosher salt

2 teaspoons Chinese five-spice powder

⊕ Heat the salt in a dry pan for about 40 seconds, stirring constantly to prevent burning. Turn off the heat and stir in the five-spice powder. Allow to cool completely before storing. Five-Spice Salt keeps its full flavor for about six months, if tightly sealed and kept dry.

Pepper-Salt

2 tablespoons fine table or kosher salt

1 3/4 teaspoons finely ground Sichuan peppercorns

1/4 teaspoon freshly milled black pepper (optional)

⊕ Prepare and store in the same way as Five-Spice Salt.

Chaat Masala

Dress crunchy fruit and vegetable combo salads with this salty spice mixture to serve with rich north Indian curries.

3 teaspoons cumin seeds

2¹/₂ teaspoons salt

1 small pinch asafoetida (optional)

1 teaspoon chili powder

1 tablespoon aamchur (dried green mango powder)

1 teaspoon dried mint, finely crumbled

1 teaspoon ground ginger

⊕ Combine the ingredients and store in a spice jar for up to 3 months.

Garam Masala

Makes ³/₄ cup

This aromatic masala is what Indian cooks prefer to a commercial curry powder blend. Sprinkle it as a finishing touch over curry or rice, or use as required in a recipe. Like all ground spices, store in a tightly capped jar away from light, heat and moisture, and use preferably within 1 month of making.

3 tablespoons coriander seeds

2¹/₂ tablespoons cumin seeds

2¹/₂ tablespoons black peppercorns

8 cloves

6 to 8 green cardamom pods

1¹/₄-inch cinnamon stick

¹/₄ nutmeg pod

⊕ Place the coriander and cumin seeds in a small pan without oil and dry roast them over medium heat until they are aromatic, 3 to 5 minutes, stirring or shaking the pan frequently so they cook evenly. The longer the spices cook, the darker they will become, and will develop rich "toasty" aromas.

⊕ Transfer to a mortar or spice grinder, add the remaining ingredients and grind to a semi-fine powder, then sift to remove any large fragments and unwanted skins. When completely cool, store in a spice jar for up to 1 month.

Thai Red Curry Paste

Makes 1 cup (Makes 2 to 4 curries)

This boldly flavored curry paste with its rich spices and aromatic herbs gives Thai curries their characteristic taste and bright scarlet color. Coconut milk melds it into a smooth and complex sauce that's unbeatable for taste. It is also a versatile flavor base that can lend rich, sharp flavors to a stir-fry, or make a spectacular sauce for a whole fried or baked fish when combined with pureed tomatoes and coconut milk. Red Curry Paste will keep for one to two weeks in the refrigerator. The best storage method is to decant it into a small jar, level the surface of the paste and cover with a film of oil to exclude air and thus prevent oxidation.

2 tablespoons coriander seeds

1/2 teaspoon caraway or fennel seeds

1 1/2 teaspoons shrimp paste

3 teaspoons black or white peppercorns

1 teaspoon chili flakes (crushed dried chilies)

3 teaspoons (about 7 small strips) fresh or dried kaffir lime rind

1 stem lemon grass, coarsely chopped

5 cilantro (fresh coriander) roots

6 shallots, peeled

3 teaspoons chopped galangal (or fresh ginger) or 1 teaspoon laos

6 to 8 cloves garlic, peeled

1 large fresh mild red chili, seeded

1 to 3 medium-sized fresh hot red chilies, seeded, or 10 Thai "bird's eye" (small, hot) chilies, soaked in hot water for 18 minutes and seeded

3 tablespoons vegetable oil

⊕ Place a wok or small sauté pan over medium heat. Add the coriander and caraway or fennel seeds, the shrimp paste and peppercorns. Cook for about 3 minutes, stirring frequently and mashing the shrimp paste. When very aromatic add the chili flakes and kaffir lime peel and heat briefly. Transfer to a mortar, spice grinder or blender (Note: A food processor is not really successful here unless it has a small bowl) and grind to a finely textured paste. Remove and set aside.

⊕ Place the lemon grass, cilantro roots, shallots, ginger or *galangal*, the garlic and the chilies in the mortar, spice grinder, blender, or in a food processor fitted with metal blades and grind to a paste, adding the vegetable oil a little at a time, to keep the machine running. Add the ground spice paste and process to a fine-textured paste. Store in a covered glass jar in the refrigerator for 1 to 2 weeks.

Madras Curry Paste

Makes 1 1/2 cups

1 cup coriander seeds

1/3 cup cumin seeds

1 teaspoon fenugreek seeds

1 teaspoon black peppercorns

2 teaspoons brown mustard seeds

2 dried red chilies

1 cinnamon stick

1 tablespoon ground turmeric

9 cloves garlic, peeled

2 tablespoons grated fresh ginger

2 tablespoons white vinegar

1/2 cup vegetable oil

Heat a sauté pan without oil over medium-low heat, add the whole spices and the dried chilies and dry roast until the spices are very aromatic, about 4 minutes. Shake the pan frequently to turn the spices so they cook evenly. Pour into a stone mortar, blender or spice grinder, add the broken cinnamon stick, and grind to a fine powder. Stir in the turmeric. Add the garlic and ginger and grind to a paste, moistening with the vinegar. Heat the oil in a nonstick saucepan and add the ground curry paste. Cook over medium heat for about 7 minutes, stirring continually. When the oil separates, pour it off and remove the pan from the heat. When cool, transfer to sterilized jars to store for 4 to 5 weeks, preferably keeping it in the refrigerator in hot climates.

Tandoori Marinade

Makes approximately 3/4 cup (4 to 6 servings)

Tandoori marinade gives piquancy and a touch of the exotic to simple grills of chicken parts or breasts, lamb cutlets or tenderloin, skewered lamb or koftas (meatballs) of ground (minced) meat.

Preparation is mimimal. Just allow a few hours for the wonderful flavors to penetrate. I prefer to remove the skin from chicken, and ensure that lamb is well trimmed of fat.

2 teaspoons grated fresh ginger

4 large cloves garlic, crushed

1/3 teaspoon hot chili sauce or powder

1/4 teaspoon ground turmeric

1 teaspoon sweet paprika

1 teaspoon garam masala (page 247)

3 teaspoons mild curry paste or powder

1/2 teaspoon salt

3 to 4 tablespoons plain yogurt

1 tablespoon fresh lemon juice

1 tablespoon vegetable oil

2 teaspoons finely minced cilantro (fresh coriander) leaves (optional)

Pinch of tandoori food coloring or a few drops of orange/red natural food dye

⊕ Place grated ginger in a piece of clean cloth, and squeeze the juice into a bowl. Add the garlic, spices, curry paste or powder and salt and mix thoroughly, then beat in the yogurt, lemon juice and vegetable oil to make a thick emulsion. Add the cilantro leaves, if desired, and as much food coloring or food dye as needed to color the marinade a bright orange/red. This marinade cannot be stored and must be used on the day it is made.

⊕ To use, place the meat in a shallow dish, spread the marinade evenly over top, then cover with plastic wrap and refrigerate for at least 3 hours. Turn the meat every twenty minutes, to ensure even coverage.

Citrus Marinade

Makes approximately ¾ cup

This sweet and tangy sauce goes magnificently with game birds, such as quail and duck or baby chickens. I marinate them for 2 hours, before roasting in a hot oven and basting them frequently. Then I reduce the marinade to make the sauce. I also use it to glaze a whole fish, crisp-fried in the Thai style.

2 limes, juice and finely grated zest

1 lemon, juice and finely grated zest

1 small clove garlic, very finely minced

½ green chili, seeded and very finely minced

1 kaffir lime leaf, center rib removed, very finely shredded

1 tablespoon fish sauce

1 tablespoon clear honey or dark corn syrup

2 tablespoons vegetable oil

⊕ Combine the ingredients thoroughly. Use within 3 to 4 days of making.

Peanut Sauce

Makes 1¹/₂ cups

Serve this mild and nutty sauce with grilled satays and fried tofu (bean curd), or spoon it over a cold Indonesian style salad of boiled potatoes, onion, tomato and cucumber. The warm sauce makes a delightful dressing for stir-fried mixed vegetables or Chinese cabbage.

1 large onion, peeled

1 small clove garlic, peeled

2 slices fresh ginger

¹/₄ to ¹/₂ small fresh hot red chili, seeded

1 tablespoon peanut oil

2 teaspoons ground coriander

1 teaspoon ground cumin

1 tablespoon soft brown sugar

1 tablespoon light soy sauce

1 teaspoon tamarind concentrate

3 tablespoons peanut butter

¹/₂ to 1 cup coconut cream

Salt and freshly ground black pepper

⊕ Place the onion, garlic, ginger and chili in a food processor fitted with the metal blades, or a blender and grind to a paste. Heat the oil in a small nonstick saucepan over medium heat and fry the onion puree for about 3¹/₂ minutes, until lightly colored. Add the spices, sugar, soy and tamarind and cook for 30 seconds, stirring, then add the peanut butter and as much coconut cream as you need. Heat until well mixed, stirring slowly with a wooden spoon. Check for seasoning adding salt and pepper to taste. Keep refrigerated. Use within one week of making.

⊕ To serve as a dip with grilled satay, spread over saucers or shallow dishes and serve at room temperature. As a dressing for vegetables or salads, the sauce should be made thin enough to pour on.

Variations: For a hotter and spicier peanut sauce, add more red chili or your favorite chili sauce, or use the Spicy Peanut Sauce recipe on page 224.

Swirl *kecap manis* (sweet thick soy sauce) over the peanut sauce to add extra flavor dimensions.

Sweet Chili Sauce

Makes 2 cups

This indispensible sauce goes with just about anything that needs dunking or pepping up. Lavish it, as the Thais do, over fried or barbecued chicken and other grills.

1/4 cup minced mild red chilies (seed at least half of the chilies before mincing)

1/4 cup rice vinegar

1 cup fine white sugar

3/4 cup water

1/4 cup glucose or 1/3 cup light corn syrup

1 tablespoon cornstarch

1 clove garlic, finely minced

1 teaspoon grated fresh ginger

⊕ Combine the ingredients, except garlic and ginger, in a small nonreactive saucepan and simmer over medium-low heat for about 8 minutes. Add the garlic and ginger and remove from the heat. When cool, decant into jars. Store, preferably in the refrigerator, for up to 2 months.

Chili-Garlic Vinegar Sauce

Makes 3/4 cup

This is great with spring rolls and Vietnamese rice paper rolls, and with grilled chicken and crisp-fried fish.

1/3 cup fine white sugar

1/4 cup boiling water

1 to 2 fresh hot red chilies, finely minced

1 large clove garlic, finely minced

1/2 cup rice or cider vinegar

1/3 teaspoon salt

2 1/2 teaspoons minced cilantro (fresh coriander) leaves

⊕ Pour the sugar into a small mixing bowl, add the boiling water and stir until the sugar has dissolved and the syrup is cool, then add the remaining ingredients.

⊕ This tangy sauce-dip should be used within 2 days of preparation.

Vietnamese Dunking Sauce

Makes ³/₄ cup

This is my version of the sauce that appears on the table at every Vietnamese restaurant. It's perfect for dunking rice paper rolls, filled rolls of rice flour dough, grilled meatballs and skewered foods. For a quick snack at home, we pour it over rice noodles, into which we have stirred blanched bean sprouts, finely shredded carrot and fresh herbs—usually mint and cilantro.

¹/₄ cup water

5 tablespoons fine white sugar

1 small red chili, seeded and finely minced

1 small clove garlic, finely minced

¹/₄ cup fish sauce

2 tablespoons finely shredded carrot

Combine the water and sugar in a small saucepan and bring to a boil. Reduce heat and simmer for 2 minutes then remove from the heat and allow to cool. Stir in the chili, garlic and fish sauce and mix well, then add the carrot. Best used on the same day it is made, but unused sauce can be kept in the refrigerator in a covered glass jar for a day or two.

Chinese Essentials

Choose any of these three easy-make Chinese sauces for dunking shellfish, steamed or poached chicken, or roast duck.

Sichuan Sauce Dip

Makes approximately ³/₄ cups

1¹/₂ teaspoons minced garlic

1¹/₂ teaspoons minced fresh ginger

1¹/₂ teaspoons minced red chili

1¹/₂ teaspoons minced scallion (white part)

1 teaspoon Chinese black vinegar or balsamic vinegar

2 teaspoons sesame oil

1 tablespoon vegetable oil

¹/₂ cup chicken stock

¹/₄ cup light soy sauce

2¹/₂ teaspoons fine white sugar

Finely ground Sichuan peppercorns or white pepper

⊕ Whisk the ingredients together in a bowl. Serve into small dishes or rice bowls for dunking. This sauce will keep for no more than two days.

Soy Green Chili Sauce

Makes ¼ cup

3 tablespoons light soy sauce

1 tablespoon vegetable or peanut oil

1 green chili, very thinly sliced

⊕ Combine and serve in small Chinese sauce dishes. Use within 2 days.

Hot Hoisin Sauce

Makes 2½ tablespoons

2 to 3 teaspoons Chinese soy chili or garlic-chili bean sauce

3 tablespoons hoisin sauce

⊕ Mix the ingredients together and serve in small Chinese sauce dishes. If it is to accompany roast duck or pork, serve with small dishes of fine white sugar. Use within 1 week.

Mint Yogurt Sauce

Makes approximately ¹/₂ cup

This creamy, tangy sauce makes a great dip for Vegetable Pakoras (page 86) and Curry Puffs, and it's a natural partner for Spiced Chickpeas (page 236) and Tandoori Chicken Tikka (page 191). Mix it with a good mayonnaise in proportions to your liking, to dress sliced boiled eggs as a simple first course or an accompaniment to any hot curry.

1 bunch fresh mint, approximately
    2 cups loosely packed picked
    leaves

1 mild green chili, seeded and sliced

2 tablespoons plain yogurt

1¹/₂ teaspoons white vinegar

¹/₂ teaspoon salt

¹/₄ teaspoon cumin seeds

¹/₂ teaspoon aniseed

¹/₄ teaspoon ground coriander

¹/₈ teaspoon hot chili powder
    (optional)

⊕ Finely chop the mint leaves and chili in a blender or a small food processor fitted with the metal blade. Add the remaining ingredients and process until well blended and smooth. Pour into a container to store for up to several days in the refrigerator.

 Note: **As a dip, this sauce is best thinned with a little extra yogurt.**

Creamy Dips with Pizzaz

Zap mayo, yogurt or sour cream with a spicy sauce to make these peppy dips in seconds. Serve them with vegetable sticks, crackers or flatbread, or use to dress hardboiled eggs, cold shrimp (prawns) or small boiled potatoes.

Sweet Chili Mayo

⊕ For every 2 tablespoons mayonnaise, add 3 teaspoons sweet chili sauce (use bottled Thai sauce, or your own sauce made from the recipe on page 253). Add finely chopped basil or Vietnamese mint. What you don't use can be kept for 2 to 3 days in the refrigerator.

Spiced Mayo

⊕ For every 2 tablespoons of mayonnaise, stir in 1½ to 2 teaspoons of bottled satay sauce, or your own sauce made from the recipe on page 252. Serve plain or add finely chopped cilantro (fresh coriander) leaves.

⊕ Best used immediately, but unused portion can be refrigerated for several days.

Spiced Yogurt

⊕ Beat plain yogurt (or sour cream) until smooth. Season with ground cumin, a pinch of hot chili powder if you like and plenty of finely chopped cilantro or a combination of grated cucumber and chopped cilantro (fresh corinader) or mint.

Sour Cream and Chili Chutney

Makes approximately 1 cup

1 cup sour cream

1½ tablespoons Chili Chutney
(page 266)

⊕ Stir chili chutney into sour cream, until smooth. Use within 3 to 4 days.

Wasabi Sabayon

Makes approximately ³/₄ cup, enough for 2 to 3 servings

A treat over grilled salmon or lobster!

3 teaspoons wasabi paste

1¹/₂ teaspoons mild horseradish cream

¹/₂ cup thin cream

Salt and freshly ground black pepper

1 medium-size egg

 Combine the wasabi, horseradish and cream in a small saucepan and bring to a boil. Remove from the heat and season generously with salt and pepper. Have ready a small electric beater. Break the egg into the sauce and immediately beat until the sauce is creamy, continuing to whip until the sauce has cooled to room temperature.

Cilantro Pesto

Makes approximately 1 cup

This fresh and nutty-flavored, Asian-style pesto can be used hot or cold in many dishes as a dressing, dip or sauce.

1½ cups cilantro (fresh coriander) leaves

2 large cloves garlic, peeled

½ teaspoon salt

½ teaspoon cracked black pepper

2½ tablespoons toasted pine nuts or chopped and toasted macadamias

¾ cup light olive oil, vegetable oil or mild peanut oil

Rinse the cilantro leaves and dry in a kitchen towel, set aside. Place the garlic, salt and pepper in a heavy stone mortar or in the bowl of a food processor fitted with the metal blade. Grind to a pulp. Slowly begin to incorporate the cilantro leaves, pine nuts and oil, adding a little of each after each lot has been thoroughly pounded and emulsified. Use only as much oil as will be absorbed by the emulsion, excess will cause it to crack and be spoiled. Store in the refrigerator for up to 1 month.

Chili Vinaigrette

Makes ½ cup

Drizzle this fiery vinaigrette over seafood or cold chicken salads, over steamed green beans, boiled new potatoes or a basic tomato, onion and cucumber salad.

2 tablespoons rice vinegar

⅓ cup corn oil

½ teaspoon sambal ulek or other chili paste

½ teaspoon minced garlic

¼ teaspoon cracked black pepper

2 teaspoons minced Thai or anise basil, or cilantro (fresh coriander) leaves

Salt and fine white sugar

Combine the ingredients in a screwtop jar, close tightly and shake until they are thoroughly emulsified. Check for seasoning, adding salt and sugar to taste and shake again until dissolved.

Wasabi Vinaigrette

Makes ¹/₂ cup

Cold cooked seafood, particularly shrimp, responds to a bright, hot wasabi dressing. I compose a salad of cold cooked noodles (soba or rice vermicelli), with peppery greens and daikon, and cover it with peeled and sliced plump shrimp so fresh they still have the taste of the sea. If you want to use powdered wasabi, make it up into a paste with water and allow it to develop for at least 20 minutes before making the vinaigrette.

2 teaspoons wasabi paste

2 tablespoons rice vinegar

¹/₄ cup olive oil (not too fruity)

¹/₂ teaspoon fine white sugar

¹/₃ teaspoon salt

⊕ Combine the ingredients in a bowl and whisk to emulsify. Use on the day it is made.

Sambals, Relishes, Pickles and Chutneys

Indonesian Chili Coconut Sambal

Makes approximately 1 cup

The Indonesians often cook quite mild dishes, relying on potent sambals to add fiery flavor highlights. Serve this with meat or vegetable curries as a side dish. In Sri Lanka, the equivalent sambal is made spectacularly hot with a mass of fresh red chilies.

5 tablespoons finely shredded, unsweetened coconut

3 teaspoons hot chili flakes (use less, if preferred)

1 teaspoon ground coriander

¹/₄ teaspoon salt

¹/₄ teaspoon fine white sugar

1 tablespoon white vinegar

¹/₄ cup mashed canned tomato, with its liquid

1 tablespoon finely minced cilantro (fresh coriander)

⊕ Place the ingredients in a food processor fitted with the metal blades, or a blender and grind briefly. It should retain some of its grainy texture. Transfer to a glass container to store for up to 4 days in the refrigerator.

Fresh Tomato and Onion Sambal

Makes 2 cups

Prepare this sambal in advance so it can be refrigerated for at least 1 hour to crisp it up and bring out its full, fresh flavors. For a creamy sauce that is wonderfully soothing on the palate after a hot curry, drain the liquid from a half cup of this sambal and replace it with a cup of plain yogurt, adding a sprinkle of anise or cumin seeds.

1½ cups seeded tomato, cut into small dice

½ cup chopped scallions (green and white parts)

½ cup seeded, unpeeled cucumber, cut into small dice

1 to 2 red chilies, seeded and minced

2 tablespoons chopped herbs of choice (mint, basil, cilantro, dill)

1 teaspoon palm sugar or soft brown sugar

1 tablespoon rice vinegar

Salt and freshly ground black pepper

⊕ Combine the prepared vegetables in a bowl. Add the chilies and herbs. Dissolve the sugar in the vinegar, pour over and stir. Add salt and pepper to taste. Use within 2 days.

Shrimp Paste and Coconut Sambal

Makes ³/₄ cup

Sprinkle this crunchy, toasty condiment over curries, rice dishes or vegetables, or use as a topping for mildly flavored vegetable dishes.

1 tablespoon compressed shrimp
    paste (blacan) or 1¹/₂ tablespoons
    dried shrimp, ground to a
    powder

6 tablespoons finely shredded,
    unsweetened coconut

¹/₂ to ³/₄ teaspoon salt

2 teaspoons hot chili flakes

⊕ Place the dry ingredients in a mortar, spice grinder, blender or a small food processor fitted with the metal blades and grind to a reasonably fine texture. Add the shrimp paste and grind again briefly to mix. It can be kept in a sealed jar for several months.

Variation: Toasted Coconut Sambal: Combine the ingredients in a dry wok or skillet and cook over medium heat until the coconut is a rich golden brown and very aromatic. Stir slowly and continually to avoid burning. As it cooks, mash the shrimp paste against the side of the pan with the back of a spoon, and stir it evenly through the coconut. When done, remove from the heat and allow to cool completely before storing in an airtight glass container. It will keep for many months in dry conditions away from light.

Chili Sambal

Makes approximately 1¼ cups

2 tablespoons sambal ulek *or minced fresh chilies**

1½ teaspoons *minced fresh ginger*

2 tablespoons *finely chopped onion*

2½ tablespoons *palm sugar or soft brown sugar*

2 tablespoons *white vinegar*

¾ cup water

✦ Simmer the ingredients in a small saucepan for 4 to 5 minutes over medium-low heat. Thicken, if necessary, by adding a thin solution of cornstarch and water and cook until thickened and translucent, stirring slowly and continually as it cooks. Remove from the heat and allow the sambal to cool, before pouring into small bowls to serve. It can be stored in jars in the refrigerator for several weeks. If you have thickened the sambal, remove from the refrigerator and bring up to room temperature, then stir up with a fork, before using.

*If using fresh chilies, cook for 5 to 6 minutes and add salt to taste.

Hotter than Hellfire Sambal

Makes approximately 2½ tablespoons

The small quantities of this recipe speak for themselves. Approach with caution!

1½ tablespoons *minced hot red chilies, unseeded*

1 tablespoon *toasted cumin seeds*

3 large cloves garlic, *minced*

2 tablespoons *vegetable oil*

½ teaspoon *salt*

✦ Place ingredients in a mortar, blender, spice grinder, or a small food processor fitted with metal blades and grind to a reasonably smooth paste. Transfer to a wok or small saucepan and fry slowly for about 15 minutes, stirring continually.

✦ Store in a small glass container, well sealed for up to 4 months, if refrigerated.

Fresh Herb Chutney

A fresh mint or cilantro chutney is the natural partner for a hot curry, or a crunchy Indian pastry.

One bunch fresh mint or cilantro (fresh coriander)

3 scallions (green and white parts)

1 to 3 fresh green chilies

2 to 3 teaspoons sugar

$^1/_2$ teaspoon salt

2 to 3 teaspoons white vinegar

Pick off the mint or cilantro leaves and discard stems. Trim scallions and cut into 1-inch pieces. Cut the chilies in half, scrape out the seeds and ribs and chop the chilies coarsely. Place onions and chilies in the small bowl of a food processor fitted with metal blades. Chop briefly. Add the mint or cilantro, sugar and salt and process using the pulse control, until fairly finely chopped. Add the vinegar and process further to make a paste. Adjust the seasonings, adding additional sugar, salt and vinegar, to taste. Keeps for 1 to 2 days only, in the refrigerator.

Variation: Add about $^1/_2$ cup sour cream or plain yogurt and process to an emulsion.

Quick Date and Ginger Chutney

Makes 1$^1/_2$ cups

1$^1/_4$ tablespoons sambal ulek or other chili sauce

3 teaspoons minced garlic

2 tablespoons grated onion

$^1/_4$ cup brown sugar

2 tablespoons white vinegar

$^3/_4$ cup water

1 cup chopped, pitted Californian dates

$^1/_3$ cup chopped crystallized ginger

Combine the ingredients in a small nonstick saucepan and simmer for about 15 minutes over low heat until thick. Remove from the heat and when cool store in a jar. Keeps for about 3 months.

Onion Chutney

Makes approximately 1³/₄ cups

I keep several jars of this chutney in my refrigerator. It's a great asset in emergencies. I use it to fill small, shortcrust pastry shells to serve as canapes, spread it over a puff pastry sheet or pizza base and top with finely sliced ham, roast chicken or lamb to bake as a quick pizza. It's the filling for the barbecued lamb on page 213, and goes superbly with just about any grill.

3 to 4 large onions
2¹/₂ tablespoons crushed garlic
2 large medium-hot green chilies
2 stems lemon grass
6 dried mild red chilies
³/₄ cup vegetable oil

2 teaspoons shrimp paste
¹/₃ to ¹/₂ cup palm sugar or dark
    brown sugar
³/₄ cup white vinegar
¹/₄ cup water
Salt

⊕ Peel and coarsely chop the onions and garlic. Slit open the green chilies and scrape out the seeds and soft fibers inside. Chop the chilies coarsely. Trim the lemon grass stems, removing the root end and the leafy tops, leaving stalks about 6 inches long. Chop them into ¹/₂-inch pieces. Place the onions, garlic, chilies and lemon grass in a food processor fitted with the metal blade, and process briefly to a coarse pulp. It is very important that the onions are not chopped to a puree.

⊕ Heat the oil in a wok or medium-sized saucepan over high heat. Add the dried chilies and fry for 30 seconds until they are a deep brown, retrieve with a slotted spoon and place in a spice grinder or mortar to grind to a paste. Add the shrimp paste to the oil and cook briefly, then add the onion mixture and the dried chili paste and cook everything together, stirring frequently, for 2 to 3 minutes. Decrease the heat and allow the onions to cook gently until they have caramelized to a deep golden brown.

⊕ Add the sugar, vinegar and water, with salt to taste and cook until it resembles a dark marmalade. While it is still hot, spoon into sterilized jars. Sealed with wax or an airtight, noncorrosive cap, the chutney will keep for many months.

Chili Chutney

Makes approximately 1 cup

5 ounces fresh red chilies

2 tablespoons water

1/3 cup white sugar

3 tablespoons white vinegar, or to
    taste

2 cloves garlic

4 curry leaves

1/2 teaspoon black peppercorns

1/2 teaspoon nigella (optional)

⊕ Rinse the chilies and dry them, then chop. Set aside. Combine the water, sugar, vinegar and garlic in a small saucepan and bring to a boil. Lower the heat and simmer until the sugar dissolves, then add the chopped chilies and remaining ingredients. Cook, stirring occasionally, over medium-low heat until the liquid has partially caramelized. Cool and store in a clean jar. Keeps for 3 to 4 months.

Pumpkin Chutney

Makes approximately 1 1/2 cups

This unusual chutney is wonderful with plain grilled meats. I sometimes serve it in a tiny tart shell or small hollowed squash with a roast of lamb or pork.

12 ounces pumpkin

2 teaspoons grated fresh ginger

1 large clove garlic, mashed

2 slender fresh hot red Thai chilies,
    unseeded

5 tablespoons white vinegar, or to
    taste

3 tablespoons fine white sugar

Salt

⊕ Peel the pumpkin and cut away the seeds and any loose fibers surrounding them. Grate the pumpkin coarsely and place in a nonreactive medium-size saucepan with the other ingredients. Cover tightly and cook over low heat for about 50 minutes. Stir the chutney occasionally to ensure it is not sticking to the bottom of the pan. When ready it will be as thick as marmalade. Check seasonings, adding salt to taste. While hot, spoon into a sterilized jar and seal tightly with wax or a plastic-lined cap. The chutney can be kept refrigerated for many weeks.

June's Chili Relish

Makes approximately 2 1/2 cups

My friend June Parker gave me this recipe for a potent chili relish. I have used it, moistened with melted butter or light olive oil, as a superb glaze for roast lamb or beef, or grilled cutlets. See sidebar for more tips.

1 cup chopped red chilies	*1/2 cup sugar*
2 teaspoons salt	*1 teaspoon sweet paprika*
1 cup white vinegar	*1 clove garlic, minced*
1/2 cup water	*2 cups white raisins (sultanas)*

⊕ Place chopped chilies in a glass or stainless steel bowl and sprinkle on the salt. Let stand for 3 to 4 hours, or overnight.

⊕ Transfer to a blender or the small bowl of a food processor fitted with the metal blades and add the vinegar, water, sugar, paprika and garlic. Grind briefly. Add the sultanas and grind again until partially chopped.

⊕ Tip into a small nonreactive saucepan and bring to a boil, then simmer on low heat for about 1 hour. Allow to cool completely before packing into sterilized jars. Keeps for many months.

*S*pread this perky, aromatic paste over a leg or racks of lamb before roasting or cooking in a kettle barbecue: 3 to 4 teaspoons *harissa*, 2 tablespoons ground coriander, 2 teaspoons ground cumin, 2 tablespoons mashed garlic, 3/4 teaspoon salt, 2 tablespoons vegetable or light olive oil. Grind to a paste, spread over the meat and allow to sit for at least 30 minutes before cooking. Makes 4 servings.

Peach Relish

Makes 2 to 2 1/2 cups

1 1/2 pounds peaches (makes 1 pound, sliced)	*1 fresh red chili, seeded and sliced*
3 1/2 tablespoons shredded ginger	*1 teaspoon garam masala (page 247) or mild curry powder*
1/3 cup white vinegar	*1 teaspoon white peppercorns, lightly cracked*
2 tablespoons fine white sugar	

⊕ Peel the peaches, remove the stones, slice or dice the peaches and place in a medium-size nonreactive saucepan. Add the remaining ingredients and simmer on medium-low heat until the chutney is thick. Stir occasionally to prevent sticking. Taste, adding salt if needed. Pack into sterilized jars while hot, leave to cool, then store in the refrigerator. Keeps for many months.

Tamarind Sauce

Tamarind sauce is the classic accompaniment to a range of Indian and Malaysian snack foods. It's superb with curry puffs and samosas, with vegetable pakoras and spiced meatballs. It is a versatile marinade and seasoning sauce, also, lending a tart-sweet flavor and smooth texture to sauces and gravies, and a tangy crust to a roast.

2 cups tamarind pulp, with seeds

3 cups boiling water

3 cups palm sugar or soft light brown sugar

⅓ cup white vinegar

1 tablespoon ground coriander

2 teaspoons ground cumin

½ teaspoon chili flakes or powder

¾ teaspoon coarse salt

1 tablespoon garam masala (page 247)

1 teaspoon minced garlic

🌐 Break up the tamarind pulp in a bowl and pour on the boiling water. Stir and mash the tamarind with the back of a wooden spoon to release the tamarind pulp from its seeds. Strain through a nylon sieve into a small nonreactive saucepan, pushing as much of the pulp through as you can. Add the sugar and place over low heat to cook gently. Add the remaining ingredients and simmer until the sauce is reduced and syrupy, about 1½ hours, stirring it frequently to prevent catching.

🌐 It can be stored in the refrigerator for several months. Pack what you don't need into small decorative gift jars.

Chili Pickle

Makes about 2½ cups

This is potent!!! Make a less-challenging pickle using milder chilies, seeded, if you prefer.

1 medium onion, very finely sliced

¾ to 1 cup light olive oil

2 cups whole Thai "bird's eye" (small, hot) chilies

1½ cups white wine vinegar

2 cups fresh mild red chilies, seeded and chopped

1 lemon, peeled, seeded, cut in half and very finely sliced

3 tablespoons tomato ketchup

In a nonreactive saucepan (stainless steel or glass), gently cook the onion in 3 tablespoons of oil, stirring, over medium-low heat until it is translucent, about 12 minutes. Add the remaining ingredients and bring slowly to a boil. Reduce heat to low and cook for 40 to 50 minutes, covered. Stir every 10 minutes to prevent the pickle catching on the pan.

Allow to cool in the pan, then pack into sterilized jars. Keeps for many months.

During my years in Asia I was never without a jar of pickled shallots on hand. I served them whole, like olives, with drinks; sliced them onto canapes; occasionally threw an impertinent handful into a rich curry of pork or duck; minced them to strew through a salad; and scattered them over my sushi and sashimi platters. Stock up at your favorite Asian food store.

Kim Chi
(Hot and Sour Cabbage Pickle)

Makes approximately 4 cups

In Korea, kim chi is made early in the season and packed in big pottery tubs to ferment. The fiery result is brought out during winter when fresh vegetables are scarce. This is a simplified recipe which can be eaten within a few days of making, but will also keep for many months in the refrigerator. Kim chi is a great accompaniment to all kinds of grilled and barbecued meat dishes.

1 pound white or Chinese cabbage
1½ tablespoons minced red chili
1 tablespoon minced fresh ginger
1 tablespoon minced garlic
1 tablespoon sesame oil

2 teaspoons salt
1½ teaspoons cracked black pepper
⅓ cup white vinegar
1⅓ tablespoons sugar

Cut the cabbage into ½-inch strips discarding the core and tough ribs and then cut across these strips so you have small squares. Rinse and drain, then place in a saucepan with just the water that remains clinging to the cabbage, and cover tightly. Cook over low heat for 6 to 7 minutes, shaking the pan frequently to turn the cabbage. Do not allow it to brown. In a nonreactive saucepan, cook the chili, ginger and garlic in the sesame oil, stirring, until softened, about 2 minutes. Add the salt, pepper, vinegar and sugar and bring to a boil. Pour immediately over the cabbage. It will not require further cooking. Stir thoroughly, then pour into a glass or nonreactive metal bowl to cool. Pack into storage containers and refrigerate. Stir occasionally to keep the *kim chi* evenly moistened.

Raita

Makes 4 to 8 servings (approximately ²/₃ cup grated)

Southern Indian dishes are often incendiary, loaded with chili and searing spices like mustard seed and pepper. Side dishes of sweet chutney serve to counterbalance the heat, and yogurt helps quell the fire and soothe away stomach irritation. Serve the yogurt plain, or flavor it with any combination of these ingredients: finely chopped, seeded tomato; mashed banana; tiny cubes of cooked potato or sweet potato; chopped fresh mint, cilantro, basil or dill; chopped scallion greens or celery leaves; fennel leaves and crushed fennel seeds; or grated onion. Or spice it up with ground or whole cumin; toasted mustard seeds; finely chopped red or green chili; garam masala or cracked pepper. This cucumber raita is a favorite!

1 to 2 small cucumbers, unpeeled

1 teaspoon grated fresh ginger

1 teaspoon ground cumin

1 teaspoon sugar

¹/₂ teaspoon salt

1¹/₄ cups plain yogurt

Garnish

Garam masala, paprika or ground turmeric

Chopped fresh mint

⊕ Grate the cucumbers over a bowl, squeeze out excess liquid and discard. Combine the ingredients and beat until well blended.

⊕ Spoon into small serving dishes and decorate with a grid of spices and herbs sprinkled in fine lines across the surface. Serve at room temperature, or lightly chilled.

Kachumber

The Indian cook rarely serves a dish without some kind of complementary side dish. Palate-refreshing kachumber *is their equivalent of our green salad, to partner grills, roasts and kebabs. It is a common element on the condiment tray, along with small bowls of yogurt, fiery pickles and sweet chutneys.*

2 medium onions

3 medium ripe tomatoes

1 medium cucumber

2 tablespoons chopped fresh mint or cilantro (fresh coriander)

$^1/_2$ to 1 fresh red or green chili, seeded and chopped

1 teaspoon salt

1 cup tamarind water or white vinegar

Sugar to taste

Plain yogurt (optional)

⊕ Prepare the salad at least 1 hour before serving.

⊕ Peel the onions and trim off the tops and bases. Use a small, sharp knife to cut the onions into very thin wedges, place in a bowl and separate the layers. Cut the tomatoes into thin wedges. Peel the cucumber, if preferred, or leave unpeeled. Cut in half, scoop out the seeds with a teaspoon and slice finely. Combine the salad vegetables, herbs and chili in a bowl.

⊕ In another small bowl whisk the salt, tamarind water or vinegar and sugar together until the sugar has dissolved. Pour over the salad and cover with plastic wrap. Set aside in a cool place or in the refrigerator.

⊕ When ready to serve, remove the salad from the marinade with tongs and assemble on a serving dish or on salad leaves. Sprinkle on a few extra chopped herbs, and if you like, spoon on plain yogurt.

Variations: Scoop out a fresh pineapple and dice the flesh. Combine with the salad and serve the salad in the pineapple skin.

Just before you serve the salad, toss through sliced banana and shredded coconut.

Add small boiled potatoes or wedges of hard-boiled egg to the finished salad.

Pickled Vegetables and Marinated Onion Rings

Makes 6 to 8 servings

Pickled vegetables are a crisp and tangy meal accompaniment that's enjoyed in one form or another all around Asia. Chinese cooks serve cold entrees of sliced roast pork or duck over a bed of pickled cucumber or mixed vegetables, its tartness perfectly partnering the sweet rich flavors of the meat. In India it serves as an exciting contrast to creamy, richly spiced curries. Tandoori roasted meats are usually accompanied by onion rings marinated, like the vegetables in this recipe, in salt, sugar and vinegar. In Malaysia and Singapore, a tiny pickled vegetable salad is considered a part of the meal. This recipe combines cucumber, carrot and onion, but you can use just one of these, or include daikon (Japanese white radish) or jícama (yam bean), see variation below.

1 medium cucumber	1 tablespoon salt
1 medium carrot	1 tablespoon fine white sugar
1 medium onion	2 tablespoons white vinegar

Cut the unpeeled cucumber into 2-inch pieces then cut into sticks, discarding the seed core. Cut the peeled carrot into sticks of similar size as the cucumber.

Peel the onion and cut into small wedges. Bring a small saucepan of water to a boil, add the onion and immediately remove from the heat. Leave the onion to steep in the hot water for 2 minutes, then drain and leave to cool.

Place the cucumber and carrots in a bowl and sprinkle the salt evenly over. Knead and squeeze for a few minutes until the salt begins to soften the vegetables, then rinse under running cold water and drain.

Add the drained onions, and sprinkle on the sugar and vinegar. Again knead and squeeze for a short time, then set aside for at least one hour.

Variations: Combine cucumber, carrot and sliced daikon (giant white Japanese radish) or jícama.

Chili Cucumbers: Use this same method to prepare whole baby cucumbers, slicing them very closely almost through, so they retain their form, and add finely chopped chili.

Marinated Onion Rings: Pickle onion rings using the same method as described above, to serve with tandoori roasted meats.

Chili Fruit Compote

Makes 3 cups

Introduce sweet notes in a hot meal with stewed fruit dishes like this mildly spiced compote with a hint of chili. It can be kept for at least a week in the refrigerator.

1 small can sliced peaches
    (14 ounces)

1 small can sliced pears (14 ounces)

12 dried apricots

6 pitted prunes, halved

6 pitted Californian dates, halved

2 whole cloves

1 small cinnamon stick

1/4 cup white wine vinegar

1/4 cup sugar

2 small red chilies, finely chopped

1 1/2 teaspoons garam masala or mild
    curry powder

1 1/2 tablespoons chopped fresh mint

Salt and white pepper

⊕ Drain the liquid from the peaches and pears into a medium-size saucepan and add the apricots, prunes and dates. Bring to a boil, add the spices, vinegar, sugar and chilies and simmer until the fruit is soft and pulpy, about 10 minutes over medium heat.

⊕ Chop the peaches and pears into small pieces, stir into the compote with the *garam masala*, salt and pepper and cook for about 20 minutes more, until the mixture is quite thick and liquid well reduced. Stir in the mint and heat briefly.

⊕ Transfer to a bowl to cool. Serve at room temperature or lightly chilled.

Garlic Chili Bread Sticks

Makes approximately 26 sticks

1¹/₂ cups all-purpose flour

1 teaspoon active dry yeast

2 tablespoons tepid water

¹/₂ teaspoon sugar

2 teaspoons minced garlic

1 teaspoon chili flakes, or hot chili powder

1 teaspoon sweet paprika

1 teaspoon salt

1 tablespoon melted ghee (clarified butter) or butter or margarine

¹/₂ cup tepid milk or water

Extra melted ghee (clarified butter), or butter or margarine

Coarse salt

⊕ Sift the flour into a bowl and set aside. Whisk the yeast with water and sugar in another small bowl and set aside for 10 minutes to activate. Stir into the flour, adding the remaining ingredients, except for the extra *ghee* or butter or margarine and salt. Knead for 10 minutes on a floured surface until the dough is smooth and elastic. Form into a ball, coat with oil and set aside in a clean bowl for about 1¹/₄ hours until doubled in bulk. Knock down and gently knead for just a few turns, then roll out on a lightly floured board into a rectangular shape, about ¹/₃-inch thick. Cut into ¹/₂-inch strips and place on a greased baking sheet. (A pizza wheel is much easier to use than a knife, on this soft dough.)

⊕ Preheat the oven to 440°F. When the bread sticks have rested and proved for another 20 minutes, brush them with a little melted *ghee* or butter or margarine and sprinkle with coarse salt. Place in the oven for about 15 minutes until cooked and golden. Cool before serving.

Peppered Flatbread

Makes 6 servings

Bought flatbread can be pepped up with a flavored butter, to serve as a snack, with dips, or as a curry accompaniment in place of Indian breads or pappadums.

6 pieces thin flatbread

Peppered Butter

4 tablespoons (¹/2 stick) butter or margarine

¹/2 teaspoon chili powder

1 teaspoon garam masala *or* mild curry powder

1 teaspoon freshly ground black pepper

2 teaspoons mashed garlic

1 teaspoon salt

⊕ Preheat the oven to 440°F.

⊕ In a small bowl combine the peppered butter ingredients, working to a smooth paste. Spread over one side of each piece of flatbread. Cut each into wedges and spread on baking sheets without overlapping.

⊕ Place in the oven to bake for about 12 minutes, until crisp. Serve hot or cold.

Sichuan Hot Sauce Noodles

Makes 4 servings as a snack, 6 to 8 accompanying other dishes

Heat your favorite noodles in a fiery sauce for a high-energy, flavor-packed snack. I prefer to use bean thread vermicelli, and serve them as part of a vibrant menu with Chinese greens, a stir-fry and something crispy—perhaps Grilled Quail with Chili and Sichuan Pepper (page 200). You can also use this sauce as the base for a vegetarian dish, using about one-third the quantity of bean threads and adding to it strips of lightly sautéed firm tofu (bean curd), and a handful of spinach leaves or broccoli flowerets.

8 ounces bean thread vermicelli
    (or 12 ounces fresh egg noodles)

2 teaspoons mashed garlic

1 tablespoon sesame oil

1 tablespoon Sichuan chili sauce or
    Chinese hot bean paste

1/3 teaspoon ground Sichuan pepper-
    corns or freshly ground black
    pepper

2 teaspoons Chinese cooking (rice)
    wine or sake

2 tablespoons light soy sauce

1 tablespoon sugar

3/4 to 1 cup chicken or vegetable
    stock*

1 1/2 teaspoons cornstarch

1 to 3 teaspoons finely chopped
    cilantro (fresh coriander)
    leaves, or scallion greens

Salt to taste

Soak the vermicelli in boiling water to soften (or cook egg noodles until *al dente*).

In a wok, or a medium-size nonreactive saucepan, gently heat the garlic in the sesame oil over medium heat for 2 to 3 minutes until it is very aromatic. Add the chili sauce or bean paste, pepper, wine or *sake*, soy sauce and sugar and stir for 30 seconds.

Combine the stock and cornstarch, pour into the pan and cook over high heat, stirring, until the sauce thickens slightly.

Drain the vermicelli or noodles, place in the sauce and toss for a few minutes until heated through and evenly glazed with the sauce. Serve onto a plate and garnish with chopped coriander or green onion.

*Egg noodles may absorb more liquid than bean threads.

Nasi Goreng

1³/₄ cups long-grain white rice

3 tablespoons light olive oil or peanut oil

1 medium onion, finely chopped

2 cloves garlic, minced

¹/₂ teaspoon dried shrimp paste, or 1¹/₂ teaspoons very finely minced dried shrimp

2 large eggs, lightly beaten

¹/₂ cup diced celery

¹/₂ cup diced carrot, parboiled and drained

¹/₂ cup small peeled shrimp

1 cup chopped fresh bean sprouts

1 tablespoon sweet soy sauce (kecap manis)

1 teaspoon sambal ulek or Chinese chili paste or sauce

Salt and freshly ground black pepper

⊕ Pour the rice into a medium-size heavy saucepan with a tight fitting lid. Add water to cover by 1 inch, cover and bring to a boil. Reduce heat to very low and cook the rice undisturbed for about 15 minutes, or until the water has been completely absorbed and the rice is dry and fluffy.

⊕ In a wok or large skillet heat half the oil over medium-high heat and cook the onion, garlic and shrimp paste or dried shrimp, stirring, until the garlic is translucent, 1 to 2 minutes. Push to one side of the pan.

⊕ Pour in the beaten eggs and cook until set, break up into small pieces with the spatula. Remove the egg from the pan. Add the remaining oil and reheat, then add the celery and carrots and stir-fry until tender. Add the shrimp, bean sprouts and the rice.

⊕ Stir and toss everything together until well mixed. Stir in the sweet soy sauce and *sambal ulek* or chili paste/sauce and season to taste. Heat for a few minutes, stirring, then serve.

Thai Fried Rice with Pepper and Crabmeat

1½ cups long-grain white rice

2 cups water

1 teaspoon salt

2 tablespoons vegetable or peanut oil

½ medium onion, very finely minced

1 cup fresh bean sprouts

2 tablespoons fish sauce

½ teaspoon fine white sugar

1⅓ teaspoons finely ground white pepper

1 cup flaked crabmeat

1 tablespoon minced cilantro (fresh coriander) leaves, or 2 tablespoons sliced scallion greens

⊕ Pour the rice and water into a saucepan with a heavy base and tight-fitting lid and add the salt. Bring to a boil, reduce heat to the very lowest setting and cook the rice for 14 minutes, or until the liquid has been completely absorbed and the rice is dry and fluffy. Do not open the pan or stir the rice during cooking.

⊕ In a wok or large skillet, heat the oil and fry the onions until lightly colored. Add the bean sprouts and sauté briefly. Add the hot rice and stir over high heat, seasoning with the fish sauce, sugar and pepper.

⊕ Lastly, stir in the crabmeat, and the minced cilantro or sliced scallions, heat until evenly warmed through, stirring constantly, then serve.

Crisp Fried Onions

Makes 2 cups

Sprinkle these liberally over curries, rice and sauces, or over salads containing chunky vegetables or seafood.

30 shallots or 10 small onions   *3 to 4 cups peanut oil*

⊕ Peel the shallots and very thinly slice them lengthways, or peel the onions, cut in half and very thinly slice.

⊕ Heat the oil in a wok or skillet over high heat, then immediately reduce the heat to medium and put in the shallots or onions. Stir with a pair of wooden chopsticks to separate the pieces and cook until they are a dark golden-brown. Remove from the oil on a wire ladle or slotted spoon and shake over the oil for a few minutes to drain thoroughly, then spread on a rack lined with a double thickness of paper towel. Drain until they are quite dry and cold and have crisped up, but do not wait too long before storing them in an airtight container. They will keep indefinitely in the refrigerator.

Crunchy Garlic Crisps

Makes about 3/4 cup

2 whole heads garlic   *3 cups peanut or vegetable oil*

⊕ Peel the garlic and cut each clove into thin slices. In a wok, heat the oil to medium, add the garlic and cook for about 20 minutes, and fry to a dark golden brown. Take extreme care in the last minutes not to overcook. If they burn, the garlic will become bitter and you will have to begin again. Retrieve from the oil with a wire ladle and drain on a rack covered with a double thickness of paper towel. When cold, store in an airtight spice jar. They will keep for many months if cool and stored away from light.

Final Flavors

Afterthoughts

I had intended to name this chapter 'Afterthoughts', but on reflection realized that what comes at the end of a hot and spicy meal is of no little consequence. The right dessert is necessary, I think, to combat afterburn and a digestive overload of rich spices and feisty flavors. In tropical Asia, where coconuts proliferate, their creamy milk is the base for a host of soothing and refreshing desserts and cold sweet soups. Elsewhere, rice or rice flour puddings and desserts based on unusual ingredients like yams, noodles, semolina and reduced milk are the traditional finale to a lavishly spiced, fiery meal.

Imagine how a deliciously icy sorbet could refresh and cool the palate after an onslaught of chili. Picture a creamy pudding soothing the digestive system and restoring equilibrium. Liken it, if you would, to the Chinese precept of 'yin and yang.' Chili heat, powerful spices, pepper, bold food combinations are the *yang* element—masculine, aggressive, dominating. The balance is *yin*—things soft, feminine, calming, soothing, non-confrontational.

But because this book is about fire and spice, I couldn't resist carrying the theme all the way through. So my coconut ice cream comes with the surprise element of black pepper to follow the initial creaminess with a tantalizing, subtle after bite. An over-the-top chocolate ice cream, similarly, has the underlying zap of chili, in a decadently rich chocolate mousse. Luscious mango sorbet has a vibrant note of chili, which can be duplicated in a pineapple sorbet, if you prefer. For pure refreshment, I've made an ice dessert with two favorite Thai seasonings, basil and lime, and on the same theme introduced fresh green peppercorns as a delightful palate stimulant. Serve either of these after a meal, or as a between-course refresher.

Cardamom's unique fragrance and subtle flavor gives delightful Asian tastes to a creamy brulee, and similarly star anise enhances an anglais served over spiced pears. Spiced rice custard is a favorite Indian recipe that I serve often at home. It's wonderfully aromatic and a perfect conclusion to a meal that's packed with zippy, zappy tastes.

Black Pepper Ice Cream

Makes 4 to 6 servings

Cracked black pepper introduces fiery flavor highlights to a creamy ice cream. It's superb served beside a slice of tart made from a tangy fruit such as rhubarb or nectarine.

1 whole star anise	2 large egg yolks
1 cup cream	1/3 cup sugar
1 cup coconut cream, unsweetened	2 teaspoons cracked black pepper

⊕ Break the star anise into points, place in a mortar and pound gently with the pestle until partially crushed. This will ensure the flavor can be fully released into the infusion.

⊕ In a saucepan, combine the cream, coconut cream and crushed star anise. Bring to a boil, then remove from the heat and allow it to infuse for at least 10 minutes.

⊕ Whisk the egg yolks and sugar until creamy, then gradually strain in the cream mixture. Return to the saucepan and cook over low heat, stirring continually with a wooden spoon, until the mixture has thickened enough to coat the back of the spoon, about 8 minutes. Remove from the heat, pour into a bowl to cool and stir in the pepper.

⊕ When it is at room temperature, pour into the bowl of an ice cream maker and churn for about 18 minutes, until firm (or according to the directions on your machine). Serve at once, or transfer to a freezer tray and cover with aluminum foil.

⊕ If you are not using an ice cream maker, freeze the mixture in a shallow container until barely firm. Beat up with a fork, then refreeze until firm. For a smoother texture, beat up a second time and refreeze.

Hot Chocolate Ice Cream

Makes 6 servings

This super-rich ice cream has a zappy chili afterbite. Serve it with poached peaches or pears, in hazelnut meringue cases, or with almond tuilles or "glass biscuits" (shards of thin toffee specked with minced pistachios or toasted pinenuts).

3 cups light cream (or half-and-half)

2 cinnamon sticks

2 whole star anise

3 Thai "bird's eye" chilies, stemmed, (seeded if preferred)

12 ounces dark unsweetened cooking chocolate

6 egg yolks

6 tablespoons dark brown sugar, or to taste

2 tablespoons coffee or chocolate liqueur

✤ Pour the cream into a medium saucepan and add the cinnamon sticks, star anise and the chilies cut in half lengthways. Bring just to a boil, then remove from the heat and allow the cream to infuse for 15 minutes.

✤ Chop the chocolate into small pieces and place in a bowl over a pan of gently simmering water. When it begins to soften, stir briefly with a wooden spoon until the chocolate is smooth, but do not allow it to overheat. Remove the saucepan from the heat but leave the bowl over the water to hold the chocolate in its melted state.

✤ Return the cream almost to a boil. In a bowl, whisk the egg yolks and sugar until creamy and smooth, pour in the hot cream in a stream, whisking continuously. Pour the mixture back into the pan and cook over very low heat, stirring slowly but continuously. Strain onto the melted chocolate and add the liqueur, stirring well.

✤ Chill the mixture in the refrigerator, or over a bowl of ice until it has cooled to room temperature.

✤ Pour into the bowl of the ice cream maker and churn according to the instructions for your ice cream machine. When set, serve immediately or transfer to a freezer container, cover and freeze. Alternatively, pour into a stainless steel tray, cover with aluminum foil and freeze. Stir up with a fork and beat until smooth, then refreeze. Beat up a second time and refreeze to firm before serving.

Chili Mango Sorbet

Makes 4 to 6 servings

Hot red chilies give this luscious mango sorbet an appealing kick. Use this same recipe to make a vibrant Pineapple Sorbet, using peeled fresh pineapple (not canned) and adding enough freshly squeezed lime juice to balance the flavor if the pineapple is very sweet.

2 fresh mild red chilies	*1 cup water*
2¹/₂ to 2³/₄ pounds fresh mangoes	*2 egg whites, whipped to soft peaks*
1¹/₂ cups sugar syrup (see sidebar)	*Freshly squeezed lime juice*

✦ Cut the chilies in half lengthways and scrape out the seeds and the soft internal fibers, to decrease the heat level of the chilies. Chop them finely.

✦ Peel the mangoes, cut off the two "cheeks" and chop them into cubes. Place in a food processor. Trim the flesh from the stones (seeds), add this to the food processor and discard the stones. Process to a smooth puree, adding half the sugar syrup. Pour into a mixing bowl and add the remaining sugar syrup, water and chopped chilies. Transfer to the bowl of an ice cream mixer and churn for 10 minutes, add whipped egg whites and churn until frozen. Transfer to a freezer container, cover with aluminum foil and freeze until firm.

✦ If you do not have an ice cream maker, combine the mango puree, sugar syrup, chili and egg whites and freeze in a shallow container. Break up with a fork, refreeze and break up again, then beat up until the mixture is smooth and light. Refreeze once again before serving.

✦ Scoop into chilled bowls to serve, garnished with sprigs of mint.

To speed up ice cream and sorbet making, keep some made-up sugar syrup in the refrigerator. In a covered glass or plastic storage container it should be fine for many weeks.

1 pound fine white sugar

2 cups water

Pour sugar and water into a stainless steel or glass saucepan and bring to a boil. Reduce heat and simmer for about 10 minutes, stirring just enough to dislodge the crystals that adhere to the side of the pan. Cool, pour into a container and refrigerate.

Lime and Basil Ice

Makes 4 servings

This tangy ice is a deliciously tingly way to cool and refresh the palate after chili fire. It is also superb as a palate refresher between courses.

3/4 cup freshly squeezed lime juice

1/2 cup water

1 cup sugar syrup (see sidebar, page 285)

2 tablespoons chopped basil leaves

1 egg white, whipped to soft peaks

⊕ Strain the lime juice into the bowl of the ice cream maker, adding the water, sugar syrup and basil. Churn for about 12 minutes, until the mixture has begun to thicken, then add the egg white and continue to churn until the ice is frozen.

⊕ Transfer to a freezer container, cover with aluminum foil and freeze.

⊕ If you do not have an ice cream maker, freeze the mixture without the egg whites, then break up the mixture, add the egg whites and beat to smooth, then refreeze. You may need to repeat the beating and refreezing to break up ice particles and ensure the ice has a fine, smooth consistency.

Variation: Green Peppercorn Ice

⊕ Replace the basil leaves with fresh green peppercorns. Place them in a small saucepan with the water, plus an extra half cup of water and a pinch of salt. Simmer for 5 minutes. Remove from the heat and retrieve 2 teaspoons of the peppercorns. Set these aside, then pour the rest, and the liquid, into the bowl of a blender or food processor. Blend to a puree, then add the sugar syrup and the lime juice and whip briefly. Fold in the beaten egg white and the reserved peppercorns, then freeze in an ice cream maker, or by following the directions above.

Cardamom Crème Brûlée

Makes 4 to 6 servings

In hot weather, a caramelized sugar glaze is best done at the last minute, to avoid melt-down. But of necessity, they can be glazed in advance, and the brûlées covered with plastic wrap and chilled thoroughly, to serve cold.

Professional chefs use a small gas blow torch to quickly caramelize the sugar on top of a brûlée. These are sold in well-stocked kitchen shops, though they are rather expensive. They are useful for flash surface searing when you require a browned or melted toffee finish. I've used one to brown the top of marzipan-coated cakes and desserts, and even for passing a quick blast of heat across the top of a pizza when the cheese has begun to firm.

2 cups heavy cream

5 black cardamom pods, or 8 green cardamom pods, peeled and lightly crushed

1 small piece cassia bark or cinnamon stick

7 egg yolks

1/4 cup sugar

Extra 1/3 cup sugar for glazing

⊕ Preheat the oven to 350°F. Pour the cream into a small stainless steel or glass saucepan and add the cardamom pods, and the cassia bark or cinnamon stick. Bring barely to a boil, then reduce heat and warm the cream over very gentle heat for about 15 minutes until the cream is well infused with the flavor of the spices.

⊕ In a mixing bowl whisk the egg yolks and sugar until light and creamy. Slowly strain the cream over the egg mixture and stir in well. Divide between ramekins or small ceramic pots of no more than 1-cup capacity.

⊕ Stand the pots in a *bain marie* (water bath) half filled with warm water. Place in the oven to cook for about 40 minutes, until the custard is set. Remove the pots from the *bain marie* and allow the custards to cool for at least 40 minutes.

⊕ Sprinkle the extra sugar thickly and evenly over the top of each custard. Place under a very hot grill just long enough for the sugar to caramelize.

Spiced Rice Custard

Makes 6 servings

1/2 cup white rice, preferably
    short-grain

4 whole cloves

2 cinnamon sticks

4 green cardamom pods, crushed

Large pinch of saffron threads

2 1/2 cups milk

2 tablespoons butter

1/2 cup fine white sugar

3 eggs, lightly beaten

2 tablespoons blanched almonds,
    toasted and chopped

⊕ Wash the rice, then soak for 10 minutes in cold water. Infuse the spices and saffron in the milk over medium heat for 10 minutes.

⊕ Drain the rice. Melt the butter in a saucepan and add the rice. Stir over medium-high heat until each grain is coated with the butter and cook for 1 to 2 minutes, stirring continually. Strain in half the milk and bring to a boil, cover, reduce the heat and simmer the rice for about 10 minutes.

⊕ Preheat the oven to 350°F.

⊕ In a mixing bowl beat the sugar and eggs until smooth, light and creamy. Strain on the infused milk and stir well. Add the almonds and the rice mixture. Pour into a shallow casserole dish or suitable heatproof dessert dish and set in a *bain marie* (water bath) with warm water to come half way up the sides of the casserole.

⊕ Place in the oven to bake for about 30 minutes, until set.

Star Anise Cream on Spiced Pears

Makes 6 servings

2 whole star anise
1 cup milk
1 cup cream

5 egg yolks
1/3 cup sugar

Spiced Pears

6 firm, ripe pears
3 cups sweet white wine
2 cinnamon sticks
2 whole star anise

3 slices fresh ginger
Zest of 1 lime
2 tablespoons sugar

To Serve

Roasted pepitas (pumpkin seeds), or
    toasted flaked almonds

Palm sugar syrup (see sidebar,
    page 290)
Fruit syrup (see sidebar)

Intensely flavored syrups made from berries or exotic tropical fruit add color and interest to dessert plates. Puree fresh ripe berries, mango, passion fruit, soursop, *sapodilla* or papaya. Dilute and sweeten with sugar syrup, then heat and thicken, if needed, with a cornstarch or arrowroot solution.

✦ Cook the pears first if you want to serve them cold. Peel and stand in a nonreactive metal saucepan. Pour in the wine and add the cinnamon sticks and star anise and the ginger, lime zest and sugar. Cover and cook on low heat for about 25 minutes, until the pears are tender. Set aside, keeping warm if you plan to serve them hot, or transfer to a glass bowl and strain on the liquid, then refrigerate to serve cold.

✦ To make the star anise cream, first break the star anise into points, place in a mortar and pound lightly with a pestle. Place in a saucepan and pour on the milk and cream. Heat to a boil, then remove from the heat and set aside to infuse for 15 minutes.

✦ Whisk the egg yolks and sugar together. Reheat the milk and cream mixture for about 3 minutes over medium-low heat and strain over the eggs. Return to the saucepan and cook gently over medium-low heat, stirring continuously, for a few minutes until it has thickened enough to thinly coat the spoon. Do not allow it to overheat, or the cream will curdle. When done, place the saucepan in a pan of iced water and stir until the cream has cooled to room temperature.

✦ To assemble the dessert, stand a whole pear in the center of each plate and surround with the sauce. Dot the sauce with the fruit and sugar syrup and scatter on the roasted pumpkin seeds. Serve.

Chocolate-Coated Ginger

Makes 18 pieces, or 6 servings

6 ounces milk chocolate or dark chocolate

4 ounces sugar-coated crystalized ginger (18 pieces)

❀ Break or chop the chocolate into small pieces and place in the top of a double boiler, or in a bowl over a saucepan of gently simmering water. Allow the chocolate to melt, stirring until it is smooth and glossy. Cover a tray or plate with baking (silicon) parchment paper.

❀ Pierce the ginger pieces, one by one, with a thin skewer and dip halfway into the chocolate. Allow excess to drip off before placing on the paper to set. Serve with coffee.

Spiced Mixed Nuts

1 teaspoon ground coriander

1/2 teaspoon ground cumin

1/2 to 1 teaspoon hot chili power

1/2 teaspoon garlic salt

1/2 teaspoon onion salt

1/4 teaspoon ground turmeric

4 ounces pecan halves

4 ounces raw cashew nuts

4 ounces whole blanched almonds

1 1/2 cups vegetable or peanut oil

Fine sea salt to taste

❀ Combine the spices and set aside. Heat the oil in a wok or medium-size saucepan for about 6 minutes over medium-high heat. Add the nuts and cook, stirring, until the cashews and almonds are golden, about 4 minutes. Remove with a wire strainer and pour off the oil from the saucepan. Return the nuts to the saucepan and add the spice mixture. Shake and stir the nuts in the spices until they are well and evenly coated. Add salt to taste. Transfer to a plate to cool, then when they are completely cold, and not before, store in an airtight container.

Palm Sugar Syrup

5 ounces palm sugar or soft brown sugar

1/3 cup water

Put the sugar and water in a small stainless steel or glass saucepan and bring to a boil, stirring to break up sugar lumps. Reduce heat and simmer gently for 10 to 15 minutes, until syrupy. Pour into a jar to store.

Metric Conversions

Solid Weight Conversions

Standard	Metric	Standard	Metric
1/2 ounce	15g	7 ounces	210g
1 ounce	30g	8 ounces-1/2 pound	240g
2 ounces	60g	9 ounces	270g
3 ounces	90g	10 ounces	300g
4 ounces	120g	12 ounces	360g
5 ounces	150g	14 ounces	420g
6 ounces	180g	16 oz-1 pound	480g

.03+oz-1 pound   480g

Liquid Conversions

Standard	Standard	Metric
1 tablespoon	1/2 fluid ounce	15ml
1/4 cup	2 fluid ounces	60ml
1/2 cup	4 fluid ounces	125ml
2/3 cup	5 fluid ounces	150ml
3/4 cup	6 fluid ounces	165ml
1 cup	8 fluid ounces	250ml
1 1/4 cups	10 fluid ounces	300ml
1 1/2 cups	12 fluid ounces	375ml
2 cups	16 fluid ounces	500ml
2 1/2 cups	20 fluid ounces	600ml

Index